Political Communication and Mobilisation

This book provides a fresh perspective on the importance of the Hindi media in India's political, social and economic transformation with evidence from the countryside and the cities. Accessed by more than 40 per cent of the public, it continues to play an important role in building political awareness and mobilising public opinion.

Instead of viewing the media as a singular entity, this book highlights its diversity and complexity to understand the changing dynamics of political communication shaped by the interactions between the news media, political parties and the public, and how various media forms are being used in a rapidly transforming environment.

It also looks at the transformations occurring in the countryside and small towns, away from the glare of the Delhi TV studios. There is commercialisation and infotainment, along with a concern for the poor and the marginalised in the Hindi media-mediated democratic transformation, which is defined here as mobilisation for electoral politics and civil society activism.

The book offers insights into how print, television, and digital media work together with, rather than in isolation from, one another to grasp the complexities of the emerging hybrid media environment and the future of mobilisation.

Taberez Ahmed Neyazi teaches at the Department of Communications and New Media, National University of Singapore (NUS). Before moving to NUS, he taught at Jamia Millia Islamia, New Delhi.

Political Communication and Mobilisation
The Hindi Media in India

Taberez Ahmed Neyazi

CAMBRIDGE
UNIVERSITY PRESS

CAMBRIDGE
UNIVERSITY PRESS

University Printing House, Cambridge CB2 8BS, United Kingdom

One Liberty Plaza, 20th Floor, New York, NY 10006, USA

477 Williamstown Road, Port Melbourne, vic 3207, Australia

314 to 321, 3rd Floor, Plot No.3, Splendor Forum, Jasola District Centre, New Delhi 110025, India

79 Anson Road, #06–04/06, Singapore 079906

Cambridge University Press is part of the University of Cambridge.

It furthers the University's mission by disseminating knowledge in the pursuit of education, learning and research at the highest international levels of excellence.

www.cambridge.org
Information on this title: www.cambridge.org/9781108416139

© Taberez Ahmed Neyazi 2018

First published 2018

Printed in India by Shree Maitrey Printech Pvt. Ltd., Noida

A catalogue record for this publication is available from the British Library

ISBN 978-1-108-41613-9 Hardback

Cambridge University Press has no responsibility for the persistence or accuracy of URLs for external or third-party internet websites referred to in this publication, and does not guarantee that any content on such websites is, or will remain, accurate or appropriate.

For my Nana

Contents

List of Figures, Tables and Maps   *ix*

Preface   *xi*

Acknowledgements   *xiii*

Chapter 1:   Introduction: Political Communication and
             Mobilisation in India   1

Chapter 2:   Under Colonial Rule: Mobilisation in the
             Hindi and English Press   28

Chapter 3:   Media and Mobilisation in Independent India   49

Chapter 4:   Localisation, Grassroots Mobilisation and
             Hindi News Media   77

Chapter 5:   Political Economy of the Hindi Press   103

Chapter 6:   The Hybrid Media System, Anti-corruption
             Movement and Political Mobilisation   137

Chapter 7:   Agenda-setting and Mobilisation in a
             Hybrid Media Environment   161

Chapter 8:   Conclusion: Politics, Power and
             Mobilisation in Digital India   186

Bibliography   *197*

Index   *225*

List of Figures, Tables and Maps

LIST OF FIGURES

1.1: Schematic model of political communication 6

1.2: Growth of the internet users in India, 2007–16 22

3.1: The blank editorial published in *Nai Duniya* on 27 June 1975 62

3.2: Percentage share of Hindi and English dailies in total dailies circulation, 1961–2016 63

3.3: Growth rate of population, daily newspaper circulation and number of literates (%), 1951–61 to 2001–11 71

3.4: Voter turnout (as a percentage of the eligible electorate) in Hindi-speaking states 74

4.1: Sub-editions from Bhopal 81

5.1: Advertising revenue for English, Hindi and vernacular print media in percentage, 2010–15 121

5.2: Advertisement on the birthday celebration of the local MLA 124

5.3: Special page on the birthday celebration of the local MLA 125

5.4: Pamphlet for special promotion offered by *Dainik Bhaskar* 130

6.1: Newspaper coverage of 'Anna Hazare' from January 2011 to February 2012 147

LIST OF TABLES

1.1: Penetration of television in India, 1984–2015 (in million) 19

1.2: Number of 24x7 Hindi and English news channels launched, 2000–16 21

2.1: Selected list of important nationalist leaders and their newspapers (editors/owners/founders) 29

2.2:	Number of newspapers in India, 1901–1910	33
3.1:	Concentration of English and Hindi newspapers (%), 1981–2016	65
3.2:	Literacy rates (%) and number of daily newspapers (per 1,000 people), 1961–2011	70
3.3:	Voter turnout in state assembly elections and number of daily newspapers per 1,000 in four Hindi-speaking states	72
5.1:	Ad spend on TV and print, 1991–2015 (INR billion)	104
7.1:	Party tweets based on a random sample of 10 per cent of tweets from each party in the 2014 Lok Sabha campaign	171
7. 2:	Delhi voters' sources of campaign information	172
7.3:	Frequency of sharing campaign information with family and friends among Delhi voters	173
7.4:	Party campaigning activities in Delhi Lok Sabha 2014: Mean number of times and forms of voter reported contact (n=1,557)	174
7.5:	Tone of news items towards the party, Lok Sabha 2014 election campaign, *Aaj Tak* primetime news (8.00 to 10.00 pm) 13 March to 12 May 2014	176
7.6:	Tone of news items towards the party leader, Lok Sabha 2014 election campaign, *Aaj Tak* primetime news (8.00 to 10.00 pm), 13 March to 12 May 2014	177
7.7:	Most Important Problem (MIP) reported by Delhi voters, 2014 Lok Sabha election	181

LIST OF MAPS

1.1:	Number of Hindi speakers per 10,000 population	2
1.2:	Literacy map of India	3
1.3:	Television households map of India	20

Preface

When I began my research on the power of the Hindi media in India, there were only a few studies available on the growth of the Hindi media and its potential impact on Indian politics. The work of Robin Jeffrey (2000) and Sevanti Ninan (2007) provided broad overviews of the Hindi media while Per Stahlberg's (2002) study provided a rich ethnographic account of the relationship between the Hindi media and politics. Anup Kumar (2011) analysed the role of the Hindi media in mobilising the public that led to the creation of a new state, the State of Uttarakhand. These studies further fuelled my interest in the role and effects of the Hindi media in the political process. At the same time, my ambition as a student of political communication led me to look at the larger theoretical question of whether media plays a role in the mobilisation of citizens and influences political outcomes.

I have been interested in the growth of the Hindi media since my days as a PhD student at the National University of Singapore (NUS). In 2010, I joined Kyoto University as a Japanese Society for the Promotion of Science (JSPS) postdoctoral fellow. This fellowship gave me time to develop an analysis of the role of the Hindi media in India's democracy, which was published in *Economic and Political Weekly* in 2011. Another book chapter titled 'News Media and Political Participation: Re-evaluating Democratic Deepening in India,' analysing the relationship between the media and politics in India, was published in a volume I co-edited, *Democratic Transformation and the Vernacular Public Arena in India*, Routledge (2014). Parts of these two publications are the basis for parts of the discussion and data presented in two chapters (1 and 3) of the book. Back in India in 2013, after I joined the Centre for Culture, Media and Governance (CCMG) at Jamia Millia Islamia (JMI), a central university in Delhi, I had the opportunity to immerse myself in India's media and politics. At CCMG, I developed two specialised courses on digital media and political communication with a focus on published research largely from western contexts to discuss developments in India.

In late 2013, I collaborated with Anup Kumar and Holli Semetko on a Delhi Assembly election study that became a pilot for our spring 2014 India Election Study that focused on the impact of campaigning in urban contexts.

Our first article from these 2014 data, published in the *International Journal of Press/Politics* in 2016, showed that both digital and non-digital sharing of campaign information are significant predictors of citizens' engagement in the campaigns run by the political parties. I would like to thank Andrew Chadwick and Jennifer Stromer-Galley for inviting us to present an earlier version of that study at the 2015 conference on 'Digital Media, Power and Democracy in Election Campaigns' in Washington, D.C. I draw on data from the 2014 India Election Study in Chapter 7. I would also like to thank Akio Tanabe and Kazuya Nakamizo at the University of Tokyo and Kyoto University in Japan respectively, for the opportunity to present our election research at a workshop organised at the Centre for the Study of Contemporary India at Kyoto University in June 2016, after the International Communication Association meetings in Fukuoka.

Indian political scientists have largely ignored the role of the media in explaining political transformation. With the exception of a few articles in *Economic and Political Weekly* (such as Verma and Sardesai, 2014), the media has not featured in empirical research. The complexity of India's media system may be the reason why so few attempts have been made to study media content, uses and effects in the political process and on public opinion, whereas in Europe and the Americas these topics are often the focus of empirical research. With many languages and ethno-linguistically bounded states, India does not have one national media system, yet the Hindi language media reaches the largest number of Indians. Hindi is spoken by some 422 million, and is the major language in eight states in India, and many non-native Hindi speakers in other parts of the country often follow the Hindi media. This book sheds light on how the Hindi media, both traditional and new, functions as an important political actor that is critical to our understanding of political transformation in India.

Acknowledgements

This book is the result of a long process of research, interactions, learning and unlearning and would not have been possible without the support of my family, friends and colleagues, who have generously given their time as I worked to complete this project. I would like to start by conveying my gratitude to my PhD research supervisor, Gyanesh Kudaisya, who discussed new ideas at length and provided his critical comments on a few chapters of the book. I am very grateful to him for his advice and encouragement. I am also indebted to Rahul Mukherji, who was a co-supervisor of my research at the National University of Singapore (NUS). He alerted me to the idea of studying the relationship between media and politics more systematically. I owe a particular debt to Holli A. Semetko, who urged me to complete this book before moving on to a new project, and offered suggestions to refine the theoretical framework.

I am also grateful to Mohan J. Dutta, who invited me to visit the Department of Communications and New Media (CNM) at NUS on a fellowship during the summer of 2015. This summer fellowship gave me the opportunity to revise chapter drafts to submit with the book proposal to the Cambridge University Press. I joined CNM in July 2017 and I am grateful to my colleagues for their warmth and collegiality and the stimulating and rigorous environment, which helped me in the final stage of proofreading the book.

This book also benefitted from the stimulating environment and the support I received from colleagues at the Centre for the Study of Contemporary India at Kyoto University, particularly Akio Tanabe and Kazuya Nakamizo. I would like to thank my colleagues at the Centre for Culture, Media and Governance at Jamia Millia Islamia for their collegiality and steadfast support, particularly Biswajit Das, Saima Saeed, Supriya Chotani, Sandeep Bhushan, Arshad Amanullah and Athikho Kaisii. In addition, my thanks to Anup Kumar and T. T. Sreekumar for their helpful suggestions and intellectual stimulation.

I extend my gratitude to a number of individuals who spent their valuable time talking to me and helping me complete the fieldwork, particularly Ganesh

Sakalle, Pankaj Srivastava, Anand Pradhan, Rabindra Nath Sahay, Devika Asthana and Askari Zaidi. At the *Dainik Bhaskar* office, I would like to extend my gratitude to Abhilash Khandekar, whose unwavering support throughout my fieldwork was extremely helpful in obtaining the required data without difficulty. I also extend my sincere gratitude to Pushpender Pal Singh, former Principal of Makhanlal Chaturvedi University, Bhopal, who always readily connected me with media professionals in Bhopal and beyond. His support helped me obtain valuable information during my fieldwork.

I have been extremely fortunate to have the help of a number of part-time research assistants in the collection of materials and bibliographic works. These include Ridhi Kakkar, Purnima Tiwari, Juhi Hasan, Shamsher Singh and Arif Nadaf. As they embark upon important ventures of their own, to each of them my sincere thanks.

A number of librarians provided ungrudging help and support, for which I am most thankful. These are far too many to be listed, although I would like to mention the staff of the National University of Singapore Library, particularly to Vimala Nambiar, who always took extra pains to provide documents that I requested. I am also thankful to the staff of Nehru Memorial Museum and Library, the Indian Institute of Mass Communication library, the Kyoto University library, the Centre for Culture, Media and Governance library (particularly Rizwana Ansari) and the University of Hawaii library (specifically Susan Johnson), who actively cooperated in the collection of relevant information.

A number of friends have over the years remained steadfast in their encouragement and support in innumerable ways. They are Sarbeswar Sahoo, Lou Antolihao, Niraj Singh, Sojin Shin, Subhasish Ray, Mohammed Naushad, Sarah Moser, Kanchan Gandhi, Romit Dasgupta, Diganta Das, Smita Singh, Priya Jeradi, Sujoy Dutta, Hussain Ahmad Khan, Pooja Lal, Rashid Ahmad, Binish Maryam, Anindita Pujari and Manoranjan Pattanayak. My childhood friends Fahim Uddin and Asif Iqbal were always a source of encouragement and support throughout my journey. Naushad Alam, whose untimely death was a great loss, was also an inspiration in the early stages of my career. I would like to thank Mohammed Shamim, my teacher and friend, who inspired me to attain higher education.

This work would not have been possible without financial support. I extend my gratitude to the Asia Research Institute for supporting my fieldwork with a generous grant. I also received financial support for my fieldwork from the Japan Society for the Promotion of Science (JSPS) Grants-in-Aid for Scientific Research Programs.

I am grateful to anonymous reviewers for reading the book carefully and offering critical suggestions, which helped me tighten the arguments of the book. I am greatly appreciative of the efforts of my copy editor, Renu Gupta, whose painstaking work helped improve the contents of the book. At Cambridge University Press, I would like to thank the commissioning editor, Qudsiya Ahmed, for constant support and patience during the publication of this book. I would also like to thank Sohini Ghosh, Anwesha Rana and Anurupa Sen for their help in the production process.

Maps used in this book were prepared by Professor Atiqur Rahman of Jamia Millia Islamia's Geography Department, for which I am particularly grateful.

Finally, my greatest debt and one that is impossible to repay in proper measure is to my parents, Mohammed Naseemuddin and Ayesha Begum, who have not only shown tremendous affection but also provided unfailing support. I would like to sincerely thank my Nana (Anwar Ahmed), my grandfather, who passed away in 2009. Without his immense and sustained encouragement, this work would not have taken the present shape. I dedicate this book to my Nana.

Most of all, I would like to thank my wife, Shagufta Neyazi, for her support and energy throughout the process of writing this book. Our young family has grown from one child, Erum, born in April 2014, right in the middle of the Indian election campaign, to two, Ayan was born in October 2016. Without the support and sacrifice of my family, this book would not have been completed.

Although I am privileged to receive such empathy and support, I take full responsibility for any errors or omissions that may have crept into this work.

1

Introduction

Political Communication and Mobilisation in India

Any generalisation about the Indian media is problematic because there are diverse media systems within the country. The Hindi language media has the widest circulation, reaching almost 40 per cent of India's total population, and the Hindi-speaking population accounts for over 40 per cent of the national population and is regionally concentrated in the northern and central parts of India. The success of the Hindi media should not be compared with other vernacular language media such as Tamil and Bengali, because the Hindi language press enjoyed state support both during the colonial period and in newly independent India that helped the Hindi media attain privileged status. Hindi, together with other vernacular media, has a far wider reach than the indigenous English media, catering to both elite and popular constituencies, and is a politically significant player. While the English language media is often described as the 'national media', its reach is limited to a much smaller percentage of the population – the English-speaking elites and the middle class. The process of political communication is, therefore, more nuanced because India's news media market is more complex and diverse than in most other countries.

Moreover, the complexities associated with the size of the political economy of India requires special focus on how ethnic, religious and sectarian diversity impacts media markets and media systems, political campaigning, protest movements and grassroots mobilisation. This is largely because of the many languages in India and the existence of numerous regional and local media systems in vernacular languages. Despite the fact that similar large economic forces operate in the globalising Indian market place, there are still stark socio-cultural differences in the media systems of different states in India and, thus, many media systems exist within one country. At the same time, the process of political communication is affected by the gap between urban and rural, as well as inter- and intra-state differences on various development indicators such as literacy, poverty, urbanisation and media availability. In contrast to many western democracies that have experienced a largely linear process of media evolution with the rise of print followed by radio then television and more recently the cell phone and the internet, India has witnessed tremendous growth across all media simultaneously over the past decade. The non-linear development of India's communication processes and the proliferation of different sources of information have deepened the fragmentation in the already fragmented media.

Map 1.1: Number of Hindi speakers per 10,000 population

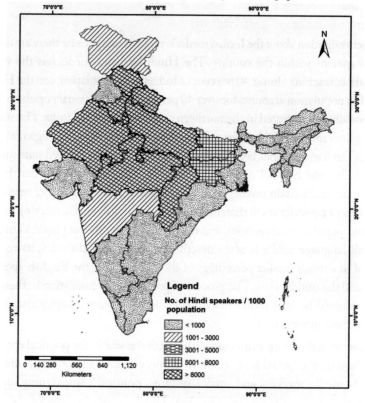

Source: Census of India. 2001a. *Distribution of 10,000 Persons by Language.*

Note: There are eight states which have Hindi speaking population more than 8,000 per 10,000, while three states have Hindi speaking population between 5,000 to 8,000 per 10,000.

Scholars writing about the Indian media tend to overlook these complexities and have focused instead on the Indian media as a singular entity (Athique, 2012; Gupta, N., 1998; Mehta, 2008; Saeed, 2012; Thussu, 2006a).[1] The lack of political autonomy is another issue that has been raised with respect to television and press (Saeed, 2012; Thakurta, 2014a; Thakurta and Chaturvedi, 2012;

---

1   There are scholarly works that are mindful of generalising about the Indian media, such as Jeffrey (2000) and Udupa (2015).

Thomas, 2014). Since the rise of television in the 1990s, there is a growing literature suggesting the rise of 'infotainment', 'Murdochisation of news' and 'commodification of news' without reference to language, in part because these trends are common across most Hindi and vernacular media. Notwithstanding these shortcomings, the news media in India has played a significant role in influencing politics and affected the transformation at the grassroots. There is a simultaneous presence of commercialisation and infotainment along with a concern for the poor and the marginalised in the Indian media. This hybrid character is clearly reflected in the Hindi media-mediated democratic transformation, defined here as mobilisation for electoral politics as well as civil society activism.

Map 1.2: Literacy map of India

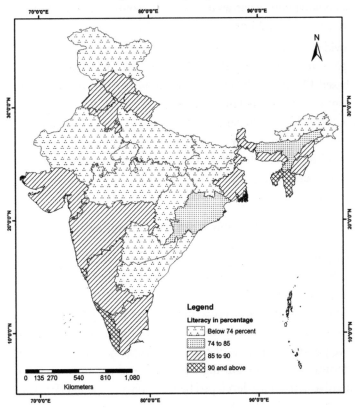

Source: Census of India. 2011a. *Literacy in India, 2011.*

Note: Most of the Hindi speaking states has average literacy rate below national average of 74 per cent.

The core argument of this book is that the Hindi media has historically played and continues to play a catalytic role as mobilising agents in the ongoing democratic transformation in India. The mobilising role of the Hindi media was first evident in colonial India where the Hindi media aligned with the freedom struggle and helped mobilise public opinion against the British. Instead of viewing the Indian media as a singular entity, this book demonstrates its diversity and complexity to understand the changing dynamics of political communication that is shaped by the interactions among the news media, political parties and diverse public. In the process, I show the ways the media in India tread the diverse space in this comparatively young democracy by encouraging political and social mobilisation while dealing with complex local realities. I also show how the new forms of media are being used by people, movements and political parties for social and political mobilisation in a rapidly transforming media environment.

I provide insights into the profound and messy, yet quiet, transformations taking place in the countryside and small towns, away from the glare of the Delhi-based TV studios. In a growing economy such as India's, what role does media play in mobilising political awareness? What role does the Hindi language media, accessed by over 40 per cent of the people, play in building this political awareness? And when nearly 30 per cent of the population is illiterate, how is the work of the media relevant to their lives? Let's first discuss the theoretical framework underpinning this book.

Media as a mobilising agent

The early pioneer of media effects research, Lasswell (1948), pointed out that mass media has three fundamental functions: surveillance of the environment, fostering consensus in society and transmission of the cultural heritage (quoted in McCombs, 2005). Although written in the post-war period, these three functions of the media are relevant even today. Pippa Norris (2000) identified three core political functions of the news media system – as a watchdog, as a civic forum and as a mobilising agent (22) – drawing upon the theory of representative democracy developed by Joseph Schumpeter (1952) and Robert Dahl (1956, 1971, 1989). The watchdog role of the media is similar to the surveillance function where media monitors the abuse of public power. Media as a civic forum should provide space for diverse and contesting viewpoints so that citizens can arrive at their own informed decisions. As a mobilising agent, media needs to enable citizens to learn about public affairs and to participate in politics. These normative ideals about the media come under strain when we tread messy empirical realities in a developing democracy. Drawing upon the work of Pippa Norris, I focus on the mobilising role of the media in political process and change. This, by no means, ignores the other two functions of the media as a watchdog and as a civic forum. By providing information to citizens, media can activate citizens politically, which is essence of mobilisation (Hansen and Pedersen, 2014; Lazarsfeld, Berelson and Gaudet, 1948; Norris, 2006; Verba, Schlozman and Brady, 1995). There are several indicators of mobilisation such as political participation, turnout, increasing interest and attention to politics, political efficacy, signing petitions, participating in protests, writing to or contacting representatives and letters to the editor.

Information can play an important role in mobilising citizens. People receive information not only through exposure to the media, both traditional and new, but also through family, friends, parties and political organisations as well as campaign literature. Several studies have highlighted the positive impact of the news media in increasing political participation and political discussion (Aarts and Semetko, 2003; Dimock and Popkin, 1997; Eveland and Scheufele, 2000; Liu, Shen, Eveland and Dylko, 2013; Newton, 1999; Norris, 1996). The literature also suggests that the type of media has a determining effect and showed that attention to newspapers and television news has a greater mobilising effect than other types of media or not following any media (Aalberg and Curran, 2012; Aarts and Semetko, 2003; Newton, 1999; Norris, 2000; Strömbäck and Shehata, 2010). Robert Putnam (1995), writing in the context of the US, showed a declining trend in social capital and civic engagement in the US, which he primarily attributed to people watching too much television. In response, Pippa Norris (1996) showed that the decline in social capital and civic engagement is not due to watching television *per se*; rather what people watch should be held responsible for the decline. Norris shows that watching news and public affairs on television, in fact, has a mobilising effect. Notwithstanding the critique of the demobilising effect of media, we have enough evidence to suggest that the media does have a positive impact on mobilisation. The schematic model of political communication developed in this book draws upon the work of Norris (2000) and could be considered a process model beginning with the generation of the messages by various actors, the processing and production of messages in the media and the effects of the messages on the receivers and continuous feedback owing to the development of newer channel of communication (Figure 1.3). The exogenous factors including social, economic and political conditions do play significant role in the entire process of political communication. This model has been adapted to suit a developing country by including not only mobilisation at national level, but sub-national moblisation taking place in the civil society. The rise of digital media has also affected the process of political communication where the messages have not only been produced by the media, but individual citizens have assumed the role of content creators once exclusively reserved for journalists leading to the convergence of the sources of information and the sites of conversation (Shah, Culver, Hanna, Macafee and Yang, 2015). The one-way model of political communication in which the voice of the authority was channelled through the mass media with limited feedback mechanisms has been replaced by an interactive communicative process. In adapting Norris's model to the case of India, these nuances in the process of political communication has been addressed.

Figure 1.1: Schematic model of political communication[2]

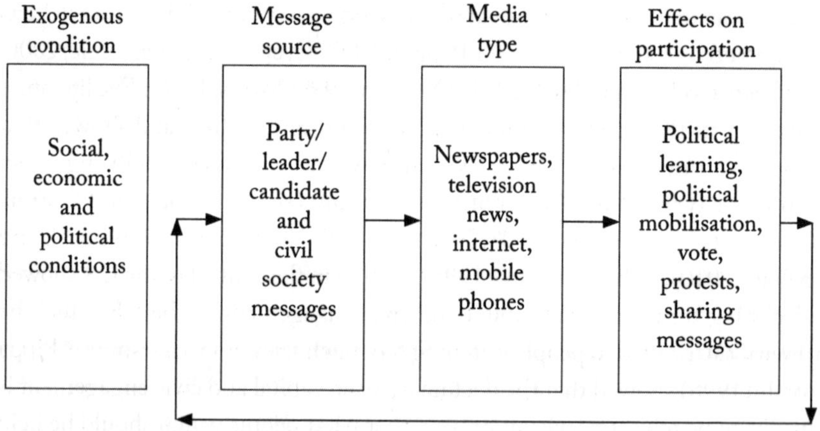

Exogenous condition	Message source	Media type	Effects on participation
Social, economic and political conditions	Party/ leader/ candidate and civil society messages	Newspapers, television news, internet, mobile phones	Political learning, political mobilisation, vote, protests, sharing messages

In this book, I focus both on mobilisation for electoral politics, which has been the main concern of political scientists, as well as grassroots mobilisation where citizens and groups from different class and caste backgrounds actively participate in mediated activities in the public arena. I examine recent developments such as the movement against corruption led by Anna Hazare that propelled him and the country into world news throughout 2011 as well

---

2   Schematic model of political communication has been adapted from Pippa Norris (2000).

as political mobilisation in the 2014 national election campaigns, and the interactions between traditional and social media and how they have changed the structures and dynamics of political mobilisation in contemporary India. The concept of a hybrid media system (Chadwick, 2013) that looks at the interplay between traditional and new media, as well as grassroots political mobilisation consisting of diverse actors, is discussed while examining the recent political and social developments. The concept of a hybrid media system addresses the emergent convergence of the sources of information and the sites of conversation and helps in further elucidating the schematic model of political communication.

Despite the higher percentage of participation in electoral politics compared with other developed democracies as evident from the record turnout during elections, Indian democracy is also marked by dysfunctional institutions and governance that affect the opportunity structures of the poor and the marginalised.[3] This puzzle has led scholars to characterise India as a procedural democracy where a patron–client relationship affects the delivery of goods and services to its citizens. Chandra (2004) argues that the post-liberalisation Indian state is distinguished by two structural features: (i) dominance, which refers to the control of the state in the delivery of goods and services affecting the lives and livelihoods of the majority of its citizens; and (ii) discretion, where public officials have tremendous discretion in allocating these goods and services to specific individuals. These observations lead to several questions about the rise of the Hindi media. To what extent has the rise of the Hindi media served to dismantle or strengthen patronage democracy? Is the Hindi media helping or hiding examples of dysfunctional governance, issues of corruption, elite capture of state resources and ethnic mobilisation? How has the growth of social media enabled political participation and helped in mobilising public opinion? These questions are addressed in this book by analysing the relationship between media and politics from colonial to post-liberalisation India.

The English media, which dominated India's national media market from independence until the late 1990s, is no longer the dominant market player (Jeffrey, 2000; Kumar, 2011; Nair, 2003; Neyazi, 2010, 2011, 2014; Ninan, 2007; Rajagopal, 2001; Stahlberg, 2002a, 2013; Udupa, 2015). English media has been displaced by the vernacular media and the Hindi news media in particular. As

---

3   The 2014 national election saw a record voter turnout of 66.4 per cent, surpassing the previous record of 64 per cent in the 1984 national election.

many as 66 Hindi news channels have been launched since 2000, more than in any other language. Similarly, according to the circulation figures for 2015, Hindi dailies lead with nearly 141 million copies or 47.7 per cent of the total circulation of daily newspapers, whereas English dailies stand a distant second with some 33 million copies or 11.4 per cent of total daily circulation (Press in India, 2015). Further, the reach of the Hindi media is not confined to north and central India where Hindi is widely used in 8 states, but it has also penetrated other parts of India. Thus, *Dainik Bhaskar* and *Dainik Jagran*, the two leading Hindi newspapers, have editions in 12 and 11 states, respectively, showing their presence beyond the 8 predominantly Hindi-speaking states. The sheer number of people who can speak Hindi or its sub-groupings form 41 per cent of India's population (Census of India, 2001b). It can, therefore, be argued that the Hindi news media has the power to influence other media such as the vernacular language press in Bangla, Odiya and Malayalam languages, though they may not change the opinions of editors or a reading public in those states. Hindi has assumed greater significance under the current Bharatiya Janata Party (BJP) government, which is trying aggressively to promote Hindi as the only national language, although this attempt has met with criticism from various quarters. This attempt by the BJP has a parallel in the colonial past and the early decades after independence when Hindi nationalists tried to impose Hindi as the national language, but met with severe criticism – a topic discussed in Chapters 2 and 3. Google has already launched the Indian Language Internet Alliance (ILIA), which aims at promoting Indian languages on the web. Further, the recent initiative by Google for tie-ups with smartphone producers in India to install Hindi keyboards on their devices shows the growing market offered by the Hindi language and its potential in mobilising people in the Hindi heartland and beyond.[4]

Despite the growing significance of Hindi in Indian politics and the massive growth of the Hindi news media, there is a dearth of systematic research on the relationship between the news media and politics within the larger context of democratic consolidation in India. With the exception of studies by Kumar (2011) and Rajagopal (2001), most studies of Indian politics have either ignored the political role of the media or viewed the media as an insignificant actor

---

4   Mobile phone producers realised the potential of growing markets in Hindi and other Indian langauges way back in the early 2000s, yet they had difficulties in getting the Indian language scripts installed because of lack of standardisation in Indian languages (Gupta, 2006; Gupta and Sornlertlamvanich, 2007).

while explaining political and social transformations in India. India's political scientists, on the other hand, have paid great attention to the study of state institutions such as political parties and the party system (Chhibber, Jensensius and Suryanarayan, 2014; DeSouza and Sreedharan, 2006; Hasan, 2004; Thatchil, 2014; Ziegfeld, 2012) and non-state institutions, such as caste, religious and community mobilisations (Chandra, 2004; Jaffrelot, 2002, 2010; Jaffrelot and Kumar, 2009; Varshney, 2000). By making media a lead player in democratic politics, this book unravels the linkages between media and politics in Indian democracy. This line of argument is consistent with the existing studies in the context of the US and Europe, where political scientists have devoted enough attention to unravel the political role of the media and its interactions with other institutions within the political system.[5]

In an interesting study on the formation of a new state of Uttarakhand, Kumar (2011) has shown how newspapers can mobilise people and could prove an effective channel in the absence of proper institutional means to communicate with the state. In this book, I examine the role of Hindi newspapers in providing a voice to the marginalised groups such as people living in rural areas and small towns, women and farmers to raise their demands in the political arena and helping them participate in the public arena. The growing political participation of the marginalised groups through the electoral process can be seen at the national level, which has been termed the 'second democratic upsurge' by Yadav (2000). I argue that Hindi newspapers have helped create a new space in which marginalised groups can participate at the local level, and are triggering social and political transformations in local society while also connecting localities with regional, national and global spheres.

This study is located in the larger context of mobilisation and political awakening that is growing at the grassroots level in India, and at an important juncture in the evolution of the Indian state when the Indian economy is increasingly driven by a private sector orientation after the economy began to open up after the financial crisis in 1991. Critics have questioned whether the neo-liberal measures have really helped improve life chances for the

---

5 Adopting an institutionalist approach, Cook (1998) argues that the media exerts institutional political power and constitute an unified institution. Similarly, Sparrow (1999) argues that the media constitutes an institutional actor within the US political system. Taking this agenda further, David Ryfe (2006) edited a special issue in the journal, *Political Communication* titled 'New Institutionalism and the News', inviting both Timothy Cook and Bartholomew Sparrow to reflect on institutionalist approach in the light of new development including the arrival of new media leading to fragmentation in the media system.

marginalised through betterment of education, health and job opportunities (Ahmed, Kundu and Peet, 2011). This is where the rise of the vernacular media, which started to discuss local issues, politics and society of its own local public, assumes significance, since media plays both an important and a critical role in evaluating the day-to-day functioning of the state and society. There have also been growing debates about the increasing influence of markets and governments in the functioning of the media. Several studies have analysed the ramifications of the corporatisation of the media and ownership concentration for democracy. Along with the increasing commercialisation of media in India, there is a cosy relationship between the government, the media and corporations, as well as the issue of opaque media ownership (Chakravartty and Rao, 2013). The phenomena of paid news, where media outlets produce content on behalf of politicians, celebrities and companies for payment that is passed off as news and not advertising, is a serious challenge that questions the independence of Indian media from external influence.

The instrumentalisation of media, where proprietors use media to advance their political and business interests outside of publishing instead of serving the public, is a major concern in the current context.[6] In some instances, enterpreneurs invest surplus capital from dubious and illegal sources, often real estate or private education, into media businesses in the hope of seeking political influence (Bhushan, 2015; Chakravartty and Roy, 2013). Despite making financial losses, the media business offers disproportionate political gains and, hence, the media business cannot be understood solely in terms of profits and losses on the books or the way conventional businesses operate. The political elites, by using their power and political muscle, have inhibited news diversity and undermined the potential of the media to offer diverse perspectives on issues. The political economy of the media and convoluted media ownership is thus more complex in the Indian context than in other nations.

The issue of media trials, where the media passes judgement on a case instead of simply reporting it, is another inherent danger particularly after the rise of 24×7 news channels. The news media sometimes influence outcomes in the justice system. The credit must go to the news media for their relentless campaign that forced justice to be given to Priyadarshini Matto's family seven years after she was raped and murdered. Similarly, it was intense media pressure

---

6 . Media capture is another expression used to explain the influence of politics and business on mass media, which I explain in Chapter 5. (For a discussion, see Mancini, 2012).

that resulted in a life sentence for Manu Sharma after he was acquitted by the lower court in the Jessica Lal murder case in 2006. Yet, trial by media cannot be defended since it undermines the authority of other institutions in the country.

In the remainder of this introductory chapter, I discuss the conceptual framework and theoretical debates related to the media and democratic political mobilisation in India. I then analyse the growth and spread of the Hindi news media and its relationship with politics. Finally, I discuss the overall transformation in the media environment and its implications for political mobilisation in India and provide a chapter outline of the book.

Political participation, media and democracy

The media plays a vital role in mobilising citizens for political participation, which is an important act of democratic citizenship and takes places both within institutional frameworks and the social norms of a country that evolve over a nation's long history and collective experience. During the evolution of a nation, certain forms of political behaviour become acceptable while other forms of behaviour are deemed unacceptable. Yet, the norms that determine the boundaries between acceptable and unacceptable political behaviour are not uniform and vary across time and nation. Studies of political participation that emerged in the post-war era were mainly concerned with the institutions of electoral democracy such as voting, party membership, or contacting a politician in advanced economies (Almond and Verba, 1963; Verba and Nie, 1972). Over the years, there has been a decline in electoral participation in these countries and a rise in non-institutionalised and extra-representative modes of participation (Hay, 2007), with people increasingly participating in social movements (della Porta, 2012), life politics and lifestyle politics (Bennett, 1998; Giddens, 1991), political consumerism (Micheletti, 2003) and postmodern politics (Inglehart, 1997). In India there has been a simultaneous rise in representative modes of participation, particularly voting, as well as non-institutionalised and extra-representative modes of participation in the form of social protest. For example, the 2014 national elections saw a record turnout of 66.4 per cent following unprecedented protest movements, including the 2011 anti-corruption movement led by Anna Hazare, national protests against the 2012 Delhi gang rape and violence against women and girls, and the 2012 anti-nuclear protests in Tamil Nadu.

Many scholars writing on Indian politics agree that there has been the consolidation of the process of democratisation over the years. Studies have focused on institutions (Kohli, 1990; Kothari, 1964, 1974; Weiner, 1989), changing voting behaviour and political participation (Frankel, 2000; Hasan, 2000; Jaffrelot, 2002; Jaffrelot and Kumar, 2009; Yadav, 1996, 2000), and how the political culture has been influenced by democratic institutions (Rudolph and Rudolph, 1987; Varshney, 2000). The process of democratic consolidation in India, unlike the experiences of Western democracies, has taken place despite the low levels of economic development, illiteracy and social divisions. In contrast to the experience of neighbouring countries in the South Asian region that have experienced authoritarian rule and military dictatorship, India has remained a successful democracy, except for a brief interlude of authoritarian rule from 1975 to 1977 that was based on ostensibly constitutional grounds and was not a military coup.

The democratic experience of India undermines conventional theories of democratisation that emphasise modernisation (Lipset, 1960), homogeneity and economic development (Barro, 1996; Dahl, 1982; Huntington, 1991; Lipset, Seong and Torres, 1993; Londregan and Poole, 1996; Mill, [1861] 1958; Przeworski *et al.*, 1996), and civil society (Diamond, 1993). The highly celebrated paradigm of modernisation theory argues that democratisation follows industrialisation. India is a classic example of a country in which democracy has not only survived but has also been consolidated with the entry of marginalised sections of society, who, in conventional theories of democratisation, were considered to be ill-equipped for adjusting to democratic functioning. India's recent economic growth also disproves the commonly held belief that was established through the experiences of East Asian countries that authoritarian regimes are needed in order to achieve rapid growth.

It must be noted that most studies of India's democratic transformation are largely concerned with the electoral politics of marginalised groups and have not paid attention to the interactions between the media and politics in the ongoing democratic consolidation. In this book, I aim to extend the definition of political participation beyond the sphere of acts intended only to influence state-related outcomes. By doing so, this study treats media as an important actor along with other actors such as political parties, pressure groups, civil society and others in the democratic transformation of India.

I argue that the Hindi media, by acting as mobilising agents, has played a key role in the process of democratic consolidation in India. The structural constraints of the English media in terms of its association with mainly the urban and English-educated sections of society restricted its domain of influence, as it could not play an effective role in the grassroots mobilisation that started in the 1980s. It was the rise of vernacular and Hindi media that facilitated grassroots mobilisation and contributed to the consolidation of the process of democratisation. The importance of the vernacular press in democratisation was also recognised by the Second Press Commission Report of 1982, which states: 'It is the Press in Indian languages, more than the English language Press, that can help in democratising communication' (21). The rise of vernacular political elites in northern India, who were leading subaltern politics, proved instrumental in the increasing role of the Hindi media in regional and national politics. The fragmentation of Indian politics in the 1980s, which saw the rise of regional political parties, has gone in parallel with the rise of the regional press. In north India, the Hindi media provided a platform to emerging political leaders to raise their voice in the public arena. In a study of Kerala, Jeffrey (2009) argues that mass mobilisation resulted in the rise of newspaper circulation. It is hard to situate the study of democratic upsurge and political mobilisation in north India since the 1980s without analysing the role of the media, especially the Hindi media, as a causal factor in mobilising people at the grassroots level. The opening up of the economy in 1991 also saw the arrival of satellite and privately-owned television networks. From just one state-controlled channel in 1990, television channels started multiplying in the 1990s and by the end of 2000, there were nearly 126 channels. Today, India has more than 900 channels, of which more than 300 channels broadcast news in 15 Indian languages.[7]

Several analysts were apprehensive that the advent of privately-operated cable and satellite (C&S) news channels would spell the death of newspapers. However, newspapers have adapted to technological innovations by changing their content, layout and design, and repositioned themselves as a vital medium of communication. The dramatic rise of Hindi newspapers has taken place in the context of the growing ascendancy of electronic media. By localising their content and bringing out regional, district and local editions, Hindi newspapers have been able to create new constituencies of readership and retained their share in advertising revenue in the face of growing competition from the electronic media.

---

7   Looking at the dramatic rise of television channels since 1991, Bajpai (2016) argues that since the time television was introduced into India in 1959, there was only one national channel for over 30 years. 25 years later, we only have 24X7 television. For a critique of television news channels with particular focus on NDTV, please see Kagal (2016).

Hindi media and mobilisation

The relationship between the media and mobilisation has to be understood within the existing political environment, as it has direct repercussions on the ways media carves out its domain of operation. Political actors often try to get positive coverage in the media because it could win supporters and bring political dividends. The media also has its own agendas, which are driven by multiple interests including political gains and profit maximisation. The Indian media system is not internally homogenous and there are vast diversities between the English language and Indian language media, national and local media, and print and broadcast media. How do we understand the political role of media in such a highly diverse system? Is it possible to mobilise people when they are exposed to diverse media and different sources of information?

The unprecedented growth of Indian language newspapers in general and Hindi newspapers in particular since the 1980s went in parallel with the greater mobilisation of the masses in north India. There was not only an increase in voter turnout, but also a simultaneous increase in political mobilisation that saw the participation of diverse groups in the non-party political process and the dramatic growth of local newspapers. Many factors beyond these are likely having an impact on political participation. My research problematises the role of the media in precipitating political participation through the concept of a hybrid media system as developed by Chadwick (2013), which looks at the relationship between media and non-media actors in any political event. Thus, we cannot understand the spectacular performance of the BJP in the 2014 national elections without understanding the contribution of the anti-corruption movement led by Anna Hazare that actually created wide discontent against the then Congress party led United Progressive Alliance (UPA) government in power in particular and against the political class in general and created a space for the rise of an alternative politics. It is in this context that the birth of the Aam Aadmi Party (AAP), which emerged from the anti-corruption movement, took place and performed extraordinarily in the 2013 Delhi assembly election. When the AAP failed to meet the expectations of the people, it further strengthened the non-Congress alternative, that is, the BJP.

To better appreciate the rise of Hindi newspapers and their relationship with politics, it is important to analyse the turbulent decades of the 1980s and the early 1990s that saw the rise of two important movements in the north India 'heartland' and changed the overall course of Indian politics: the Ram

Janmabhumi–Babri mosque controversy, popularly known as the Ayodhya movement, which eventually helped the right-wing 'Hindutva' forces gain national significance, and 'Mandal' politics that allowed marginalised groups, especially the lower castes, to assert their rights in the political and public arena.

These two important movements were preceded by the farmers' mobilisation, which politicised agricultural issues (Varshney, 1998). The politicisation of the farmers' issue in the late 1970s also helped the Hindi newspapers. Despite constituting nearly 70 per cent of the Indian population, the farmers' issue remained at the margin of political discourse in the post-independent India.[8] Chaudhary Charan Singh, who became deputy Prime Minister in the Morarji Desai-led Janata Party in 1977, played an important role in the mobilisation of farmers. The debates between rural and urban or India versus Bharat received renewed attention and changed the discourse in Indian politics. The Bharatiya Kisan Union (BKU) farmers' movement led by Mahendra Singh Tikait brought to prominence the issue of farmers including deteriorating agriculture-industry terms of trade and disparities between rural and urban standard of livings (Gupta, A., 1998; Hasan, 1995; Jeffrey, 2002). In the wake of economic reforms in the 1980s and more prominently after 1991, the agricultural issues was further politicised and resulted in the mobilisation of farmers in rural areas. The mobilisation occurred because the Indian state began withdrawing subsidies and reducing farm loans.[9] This also helped Hindi newspapers increase their influence and political importance since they have presence in small towns and rural areas, while English newspapers mostly have an urban base. Interestingly, despite sharing common concerns, Indian farmers have never been a cohesive force and remained divided across caste, religion, ethnic and linguistic identities. The rise of Mandal politics and the Ayodhya movement in the late 1980s and early 1990s sidelined agricultural issues, which also shows how dominant these two movements were in national politics.

The Ayodhya movement is arguably the most important political event of independent India. According to the Hindu holy epic, the *Ramayana*, Lord Ram was born in Ayodhya. Supporters of the Ayodhya movement allege that the first Mughal emperor Babar built the Babri Mosque by destroying the

---

8   Despite numerous strength, the Indian farmers do not consitute an homogenous group and they are divided along regional, linguistic and caste identities, which have prevented them from organising around farmers' issues.

9   A detailed analysis is provided in Chapter 5.

existing temple in 1528 and they demanded that the temple be rebuilt at the original site. The Ayodhya movement to rebuild the temple gained momentum in the late 1980s and early 1990s, which eventually led to the destruction of the Babri Mosque on 6 December 1992. Research demonstrates that when the Ayodhya movement accelerated in the 1980s, the Hindi press played a leading role by misreporting the events, which resulted in the rising circulation of Hindi newspapers.[10] During the same period, another important political controversy, popularly known as the Mandal movement, emerged in the north India. This movement was a result of a controversial decision of the V. P. Singh-led coalition government that tried to implement a 27 per cent reservation in government sectors in 1989 for people belonging to Other Backward Classes (OBCs). The recommendation for reservation came from the Mandal Commission that was set up in 1978 by the Janata Party-led government to identify socially and educationally backward caste and class groups to consider quotas and reservation of seats for them in government sectors.[11] But the BJP and the Congress party were against the implementation of the Mandal Commission Report. The protest against the implementation of the recommendations by upper caste groups drew wide attention after a Delhi University student Rajiv Goswami attempted self-immolation on 19 September 1990. This incident of self-immolation inspired other students to try similar example. There were widespread protests by upper caste groups across northern India leading to disturbance of public services and violent demonstrations, killing more than 50 people (Guha, 2008). The Hindi media, while reporting the event, were divided in their editorial stand. Many Hindi newspapers in their editorial opposed the Mandal reservations for backward castes in the name of supporting merits. But the newspaper like *Jansatta*, a Delhi-based Hindi daily, supported the Mandal reservations for backward castes (for details see Ninan, 2007).[12] These two movements, originating in the Hindi heartland, dominated national politics for more than a decade.

The emergence of the Ayodhya movement in the late 1980s had already cast

---

10 For a detailed study of the leading role of Hindi newspapers in the controversy, see Engineer (1991); Hasan (1998); Nandy, Trivedy, Mayaram and Yagnik (1995); Rajagopal (2001).

11 By the time the Mandal Commission submitted its report, the Janata Party-led government had fallen. The Congress governments that followed tried to give it a quiet burial. The recommendation resurfaced after a National Front government came to power in 1989. For details see, Guha (2008); also Jaffrelot (2002); and Shah (2013).

12 Ironically, the *Indian Express*, a leading English daily and a sister publication of *Jansatta*, urged the people in its editorial to protest against the Mandal reservations.

doubt on the claim of the English press as 'national' that could speak on behalf of the 'nation' (Rajagopal, 2001). It was the Hindi press that was spearheading the movement and the English press was largely responding to what was being reported by the Hindi press. This shows that the growth of Hindi newspapers was accompanied by major social and political upheavals in Indian society. On one hand, there were significant transformations in the form of growing literacy, improved transportation and an information and communications revolution. On the other hand, Indian society was witnessing the grassroots mobilisation and the rise of identity politics based on caste and religion. The increasing circulation of newspapers was partly driven by the rise in literacy. The information and communications revolution, in addition to improved road transportation, not only facilitated the diffusion of production and distribution centres but also ensured that newspapers are delivered to readers even in remote places early in the morning. Importantly, mounting political mobilisation outside the institutionalised arena spurred desires among the masses to orient themselves with the ongoing development. This is where newspapers played an important role not only in providing information, but also in mobilising them for or against the ongoing political developments in the country. All these developments directly or indirectly facilitated the growth and expansion of Hindi newspapers.

However, the rise of Hindi newspapers has not been unanimously welcomed by Indian scholars. Many scholars view it along with the rise of communal and identity politics in India as responsible for creating 'split public' – split between communal and secular, progressive and reactionary, orthodox and modern public – and hence, doubted its role as a vehicle of democratisation.[13] We cannot overlook the role of the Hindi press in the Ayodhya movement that resulted in the rise of Hindutva politics and the BJP. From just two seats in Parliament in 1984, the BJP went on to win 85 seats in 1989 and 120 seats in 1991. At the same time, we cannot ignore the ways in which lower caste and class mobilisation led to a major political transformation in the Hindi heartland, particularly in Uttar Pradesh and Bihar, which led to the emergence of lower caste political parties. Yet, the two other Hindi-speaking states of Madhya Pradesh and Rajasthan didn't witness major changes in the social base of political

---

13 Rajagopal (2001) has used the term 'split public' to describe the division between an elite that read the English language press and a substantial but different public that read the Hindi language press. For a detailed analysis of how Hindi newspapers played a dubious role in polarising society during the Ramjanmabhumi controversy, see Engineer (1990, 1991) and Nandy *et al.* (1995).

power, and state politics was still dominated by national political parties such as the Congress and the BJP. A puzzle for students of comparative politics and comparative media studies is why political mobilisation of lower castes and groups was successful in Uttar Pradesh and Bihar but not in Madhya Pradesh and Rajasthan. At the same time, we must note that the rise of the Hindi media after the 1990s has been facilitated by several factors other than epochal events such as the Ayodhya and Mandal Movements of the late 1980s and early 1990s. The growth of Hindi newspapers has provided an alternative platform of participation to those who have been overlooked by English newspapers, a subject discussed in detail in Chapter 4.

Changing media, changing India

The decade of the 1980s also saw the growth of television which coincided with the rapid growth of newspapers. This simultaneous growth is in contrast to the experience of developed nations where the growth of television precipitated the decline of newspapers.[14] Much has already been written about how television changed the mediascape in India and created new ways of carrying out cultural politics.[15] During the 1990s, television spread rapidly, reaching most rural villages and low-income households. India in the 1990s became a television society, which is evident from the penetration of television into the hinterland and the total number of households owning a television. From just 3.6 million television households in 1984, it increased to 30.8 million in 1991, 57.7 million in 1996 and reached 79 million by 2001 (Table 1.1). In 2015, there was a total of 167 million television households.

---

14 In the US, the household penetration (average daily circulation as a percentage of households) of newspapers peaked early in the 1920s at 130. But by 2001, newspaper household penetration was down to 54 per cent. For details, see Meyer (2004, 5). The decline may not be directly related to the growth of television, but is affected by other factors such as the emergence of new media.

15 For example, Mankekar (1999) and Rajagopal (2001). While these two works provide an authoritative account of the rise of Indian television and its manifestation in national politics and culture, they were written without taking into account the advent of satellite channels. Ninan (1995); Page and Crawley (2001); and Butcher (2003) deal with satellite channels, but were written much before the rise of 24-hour news channels. In another study, Shanti Kumar (2005) analyses how the arrival of satellite and cable television has transformed the cultural imaginations of national identity. However, his study also overlooks the rise of 24-hour news channels. In an earlier study, Kirk Johnson (2000) has explored how the arrival of television changed social relations in an Indian village.

Table 1.1: Penetration of television in India, 1984–2015 (in million)

Year	Total no. of TV homes	C&S homes
1984	3.6	NA
1989	22.5	NA
1991	30.8	NA
1996	57.7	18
2001	79	40
2006	112	68
2011	142	126
2015	167	161

Source: Cited in Vanita Kohli (2006, 62). Figures for 2011 and 2015 are from TAM Media Research (2016).

Note: C&S = Cable and Satellite.

The decade of the 1990s also witnessed major transformations in Indian society and politics. After the liberalisation of the economy in 1991, private satellite channels began entering the Indian market. The first phase of expansion of satellite channels started with the entry of Cable News Network (CNN) into India during the Gulf War of 1991 and lasted until 1998. During this period, the growth was mostly witnessed in the entertainment sector with programming largely in English and, thus, mainly accessed by the English-speaking urban middle and upper middle class. With the exception of *Zee TV*, most foreign satellite channels broadcast programmes in English. But soon they realised that the potential and real market lay in the local language market. In the second phase of expansion of satellite channels beginning in 1998, there was an efflorescence of news and current affairs channels. It was the success of *Zee TV* that persuaded *Star TV* and *Sony TV* to localise their content by producing programmes in the vernacular that targeted the Indian middle class.

Map 1.3: Television households map of India

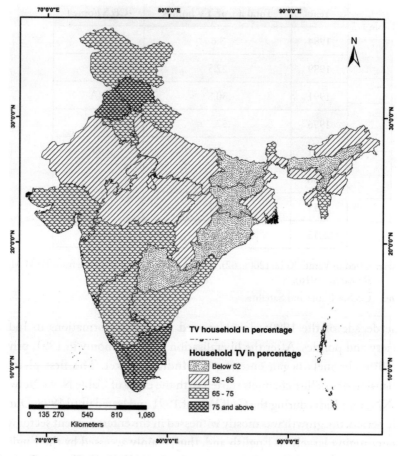

Source: Census of India. 2011b. *Houses, Household Amenities and Assets–2011.*

Note: Most of the Hindi speaking states have TV households below national average of
47.2 per cent.

Until the end of the 1990s, the 24X7 news channels were in English, with
the exception of Zee News, which was in Hindi. With the successful launch
of *Aaj Tak*, a 24-hour Hindi news channel, in December 2000, media circles
realised the potential of the Hindi news market which had been considered less
lucrative. The Hindi news media market underwent a massive transformation,
with the launch of as many as nineteen 24X7 Hindi news channels within a
span of seven years (Table 1.2; also, Mehta, 2008). The total number of Hindi
news channels mushroomed to 22 in 2005, which went up to 66 by 2016, as

shown in Table 1.2, more than in any other country. In comparison, only 26 English news channels were launched during this period.

Table 1.2: Number of 24X7 Hindi and English news channels launched, 2000–16

Year	No. of Hindi news channels	No. of English news channels
2016	2	0
2015	1	0
2014	3	2
2013	2	1
2012	2	0
2011	5	3
2010	3	1
2009	9	1
2008	7	4
2007	8	3
2006	3	2
2005	5	2
2004	6	3
2003	4	2
2002	2	1
2001	4	1
2000	1	0
Total	**66**	**26**

Source: Ministry of Information and Broadcasting (2016). Government of India, New Delhi and Mehta (2008).

In the twenty-first century, the media landscape was further transformed and democratised with the arrival of new communication and digital technology, such as the internet and mobile phones. By taking advantage of these new technologies, the vernacular population has begun to use them to mobilise public opinion; this is discussed further in Chapter 6. The tremendous growth of mobile phones along with the decline in mobile tariffs and handset prices since the mid-2000s opened up another opportunity to use technology to mobilise public opinion. The latest data released by the Telecom Regulatory Authority of India (TRAI) in July 2016 shows that the number of mobile phone subscribers has increased to 1033.16 million, which is nearly 79.9 per cent of India's total population as estimated in 2016.[16] Similarly, the internet has been growing rapidly particularly since 2011. It took over a decade for the internet to reach the figure of 100 million. However, the next over 300 million internet users have been added just within a period of five years (See Figure 1.1). In this context of the simultaneous growth of different media, the concept of a hybrid media system in which political life is mediated through a web of networked actions involving offline and online communication as well as grassroots activism becomes relevant. The evolving hybrid media environment in India has not only enabled its public and citizens to participate in a web of networks with the outside world, but also opened up new opportunities to mobilise public opinion, a topic discussed in detail in Chapters 6 and 7.

Figure 1.2: Growth of the internet users in India, 2007–16

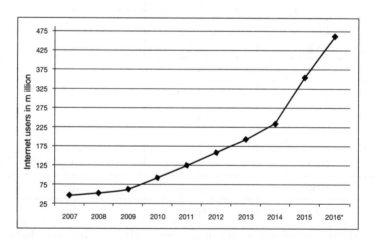

Source: Internet Live Statistic (2016).

Note: *Estimate for July 2016.

---

16   India's total population in 2016 stands at 1293.057 million, as estimated by International Monetary Fund (IMF, 2015). According to TRAI (2016), out of 1033.16 million subscribers base, the total active subscribers were 932.51 million as of May 2016. Although TRAI claims that active mobile penetration has reached 72.10 per cent of the total population based on actual and active subscribers, we need to treat this figure with caution, since a number of individuals have multiple subscriptions.

At the same time, the rise of the media and the emergence of new politics have not helped all groups equally and there are people who continue to remain at the margins of development. The process of development also requires offering land to private capital. The poor and marginalised have been displaced by private capital in the neo-liberal state that has made development its prime objective. At the same time, a wide range of inequalities between rural and urban areas remain as well as inter- and intra-state differences on various development indicators such as literacy, poverty, urbanisation and the availability of mass media, which have affected the process of political communication. The critical question here is to analyse whether the marginalised voices are getting adequate space in the emerging media environments.

Plan of the book

In a developing country, what role does the media play in mobilising political awareness? In a country where a large proportion of the population speaks Hindi, what role does the Hindi language media play in this sphere? How are print, television and the internet facilitating social and political mobilisation? Are these three media working in isolation or do they complement one another? To answer these questions, the book draws upon data from fieldwork, a content analysis of the Hindi news media, policy documents and historical texts as well as public opinion data. The data for the book was collected over many years during my fieldwork in Madhya Pradesh and Delhi in September–December 2006 and again from December 2007 to January 2008. I conducted two more field studies in September 2011 and December 2012 to January 2013, and conducted several personal interviews with journalists and politicians. Most of the interviews were conducted in Hindi, which were later translated by myself. My analysis of anti-corruption movement led by Anna Hazare uses data from newspapers and social media and my fieldwork to understand the nature of the emerging hybrid media system in India and its potential for mobilisation in the future. And while discussing the 2014 Lok Sabha campaigns I use a content analysis of newspaper and television news along with media-focused survey data on the campaign. The combination of archival, content analysis, interviews and opinion survey provides a more comprehensive understanding of the role of media in mobilisation, which might not be possible by depending on just one method.

In Chapter 2, 'Under Colonial Rule: Mobilisation in the Hindi and English Press,' I discuss the ways in which Hindi and English news media framed colonial rule and helped mobilise public opinion. The press in India played an important role in framing the freedom struggle, not least because of the larger context of the debate between the Hindi and the English press on the issue of colonial rule. By aligning themselves with the freedom struggle against the British, Hindi newspapers were able to establish themselves as a significant vehicle for political communication during the colonial period. They stood in contrast to newspapers owned by the British and Anglo-Indians in the way they framed the freedom struggle versus the colonial rule. However, Hindi newspapers were unable to contest the overall dominance of English newspapers because of the association of English with the language of modernity and moderns, which informed the subsequent development of Hindi and English newspapers in independent India.

Chapter 3, 'Media and Mobilisation in Independent India,' analyses the role of the Hindi news media in political mobilisation in independent India. The English media, which was mainly confined to the urban and English-educated sections of society, could not play an effective role in the grassroots mobilisation that started in the 1980s. It was the resurgence of Hindi newspapers in the 1980s that challenged the dominance of English newspapers in the social, cultural and political, if not economic, spheres in independent India. Such an assertion became possible because of important social, political and economic transformations during the 1980s and 1990s in which Hindi newspapers seized the opportunity and seriously challenged the continuing dominance of English newspapers. The rise of vernacular political leaders in northern India who were spearheading plebeian politics proved instrumental in increasing the role of the Hindi media in regional and national politics. The Hindi media provided a platform for the emerging political leaders of north India to raise their voice in the public arena that further contributed to the consolidation of Indian democracy. The chapter draws on data on voter turnout in the Hindi belt and newspaper circulation to analyse the relationship between formal politics and the media. At the same time, the chapter explores the reasons for the subservient position of Hindi media in comparison to the English media following independence and how the Hindi media started to assert its rightful place in the changing political environment from the 1980s.

In Chapter 4, titled 'Localisation, Grassroots Mobilisation and Hindi News Media,' I focus on 'micro politics' by analysing the process of localisation and how it has affected grassroots democracy. The process of localisation started by Hindi newspapers involved decentralising production, distribution and consumption. Localisation helped Indian language newspapers retain their advertising revenue in the face of competition from television news channels and new media. Until the 1970s, Hindi newspapers were produced just like English newspapers, mainly from urban centres where most of the English readers lived. It took more than three decades for Hindi proprietors to go looking for readers in the smaller towns and rural areas. Hindi newspapers started to localise in the 1980s, which was greatly facilitated by new technology. Localisation not only provided appealing, customised news to local societies, but also helped Hindi newspapers highlight the concerns of a vast number of heterogeneous Hindi-speaking public in the public arena. Localisation has also helped in mobilising beyond the locality, particularly after the arrival of the internet. The empirical evidence from my fieldwork reflects the simultaneous trivialisation and sensationalisation of news, as well as a concern for marginalised groups, which is seen in the focus on the politics of the livelihood of its own local public. This hybrid character of localisation mediated by Hindi newspapers is examined in this chapter.

In Chapter 5 titled 'Political Economy of the Hindi Press,' I analyse the political economy of the Hindi press with a focus on advertising and ownership. The rise of Hindi newspapers is linked to the rise of new social classes within previously marginalised sections of society. The chapter shows how economic liberalisation in India that made the private sector an important player in the Indian economy led to the rise of advertising markets that made the middle class the nucleus of its growth. There was the rise in consumerism along with the expansion of Hindi newspapers driven by growing advertising revenues from small towns and rural pockets. Contrary to the pattern of large English newspapers often owned by big business houses having other business interests, Hindi newspapers have been owned largely by those having primary interests in the Hindi media business who then went on to diversify their business by venturing into non-media business. In this chapter, I also discuss the issue of paid news in which many news media were found to be involved and how this has posed a challenge to the credibility of the media as the fourth estate.

In Chapter 6, 'The Hybrid Media System, Anti-corruption Movement and Political Mobilisation,' I examine the interface and connection between traditional and new media, which has been termed a hybrid media system (Chadwick, 2013) and show how this is opening up new avenues to conduct the business of politics. Through a case study of the agitation launched by the Indian social activist Anna Hazare over the issue of the Jan Lokpal Bill that seeks to combat corruption, this chapter analyses the role of the Hindi and English media as well as social media in highlighting the issue of corruption. The chapter demonstrates the changed tactics of protest movements in the post-broadcast era, in which activists and protestors have extensively used the internet and mobile phones to realise shared grievances, mobilise support against injustice and change state–society relations. The emergence of a hybrid media system offers both opportunities to social movements to mobilise public opinion rapidly ('virality') as well as involves the danger of disappearing equally rapidly ('ephemerality'). This virality and ephemerality might, in the process, help the movements or vested interests achieve their goal.

In Chapter 7 titled 'Agenda-setting and Mobilisation in a Hybrid Media Environment,' I examine the hybrid logics involved in Narendra Modi's election campaign that creatively combined the logic of older and newer media and integrated it with traditional campaigns that use grassroots mobilisation, rallies and volunteer activism both within and outside India. The 2014 election campaign was not just about Narendra Modi, but about a new era in political communication practices in India where professional campaign managers, journalists, volunteer activists, entertainment media and ordinary citizens together played an important role. In this chapter, I use post-election survey data from Delhi and a content analysis of media data to discuss the processes of influence and political communication in the 2014 national election.

In the concluding chapter, 'Conclusion: Politics, Power and Mobilisation in Digital India,' I discuss the future of political mobilisation in India in the context of the continued growth of digital media and the current government's ambitious plan of connecting the whole country with digital networks by 2019. The chapter summarises the key findings from themes addressed in the preceding chapters and raises current issues for public policy and political mobilisation. Power in digital India will be exercised by those who are successfully able to steer the flow of information in their favour. It would, however, be difficult to control the flow of information because of the emergence of a hybrid media system, which have seen mass participation in the creation of online content and demonstrated that political elites alone no longer constitute political events.

Rather, non-political elites will equally contribute to shaping political events, which has transformed power relationships in news production, and steered the information flow. The case of WikiLeaks is a clear rupture in the evolution of news making and political mobilisation and shows how digital technologies can enable even a small group of individuals to wield substantial organisational power. The concluding chapter discusses how the rise of digital media can alter power relationships and the future of political mobilisation in India.

2

Under Colonial Rule
Mobilisation in the Hindi and English Press

The press in India played an important role in framing the freedom struggle, not least because of the larger context of the debate between the Hindi and the English press on the issue of colonial rule. Hindi newspapers, which were mainly owned by Indians, stood in contrast to the newspapers owned by the British and Anglo-Indians in the way they framed the freedom struggle versus colonial rule. By aligning themselves with the freedom struggle against the British, Hindi newspapers were able to establish themselves as a significant vehicle for political communication during the colonial period. Yet, Hindi newspapers remained concerned with social and religious issues until the establishment of the Indian National Congress in 1885. Hindi newspapers were unable to contest the overall dominance of English newspapers because of the association of English as the language of modernity, which informed the subsequent development of Hindi and English newspapers in independent India. This chapter analyses the ways in which Hindi, other vernacular press and English newspapers framed colonial rule and helped mobilise public opinion.

Despite being region specific, the reach of the vernacular press was much greater than the percentage of the literate population due to the tradition of public reading of these newspapers on the street. These public readings contributed towards educating and mobilising the non-literate masses. In this manner, 'much propaganda first appearing in print was passed on orally' (Pandey, 1975, 207).[1] The interactions between print and orality show the hybrid nature involved in mobilising public opinion that was present even during the colonial period.[2] The power of the press was not only used by

---

1 Chandra, Mukherjee, Mukherjee, Panikkar and Mahajan (1988) describe the spread of the culture of reading newspapers to village communities in early 1870s.

2 In this sense, we cannot ignore the role of social communication that was interacting with written words. Bayly (1996, 2) argues that 'the density of social communication … help to explain why political leaders in a poor country with a relatively low rate of general literacy should have been able to create widely diffused and popular nationalist movement so early'. In the hybrid nature of this mobilisation in a predominantly illiterate society, we cannot ignore the role of visuals, not only because it bridges the divide between literacy and illiteracy, but also because it helps overcome 'linguistic boundaries, and possesses sufficient ambiguity to appeal to people in various socio-economic and power positions' (Freitag, 2007, 94; also see Pinney, 2004).

the Indian National Congress, which was looking for various platforms for propaganda, but even a revolutionary like Bhagat Singh used the press for spreading nationalist sentiments.[3] Importantly, most of the national and provincial leaders in colonial India owned or were associated with newspapers which shows the importance attached to the press even in a predominantly illiterate society (Table 2.1).[4]

Table 2.1: Selected list of important nationalist leaders and their newspapers (editors/owners/founders)

Name of leader	Name of newspaper	Language	Place	Frequency	Year of establishment
Abdul Hameed Ansari	*Inquilab*	Urdu	Bombay	Daily	1937
Maulana Abul Kalam Azad	*Al-Hilal*	Urdu	Calcutta	Weekly	1912
Krishnachandra Banerjee	*Bangabasi*	Bengali	Calcutta	Weekly	1881
Surendranath Banerjee	*The Bengalee*	English	Calcutta	Daily	1879
Pandit Gopabandhu Das	*Samaj*	Oriya	Cuttak	Weekly	1919
RR Diwakar and RS Hukerikar	*Karamveer*	Kannada	Hubli	Weekly	1921
Mahatma Gandhi	*Young India*	English	Ahmedabad	Weekly	1919
	Harijan	English, Hindi Gujarati	Ahmedabad	Weekly	1932
	Navajivan	Gujarati	Ahmedabad	Weekly	1919
Sisir Kumar Ghosh	*Amrita Bazar Patrika*	Bengali/ English	Calcutta	Weekly	1868
Shiv Prasad Gupta	*Aaj*	Hindi	Benares	Daily	1920
Gopal Krishna Gokhale	*The Hitavada*	English	Nagpur	Daily	1911

---

3   Contesting the dominant narrative that the most popular 'hat photograph' of Bhagat Singh was taken by the British, Maclean (2011) argues that Bhagat Singh 'explicitly had it taken as a political tactic, before provoking the government of British India to seal his fate – to hang him by the neck until dead' (1053–54). In this sense, the portrait should be seen as a means of revolutionary propaganda, because it travelled well beyond the literate population and had a lasting impact on the political climate of the early 1930s since the portrait was included as a part of a 'sophisticated media campaign' and it subsequently morphed into an emblem of anti-imperialism.

4   In 1941, the overall literacy rate in India was 16.1 per cent. Kaul (2002) in her study shows the cause of empire was carried forward by imperial press and many editors viewed their papers as vehicles for imperial publicity.

Name of leader	Name of newspaper	Language	Place	Frequency	Year of establishment
G. Subramania Iyer	*Hindu*	English	Madras	Weekly	1878
	Swadesamitran	Tamil	Madras	Weekly	1882
Maulana Mohammad Ali Jauhar	*Hamdard*	Urdu	Delhi	Daily	1913
Maulana Mohammad Ali Jauhar	*The Comrade*	English	Calcutta	Weekly	1911
Madan Mohan Malviya	*The Leader*	English	Allahabad	Daily	1909
	Hindustan	Hindi	Delhi	Daily	1936
Ramgopal Maheshwari	*Nava Bharat*	Hindi	Nagpur	Weekly	1934
Sir Pherozeshah Mehta	*Bombay Chronicle*	English	Bombay	Daily	1910
P. Kesava Menon	*Mathrubhumi*	Malayalam	Kozhikode	Daily	1923
Jawaharlal Nehru	*National Herald*	English	Lucknow	Daily	1938
Jawaharlal Nehru/ Hayatullah Ansari	*Qaumi Awaz*	Urdu	Lucknow	Daily	1945
Motilal Nehru	*Independent*	English	Allahabad	Daily	1919
Bipan Chandra Pal	*Bande Mataram*	English	Calcutta	Daily	1905
Sri Krishna Dutt Paliwal	*Sainik*	Hindi	Agra	Daily	1916
Kasinathuni Nageswara Rao	*Andhra Patrika*	Telugu	Bombay	Weekly	1909
Raja Rampal Singh	*Hindosthan*	Hindi	Kalakankar	Daily	1885
Bal Gangadhar Tilak	*Mahratta*	English	Poona	Weekly	1881
Bal Gangadhar Tilak	*Kesari*	Marathi	Poona	Daily	1881
Ganesh Shankar Vidyarthi	*Pratap*	Hindi	Cawnpore	Weekly	1930

Note: These are only selected list of leaders and their newspapers and should not be treated as representatives list. A number of leaders listed were also associated with other newspapers. A number of newspapers began as weekly but was later transformed into dailies and many of them were short-lived.

By the end of the nineteenth century, Hindi had emerged as powerful vehicle of mass communication that had direct ramifications for the development of

Hindi newspapers. Hindi emerged as the language of emergent nationalism. However, Hindi newspapers in their initial years, especially in the first half of the nineteenth century, were largely concerned with social and religious issues such as *sati* or the burning of widows, child marriage, untouchability and education.[5] It was only later that Hindi newspapers aligned themselves with the freedom movement against the British and helped in developing national awakening. The growth of Hindi newspapers also contributed to the development of more productive interactions between the elites and the mass public, which contributed to the formation of public opinion. Yet, by no means were Hindi newspapers a homogenous entity in terms of their internal politics and ideological perspective and they held both progressive and conservative viewpoints; some of them supported Hindu right wing politics, advocated Hindu revivalism and adopted a conservative approach on the position of women in society, while others supported the cause of peasants and advocated women's participation in public life.[6]

To appreciate the trajectory taken by Hindi newspapers in independent India, we need to go back to the history of Hindi newspapers. In the late nineteenth and early twentieth centuries, political journalism in general was not meant to cater to market needs for information, but was used to serve the owner's political agenda and the press acted as political agents (Gould, 2004). The growth of the Hindi press in colonial India can be divided into three phases. In the first phase from 1854 to 1900,[7] the Hindi press was mainly concerned with social, religious and cultural issues, though the establishment of the Indian National Congress in 1885 led to some concern about colonial rule. The second phase, from 1901 until 1918, not only saw the Hindi press increase its focus on political issues along with social issues, but there was also the growth of Hindi dailies. In the final phase from 1919 until independence

---

5   There were differences within Hindi newspapers with respect to their positions on these issues. For details, see Jagannathan (1999) and Orsini (2002).

6   While Hindi newspapers continued to frame colonial rule negatively, they were divided in their stand on various issues including the protection of cows, the role of women in society and the value of English education. Several Hindi newspapers also supported Hindu revivalism and the *Shuddhi* Movement, which aimed at reconverting Hindus. For example, two important Hindi journals, *Kavi Vachan Sudha* and *Hindi Pradip*, advocated Hindu revivalism in the later period along with attacks on British education and taxation policies (Bayly, 1975). For a rich account of the diversities and complexities of Hindi journalism in relation to various social, cultural and political issues, see Orsini (2002).

7   I have started with 1854 because of the publication of first Hindi daily, *Samachar Sudhavarshan* in that year.

in 1947, Hindi newspapers overtly aligned themselves with nationalist causes and there was a mushrooming of Hindi dailies.

While examining the growth of Hindi newspapers in colonial India, I compare them with English newspapers in order to highlight the differences in the ways Hindi and English press framed colonial rule. At the same time, I touch upon the larger debates between Hindi and English languages, particularly after the rise of nationalism, and their impact on the growth of the Hindi press. Importantly, the rise of Hindi newspapers parallels the rise of the Indian National Congress and nationalism, which ultimately resulted in India attaining independence in 1947.

Mobilisation for social issues: 1854–1900

Kolkata was home to the first newspapers in the country, with a thriving weekly newspaper in the late eighteenth century. *Bengal Gazette*, an English language weekly, started by a Briton, James Augustus Hicky, on 29 January 1780, was the first newspaper in India. The first Hindi newspaper in India, *Oodunt Martand*, also a weekly, was launched on 30 May 1826 from Kolkata, nearly five decades later. The first Hindi daily, *Samachar Sudhavarshan*, was also launched in Kolkata in 1854 by Shyam Sundar Sen. This was a bilingual newspaper containing news in both Hindi and Bengali. It published market and shipping information with minimal focus on political news. *Samachar Sudhavarshan* devoted substantial space in highlighting traditional customs and carried commentaries about efforts on social reforms (Mishra, 2011). Bharatendu Harishchandra, the father of modern Hindi, started *Kavi Vachan Sudha* in 1867, which is considered an important Hindi newspaper that subsequently went on to appeal to Indians to use Indian-made products (Gopal, 1990). *Bharat Mitra* was started in 1877 as a literary journal, and was later converted into a daily that became an influential paper which went on to set the standards for Hindi journalism. Balmukand Gupta, the editor of *Bharat Mitra*, made a significant contribution, along with Mahabir Prasad Dwivedi of *Saraswati*, to Hindi journalism and to the enrichment of the Hindi language (Natarajan, 1962). Several Hindi newspapers were started in the latter half of the nineteenth century, but they did not survive for long. It was common for a newspaper to appear suddenly and then close equally suddenly. This phenomenon continued through the second half of the nineteenth century to the beginning of the twentieth century. Table 2.2 shows that there was no linear growth in the number of newspapers from 1901 to 1911; while there were 708 newspapers in 1901, it declined to 657 in 1902. Similarly, while there were 747 newspapers in 1905, the number declined to 726 in 1909. Yet another feature of Hindi newspapers and other vernacular newspapers during this period was their concentration in the capitals of presidencies and district towns that were witnessing growing political consciousness.[8]

Table 2.2: Number of newspapers in India, 1901–1910

Year	No. of newspapers
1901–02	708
1902–03	657
1903–04	709
1904–05	713
1905–06	747
1906–07	744
1907–08	753
1908–09	738
1909–10	726
1910–11	658

Source: Reed (1914). *Indian Year Book.*

Notwithstanding their unexpected growth and limited reach, Hindi journalism was growing steadily and started to make a mark in Indian journalism. A literary magazine that set the standards for Hindi journalism was *Saraswati*, which was started in 1900 from Allahabad in present-day Uttar Pradesh by Swami Shri Chintamani Ghosh (Chaturvedi, 2004). The literary style of the magazine underwent a transformation after Mahabir Prasad Dwivedi took over as editor in 1903. It standardised the style and pattern of Hindi journalism, developed literary criticism, and cultivated a style in prose and poetry that later became the torchbearer for Hindi journalism (Chaturvedi, 2004).

Another important Hindi newspaper was *Hindi Bangavasi* launched in 1890 by Pandit Amritlal Chakarvarti from Kolkata, which played a significant role

---

8 The exception was Bengal, where purely village-based newspapers appeared (see Gupta, 1977).

in the freedom struggle. Most of the important Hindi journalists of Kolkata, such as Balmukund Gupta, Baburao Vishnu Paradkar, Pandit Ambika Prasad Vajpayee and Pandit Lakshmi Narayan Gande, were associated with the paper (Jain, 2006).

In the final year of the nineteenth century, there were only 20 Hindi newspapers (Jain, 2006, 19). The lack of formidable leaders in the Hindi-speaking areas in the latter half of the nineteenth century could be attributed to the lack of political focus and the slow growth of Hindi newspapers.[9] An organised way of expressing public opinion was hardly visible before the establishment of the Indian National Congress. Barrier (1974) argues that major criticisms of the Raj in the vernacular press started to emerge only towards the end of the nineteenth century. In this context, he writes, 'although newspapers previously had launched sporadic attacks on the British, the first substantial signs of the new militancy among journalists surfaced just prior to 1900. Tilak's *Kesari* lambasted the government; for that he was prosecuted …' (9).

The Press Act of India, popularly known as the Gagging Act, promulgated soon after the Sepoy Mutiny of 1857, was aimed at both the English and Indian language press.[10] The Act also earned the wrath of European Community for not distinguishing between 'loyal British' and 'disloyal native' press (Kalpagam, 2002). This Act prohibited owning printing presses without a licence and empowered the government to prohibit the publication or circulation of any newspaper, book or other printed matter, without making any distinction between English and the Indian languages (Karkhanis, 1981). The Act, though, remained in force only for one year.[11]

It was not until the enactment of the Vernacular Press Act of 1878, which made a clear distinction between the English press and the vernacular press, that

---

9　The only important figure before the establishment of the Indian National Congress in 1885 was Pandit Madan Mohan Malviya. I show in the next chapter how the rise of important political leaders in the Hindi heartland in the 1980s helped Hindi newspapers grow rapidly. There is, thus, a close link between the growth of leadership and media.

10　The first press ordinance in India was issued in 1823 by Governor-General, John Adam, popularly known as Adam's Press Ordinance. The ordinance required that all matters printed in a press or published thereafter should be printed and published under licence from the Governor-General-in-Council signed by the Chief Secretary of the government. The press regulations were particularly directed at Rammohan Roy's *Mirat-ul-Akhbar*, a Persian newspaper. The reactions from the British could be considered the first significant threat they felt from the emerging vernacular press (For details see Rau, 1974).

11　Indian newspapers here refer to all newspapers, including English newspapers owned by Indians. By 1858, there were only 25 Indian newspapers (Chatterjee, 1929).

the distinction became codified. There were growing invectives in the Indian language newspapers as well as in English newspapers against the government after the famine, also known as the Great Famine of 1876–78 that affected south and southwestern India and resulted in an estimated death toll of 5.5 million Indians. The declaration of war in Afghanistan in 1878 (Second Anglo-Afghan War, 1878–1880) saw a sharpening of attacks against the colonial government in Indian language newspapers. While justifying the discrimination against the vernacular press, Sir Ashley Eden, Lt-Governor of Bengal, who was at the centre of controversy for the Act, argued in his speech in the Council that the English language newspapers were written 'by a class of writers for a class of readers whose education and interests would make them naturally intolerant of sedition'(quoted in Rau, 1974, 87). The Vernacular Press Act outlined more stringent control of publications and furnished the British Raj with effective measures to punish and suppress seditious writings. [12] The Act for the first time made provision for pre-publication censorship through the levying of security and forfeiture of bond (and possibly imprisonment) on those members of the press whose printed material was deemed 'objectionable' by the local officials (Ryan, 1990, 56). Yet the colonial administration was reluctant to impose heavy censorship as it would deny useful information to the government and understand public sentiment (Bayly, 1996).

It was also the fear of the vernacular newspapers and their potential in mobilising public opinion that the colonial government started weekly translation of selected articles from these newspapers. The practice of translation from vernacular press in turn reflects the role of the vernacular press in generating critical public opinion against the British government. The *Report on Native Newspapers* sometime also covered cartoons (Boyce, 1988). Although the report dates back to 1840s, it was regularised in the 1870s (Kamra, 2011). The report was used as a mechanism of political surveillance and counter-intelligence (Bayly, 1996). The regularisation of the report in the 1870s paralleled with growing influence of the vernacular newspapers reaching beyond elites of the society.

The establishment of the Indian National Congress in 1885 was an important impetus for the rise of nationalism. The first meeting of the Indian National

---

12 It was said that the Vernacular Press Act was aimed primarily at the *Amrit Bazar Patrika* brought out by Shishir Kumar Ghosh. However, Shishir Kumar Ghosh began publishing the newspaper in English instead of Bengali, even before the Act came into force (For details, see Rau, 1974).

Congress was held on 28 December 1885 in Mumbai in which representatives from different regions and presidencies were present. Baba Ganga Prasad Verma who was associated with the development of the Urdu and Hindi nationalist press in the North-Western Provinces (NWP) attended.[13] Besides, there were founders and editors of leading newspapers in the session. The presence of editors and owners of newspapers in the meeting shows not only the close linkage between media and politics during colonial times, but was also indicative of how nationalist leaders could harness newspapers and periodicals in their later campaigns to mobilise public opinion. The Indian National Congress held three meetings in NWP before 1900; the first session in 1888 and the second session in 1892 were held in Allahabad, while the third one in 1899 was held in Lucknow.[14] Several important figures from the NWP joined the Indian National Congress; notable among them were Pandit Bishan Narain Dar, Pandit Madan Mohan Malviya, Babu Ganga Prasad, and Pandit Ayodhya Nath (Bhatnagar, 1947, 2003). Pandit Madan Mohan Malviya went on to play an important role in promoting Hindi in the Devanagari script, campaigned for cow protection and came to be regarded as an important Hindu leader.[15] Malviya's most important contribution is the establishment of Banaras Hindu University (BHU). The coming into prominence of leaders from Hindi-speaking areas and the meetings of the Congress in NWP contributed to the growing focus in Hindi journalism on nationalist and political causes.[16] These developments helped Hindi newspapers enter the twentieth century with a renewed focus on political causes alongside their preoccupation with social, cultural and religious issues.

Moblisation and early nationalism: 1901–18

The formation of the Indian National Congress, a political institution in parallel with British India, heralded new thinking among Indians who started demanding democratic rights. At the start of the twentieth century, nationalism

---

13 NWP consisted of all of present-day Uttar Pradesh except for Lucknow and Faizabad. For details, see Bayly (1988).

14 For a detailed list of all Congress sessions from 1885 to the present, see the official website http://inc.in/INCSessions.aspx.

15 Pandit Madan Mohan Malviya's main interest was establishing a Hindu university in Banaras, which was realised in 1916. For this, he was dependent upon patronage from the British, the princes and Marwaris. For a detailed account, see Medha Kudaisya (2006).

16 Besides starting to highlight nationalist issues, some of the other press topics during the 1890s were the Age of Consent Bill, cow slaughter and plague rules. See Codell (2004, 115).

was still limited and could not be converted into a mass movement until the arrival of Mahatma Gandhi. Kamra (2011) argues that the rise of early nationalism, as manifested in the struggle between the Indian press and the colonial government 'is written in the formidable history of censorship laws that effectively criminalised dissent but, predictably, produced effect that were beyond the control of the government (2011, 5).' As noted, there were many censorship laws aimed at disciplining Indian newspapers. More stringent regulations were placed against the Indian press in this period of early nationalism, explained later in the chapter. There were sporadic attempts in Hindi journalism to criticise the British government, but it wasn't developed as a coherent ideology. There were a limited number of Hindi dailies at the end of the nineteenth century, which translated into limited scope for the mobilisation of public opinion among the Hindi public. This started to change in the early twentieth century with the rise of vernacular periodicals. Another interesting feature of early Hindi journalism was the presence of bilingualism, with Hindi columns printed along with Urdu or Bengali.

The consolidation of Hindi journalism resulted in a purging of the influence of other languages, particularly Urdu and Persian. *Hitvarta*, launched in Kolkata in 1903, was considered the Hindi version of the Bengali newspaper *Hitvadi*, whose editor was Kaliprassan Vishwarath (Mehta, 2006). The freedom fighter Rasaram Ganesh Deshkar became *Hitvarta's* first editor. *Hitvarta* not only fought for freedom, but it also reflected a concern for the future of the Hindi language and supported the creation of a separate identity for Hindi, which meant purging Hindi of the influence of Persian and Urdu (Chaturvedi, 2004, 119–20). Shree Deshkar, who became the second editor of *Hitvarta*, supported the Sanskritisation of Hindi by arguing that if Sanskrit words were substantially present in the Bangla and Marathi languages, then Hindi should not be devoid of Sanskrit words. The question of why Hindi should be stripped of Sanskrit words was also posed to Mahabir Prasad Dwivedi, the editor of *Saraswati*, who preferred to remain silent on the issue (Chaturvedi, 2004, 119).

Two important Hindi newspapers started from Madhya Bharat (now Madhya Pradesh) were *Chhattisgarh Mitr* and *Karamveer*. Madhavrao Sapre, a noted Hindi literary figure, launched *Chhattisgarh Mitr*, a monthly newspaper, from Bilaspur in 1900. This newspaper was considered a pioneer that set the tone for journalism in Madhya Bharat (Chaturvedi, 2004, 115–16). Similarly, *Karamveer*, started by Madhavrao Sapre from Jabalpur in 1919, had Makhanlal

Chaturvedi as its first editor. It was not only a nationalist newspaper, but it also published Hindi literary works by eminent local writers (Chaturvedi, 2004, 145–46).

Hindi newspapers were not only voicing the nationalist cause, but were also speaking for including larger sections of society in the movement, primarily peasants and women (Orsini, 2002, 319). In this, Ganesh Shankar Vidyarthi, a leader of the Indian National Congress, through his Hindi newspaper *Pratap*, played an important role in espousing the cause of peasants and became an important critic of the pre-Gandhian Congress that was aloof from the masses. Through the editorial of *Pratap*, Vidyarthi urged readers to focus on the villages (Orsini, 2002).

The growth of Hindi newspapers, along with English newspapers, was taking place within a charged political climate. Opposition to British rule was quite discernible in Hindi newspapers. However, the division between the moderates, led by Gopal Krishna Gokhale, and extremists, led by Bal Gangadhar Tilak, put Hindi and other nationalist newspapers in flux. The other important moderates included Sir Pherozeshah Mehta, Sir Dinshaw Wacha and Dadabhai Naoroji, while the extremist camp had Bipin Chandra Pal, Lala Lajpat Rai and Aurobindo Ghosh. Both groups wanted freedom but through different approaches; the moderates were in favour of dialogue and discussion with the British and adopted non-violent means, while the extremists adopted agitation including violence as their primary means to free the country. The twenty-third session of the Indian National Congress in Surat in 1907 witnessed previously unseen uproar and violence between the two groups and led to an irreconcilable division between the moderates and the extremists. The future of the freedom struggle appeared to be at stake, with nationalist newspapers being under pressure to take a stand in support of one or the other party (Barns, 1940, 324).

After the division between the moderates and extremists, Tilak continued his violent denunciations of the British through columns in *Kesari* and *Deshasewak* of Nagpur. The rising popularity of Tilak's campaign threatened the British, who passed the Newspapers (Incitement to Offences) Act VII in June 1908, which empowered the authorities to confiscate the printing press and take judicial action against the editor of any newspaper involved in incitement to murder and acts of violence (Barns, 1940).

Yet another piece of legislation known as the Indian Press Act, 1910 was even wider in scope as it not only dealt with incitement to rebellion, but identified specific content deemed to be seditious, which was defined as bringing charges of contempt against the British government or Native Prince or to intimidate public servants or private individuals (Reed, 1914). The Act also empowered the authorities to demand security from any newspaper found to publish content that was considered offensive. In short, the 1910 Indian Press Act aimed at keeping the press within limits and allowed only legitimate discussion as defined by the British authorities. According to Barns (1940), the 1910 Act was largely the result of discontent over the partition of Bengal in 1905 and the British government's fear that there would be a country-wide sedition movement as anarchic ideas were gaining ground (327).

The outbreak of World War I in 1914 made the British more anxious because they needed the support of India. India supported the British government in the hope of getting self-determination after the war. This support for the British was no means unanimous, as several leaders such as Dr Annie Besant and Bal Gangadhar Tilak showed their displeasure. The nationalist newspapers once again got a cause to support. In the wake of the emergency created by the war and to meet the challenges, the British government passed the Defence of India Act in 1914. During the war, several newspapers forfeited their security because their content was deemed seditious by the British government.

Several Hindi newspapers appeared during World War I to meet the rising demand for news. The demand for news meant that weeklies were converted into dailies. *Viswamitra* was an important newspaper that was started in 1915 by Babu Mulchand Agarwal from Kolkata. In 1941, it started being published in Mumbai and Delhi, and later from Kanpur and Patna. It was the first daily newspaper to be published simultaneously from five different locations (Jain, 2006, 104–05).

Not only the political climate but also institutional development contributed to the consolidation of Hindi journalism and helped Hindi interests to be pursued more vigorously. Hindi journalism received a further boost with the establishment of several institutions dedicated to promoting Hindi. The establishment of the Hindi Sahitya Sammelan in 1910, the Dakshin Bharat Hindi Prachar Sabha in 1918 and the Rashtra Bhasha Prachar Samiti in 1930 were important organisations, meant to promote Hindi. The establishment of academic institutions such as BHU in 1916, Kashi Vidya Peeth in 1920, Gurukal University Kangari in 1902 and Hindi Mahila Vidyalaya in 1922 helped generate intellectual activities and promote a Hindi literary sphere.

However, they proved to be inadequate to face the challenge posed by Western-inspired English language academic institutions during the colonial period. This ultimately resulted in a protest by the Hindi intelligentsia and the demand to replace English by Hindi as the medium of instruction in institutions of higher learning (Sharma, 1969).[17] These political developments with a clear ideological orientation proved instrumental in the subsequent development of Hindi journalism and its political influence.

The vernacular turn and mobilisation: 1919–47

With Mahatma Gandhi's rise to power in the Indian National Congress and the country, the mobilisation strategies of the nationalist leaders took a vernacular turn. The Indian National Congress before the rise of Gandhi functioned in English, which was indifferent to the sentiments of various linguistic groups and made it difficult to reach out to the masses. The vernacular turn saw the reorganisation of the Indian National Congress along linguistic lines. Gandhi made clear his idea that English could not be the language of the masses and the only way to reach and influence the masses was through a national language or in a mother tongue.[18] The British system of governance divided India into a number of provinces, of which the three largest were the 'Presidencies' – Bombay, Madras and Bengal. This system of administrative division was indifferent to language and the linguistic sensitivities of the people, which resulted in growing discontent among the masses whose linguistic identities were subsumed under broader arrangements. In 1920, Gandhi suggested reorganising the Indian National Congress's political machinery

---

17 King (1997) also argues that all these measures brought no change in the position of the vernaculars. University officials, both British and Indian, did not consider Urdu and Hindi worthy of inclusion in regular degree courses as subjects in their own right until 1923, and never contemplated their use as mediums of instruction (93).

18 Though other vernacular languages got support because of Gandhi's idea of organising the Indian National Congress along linguistic lines, these vernacular languages cannot be compared with Hindi. This is because the Hindi language was being projected as the only national language and was getting the support of important political leaders including Gandhi. Defending the cause of Hindi was labelled as 'cultural cause', which largely contributed to garnering the support of varied constituencies consisting of what Orsini (2002) calls 'Hindi politicians' (see also Kumar, K., 2005). What made such an alliance of political figures formidable, according to Orsini, was the fact that it consisted of three different axes. '… a political axis between right and left, and two cultural axes, one between Hindi and English, which partly overlaps with, but is also distinguished from, another axis between popular and elite' (342). Such an alliance among political figures to support the cause of Hindi continued during the postcolonial period (see Kudaisya, G., 2006).

according to language and, thus, 21 Provincial Congress Committees (PCCs) were created.[19] From then onwards the proceedings of the Indian National Congress were conducted in vernacular languages rather than in English and all publicity materials were published in the vernacular languages as well as in English. Mahatma Gandhi was confident that with the development of a national consciousness in the vernacular, English would lose its influence.

In this vernacular turn, Hindi assumed a significant position because of the support accorded to it by important nationalist leaders including Gandhi.[20] The support from Gandhi proved beneficial for Hindi journalism and the Hindi newspapers also started aligning themselves with the nationalist cause more aggressively. Under the influence of Gandhi, the All India Congress Committee in 1920 adopted Hindi as the *lingua indica* at its special session (Mishra, 1971). Gandhi was one of the main proponents of Hindi and he wanted it to be declared the national language. Though Gandhi himself was Gujarati, he lent his support to Hindi. He believed it would appeal to people from all over India and encourage them to abandon their narrow linguistic loyalties and associate themselves with the larger identity of the nation. In this context, Lelyveld (1993) argues that Gandhi's support to Hindi was not only to create linguistic autonomy and freedom from the domination of the English language, but also to create a unifying language that would bridge the diversities of region and religion and other lines of cultural and linguistic division (190). It was for this reason that Gandhi opposed Sanskritised Hindi and supported Hindustani, a blend of Hindi and Urdu, as the possible national language. He was very critical of the Indian National Congress for using English during its proceedings.[21]

---

19 It was Bal Gangadhar Tilak who in 1891 first propounded the reorganisation of administrative boundaries according to linguistic differences. For details, see King (1997, 59). Also, for a detailed discussion on the historical development of linguistic nationalism in India, see King (1994, 52–96).

20 Bal Gangadhar Tilak was the first leading man of non-Hindi provinces who advocated the installation of Hindi as the all-India language of independent India that could be a substitute for English. In December 1905, he told a conference of the Nagari Pracharini Sabha at Benares: 'If you want to draw a nation together, there is no force more powerful than a common language for all.' See Gopal (1966, 175).

21 For example, Gandhi, on 21 January 1920, wrote in *Young India*, 'the nation has very materially suffered by reason of the proceedings of the Congress having been conducted almost entirely in English except during the last two years. I further wish to state as a fact that, barring the Presidency of Madras, everywhere else the majority of the visitors and delegates to the National Congress have always been able to understand more Hindustani than English. The astounding result, therefore, has been that the Congress has been national throughout all these long years only as a spectacle, but never for its real educative value. ... And as national consciousness develops and as the appetite

Despite the support provided to Hindustani by Mahatma Gandhi, the language did not appeal to people beyond the north India region. Supporters of Hindi were not ready to accept Hindustani as the national language because, for them, Hindustani, 'as a spoken idiom of the common man, is inadequate for serious discourse, as in education and parliament' (Kumar, K., 2005, 149). Hindi thus became the victim of its own supporters because Sanskritised Hindi was not acceptable to South Indians, nor to large numbers of neo-literate masses across north India, not to speak of Muslims. In this respect, Kumar, K. (2005) remarks that 'the enormous nationalist program of the north Indian literati to provide independent India with a national language became a victim of the religious and cultural split in the Hindi heartland' (152).

The emergent nationalism and the debates between Hindi and English were bound to have a significant impact on the development of Hindi journalism. In 1920, *Aaj* was started by Shiv Prasad Gupta, a philanthropist and a political activist from Banaras. It was a newspaper that subsequently played a prominent role in the freedom movement. Through its categorical support to the national cause, *Aaj* became a bulwark of the Indian National Congress and its main forum for spreading the message of freedom to the Hindi-speaking masses of the United Provinces (present-day Uttar Pradesh and Uttarakhand), Bihar, Madhya Bharat and Nepal. It set the tone and style for Hindi journalism and was acclaimed for its impartial and objective reporting and for its illuminating and fearless editorials (Chaturvedi, 2004). *Aaj* was the only major Hindi daily that survived in independent India. It is perhaps ironic that the same newspaper in the late 1980s would play a leading role in polarising society along communal lines by aligning itself with Hindutva forces.

The Indian Press Act of 1910 was repealed in 1922 and the political climate became more conducive. With the rising vitriolic communal content towards the late 1920s, British officials were getting restive. Yet, no action was taken until the launch of the Civil Disobedience campaign in 1930 when a Press Ordinance was promulgated (Israel, 1994). Finally, in 1931 a new Press Act was passed. Unlike the earlier press act that curbed the freedom of the press and disallowed criticisms of the Raj, this new act was more to contain contents that instigated violence (Israel, 1994). In the 1930s, newspapers were quite influential in guiding the trend of nationalist politics and played

---

for political knowledge and education grows, as it must, it will become more and more difficult, and rightly so, for a speaker, no matter how able and popular, to command the attention of a popular audience if he spoke in English' (19–20).

an important role in political mobilisation (Kudaisya, G., 2006, 159). There was a tremendous spurt in press propaganda (Pandey, 1975). According to Pandey (1975), vernacular newspapers and journals in the 1930s often carried slogans such as 'Read this yourself, read it to others, and give it to a peasant' (208). The growing fear of vernacular newspapers caused the British officials to start the *Native Newspaper Reports* to monitor the tone of the newspapers. It would therefore be erroneous to judge the influence of newspapers in this period by their circulation figures.[22]

There were several other important Hindi newspapers that appeared in the 1920s and 1930s, such as *Swatantra, Arjun, Calcutta Samachar, Lokmat, Vartman, Milap, Lokmanya, Navbharat, Adhikar, Agragami* and *Dainik Navjyoti*. Most of the Hindi newspapers were running at a loss, because their prime motive was to fight the colonial power and spread nationalist feeling. Kumar (1990) remarks that in colonial India,

> ... journalism acquired a distinct cultural function, far wider than the function it has performed in England two hundred years earlier at the beginning of the eighteenth century, in the context of a rising urban middle class. In the Hindi region at the beginning of the twentieth century, journalism performed the role of pulling together into a sense of community a heterogeneous town-based society. ... Heterogeneous though this educated town-based society was in terms of its economic character, it was mainly upper-caste, dominated by Brahmins and Kayasthas (1247).

The last characteristic of Hindi journalism as being dominated by the upper caste has not changed even today, which we will see in Chapter 4. Another important characteristic of Hindi newspapers that we have noted during the colonial period is that a large number of Hindi newspapers, including the first newspaper, were started from non-Hindi speaking areas such as Kolkata. Because Kolkata was the colonial capital until 1911, newspaper editors thought they could influence government policies by being based in Kolkata. Hindi newspapers also served as a medium for those aspiring to enter public life. Another notable characteristic of Hindi newspapers during the colonial period was their structure. Newspapers proprietors used to be their editors. This 'owner as editor' characteristic of Hindi newspapers continued in independent India and affected the growth of Hindi newspapers to a large extent.

---

22 In 1928, the combined circulation of all daily newspapers stood at only 4,00,000 for a population in excess of 45 million (Kudaisya, G., 2006, 160).

Framing colonial rule: Hindi vs. English press

Despite the fragmentation within Hindi newspapers, there was unanimity in framing the colonial rule negatively. In fact, two themes came to form the leitmotif of public discourse in the Hindi newspapers; first, the exploitative character of the colonial state; second, colonial state's indifference to the welfare of the native people. The intensity of debates on these two themes, though, varied between the papers (Kalpagam, 2002, 45). Hindi newspapers in the colonial period had a short life, but they were mushrooming continuously. This feature of the Hindi press is concomitant with individual efforts directed at starting a newspaper. Any organisational effort to launch Hindi newspapers was barely noticeable, which also reflects fragmentation at the structural level. Yet, Hindi journalists were deeply patriotic and adopted journalism as a mission. For this reason, Hindi newspapers were largely used for propaganda and opinion, rather than news (Pandey, 1975). This feature of Hindi newspapers also affected their growth in the initial years after independence, which is discussed in the next chapter. It was this sense of patriotism of Hindi journalists that helped the Hindi press be associated with the freedom movement and the politicisation of the public sphere in the colonial period. No wonder that time and again the British imposed censorship laws on vernacular newspapers.[23]

While all Hindi and other vernacular newspapers were essentially nationalist in their orientation, there were divisions within the English newspapers in terms of their political agendas. There were three kinds of English newspapers. First, there were British-owned newspapers that were mostly supportive of British rule in India. These included *Indian Daily News*, *Empire* and *Englishman*.[24] But there were a few British-owned newspapers that were critical of the colonial government. The *Statesman*, established by Robert Knight in 1875, fell in this category (Kamra, 2002, 46). Second, were Anglo-Indian English newspapers such as the *Statesman*, the *Englishman*, the *Times*

---

23 Especially after the 1857 Mutiny, the vernacular press came under the strict scrutiny of the British government, as noted above. However, the division between nationalist press and pro-British press was already sharp after the Mutiny of 1857. In this context, Narain (1970) writes, 'the holocaust of 1857, created sharp division in the Indian press. English journalists with one voice began to cry blood for blood and evinced bitter racial prejudice. Indian editors had to retaliate either by way of defending themselves or out of their sympathy with the "rebels". The journalists in India came to be divided based on their nationalities' (47).

24 After the World War I, the ownership of the *Indian Daily News* and the *Empire* passed into Indian hands. See Israel (1994, 16).

of India, the *Pioneer,* the *Mail* and the *Times.*[25] They were largely defensive of British rule and there was 'consensus about the legitimacy of the Raj and its continuing creative role and mission' (Israel, 1994, 4; also see Kamra, 2002, 37–109). English newspapers, whether British-owned or Anglo-Indian, were limited in their reach and they catered to the elite constituency. Nevertheless, the Indian elite press was better off than its vernacular country cousins, as they were largely supported by a range of merchants and planters and indirectly by the government through purchase and advertisements. But even Anglo-Indians who owned newspapers were denied the substantial support that was available to British-owned newspapers in India (Israel, 1994).

The third and final category of English newspapers was nationalist and owned by Indians. These newspapers were critical of the colonial government and supported the cause of *swaraj. Amrita Bazar Patrika, Bengalee* and *Indian Mirror* in Kolkata, the *Tribune* in Lahore and the *Hindu* in Madras were important nationalist newspapers that were started in the second half of the nineteenth century.[26]

It was the establishment of the Indian National Congress in 1885 that encouraged newspapers to frame colonial rule in an even more negative tone and report the rising aspirations of Indians for greater freedom. Thus, most of the nationalist newspapers framed the first Indian National Congress meeting positively; the *Amrita Bazar Patrika* expressed delight at an event that brought leaders from different parts of the country to deliberate upon India's fallen condition, while *Bengalee* saw in it the awakening of a new spirit in India (Karkhanis, 1981).

The early twentieth century saw the rise of several nationalist English newspapers. The first notable nationalist English newspaper in north India was the *Hindustan Times* started by G. D. Birla in 1924 from Delhi.[27] It had a good beginning as it received the blessings of Mahatma Gandhi and other

---

25 Ownership of the *Statesman* and the *Times of India* passed to Indians and subsequently the *Times of India* became the leading English newspaper of India.

26 The *Hindu* and its founder and editor, G. Subramania Aiyer not only championed nationalist cause, but also espoused for social reforms within the Hindu society and sought to raise the age of marriage, advocated widow remarriage, wished for a better place in society for Dalits and demanded the abolition of caste, child marriages. For details see the *Hindu*. 2003. 'Willing to Strike and Not Reluctant to Wound.' 13 September 2003, available at https://archive.fo/z67Ur, last accessed on 24 December 2016.

27 For a detailed history of the *Hindustan Times*, see Jha and Das, 2000.

Indian National Congress leaders (see Sahni, 1974). There were also small and short-lived nationalist newspapers. Motilal Nehru's *Independent* and Jawaharlal Nehru's *National Herald* were important English nationalist newspapers. Another important nationalist newspaper was *Bombay Chronicle* started by Sir Pherozeshah Mehta from Mumbai in 1907. B. G. Horniman, the first editor of the *Bombay Chronicle*, was one of the few Britons who supported India's cause and Home Rule. Because of his persistent support for India's independence and vehement criticism of British policies, he was finally deported to England in 1919.[28] The *Leader*, started in 1909 by Pandit Madan Mohan Malviya, can also be regarded as an important nationalist newspaper; however, it was often critical of the Indian National Congress policy as much as it was of the colonial government (Kamra, 2002, 44). The paper is also remembered for its editor, Y. M. Chintamani. Other nationalist newspapers included *Basumati, Swarajya* and *Liberty*. The *Indian Express* established in 1931 in Madras was another important nationalist newspaper.

Despite their limited reach, Israel (1994) believes that it was the English newspapers that helped in creating national awareness as 'their readership included opinion and decision makers in the nationalist movement and in the Government'. 'English was considered essential for any national role and the establishment or control of an English language paper often signalled a politician's desire to move on to the All-India stage.' He goes on to argue:

> In significant measures, the ideal of an All-India nation state that emerged out of the Indian nationalist struggle was imagined in English print. There were a variety of reasons to publish in English. It was the 'national' language, the only medium that reached beyond regional borders – especially those that separated the north and south (21).

It is difficult to agree with Israel as it is well documented that the Indian Nationalist Movement became a mass movement only after the arrival of Gandhi, who started using vernacular languages to reach the masses. The growing significance of the vernacular press can also be measured by the sense of unease that it was able to create among the British, who started passing various censorship laws especially after the Mutiny of 1857 to check the inflammatory content of these nationalist newspapers. Even though English

---

28 For details on the role of the *Bombay Chronicle* in the Indian freedom struggle, see Israel (1994, 216–45).

newspapers were considered 'elite' newspapers and were better supported through advertisements, they were unable to reach the vast semi-literate and illiterate population. Public readings of English newspapers didn't help transmit the contents of newspapers, as they required translation. This was not the case with Hindi and other vernacular newspapers, the public readings of which were often a vital means of reaching the non-literate masses and hence, mobilising public opinion.

Conclusion

In this chapter, I show the close links between the rise of nationalism and Hindi newspapers. The rise of the Indian National Congress began to instil a nationalist consciousness and the vernacular press, particularly the Hindi press, became its vehicle. The content in the vernacular press, which was earlier largely occupied at bringing social reforms in the Indian society, began to be openly and primarily political and critical of the colonial government. Even before the formation of the Indian National Congress, the colonial government was aware of the threat from the vernacular press and often passed repressive ordinance aimed primarily at the vernacular than the English press and suppressing native voices. There were several nationalist English newspapers during the colonial period, but they proved inadequate in mobilising the masses since English was the language of a limited section of the middle class. This realisation also resulted in most of the nationalist leaders simultaneously writing for or publishing both English and vernacular language newspapers to reach out to the larger masses and influence public opinion.

It was the rise of Hindi newspapers that provided a fertile ground for meaningful interaction between the elites and mass public. The educated class who often became the leaders of the people would get news from the newspapers, which would then be transferred to the general public through meetings and even through public readings of newspapers to the illiterate masses. In this way, newspapers helped disseminate the views of leaders and other matters from one area to another and from one level to another (Pandey, 1975). The hybrid interactions between the English and the vernacular language newspapers, the educated and non-literate and the British and native formed the leitmotif of mass mobilisation. The vernacular turn taken by the Indian National Congress after the rise of Gandhi that resulted in the reorganisation of the Congress along linguistic lines proved instrumental in the rise and consolidation of mass nationalism. Yet, in this vernacular turn Hindi assumed greater significance than other Indian languages because of the support provided to Hindi by Gandhi and other national leaders.

3

Media and Mobilisation in
Independent India

With India's independence from colonial rule in 1947, the political environment under which the press had to operate was transformed, because most of the authoritarian laws and regulations used by the British to suppress the press were removed. India's first Prime Minister, Jawaharlal Nehru, was an advocate of freedom of speech in general and freedom of press in particular. The Indian press, however, was not merely a passive supporter of the programmes and policies of the Indian state. In this chapter, I analyse the changing political environment under which the press had to operate in newly independent India, and explore the reasons for the subservient position of the Hindi media relative to the English media in the country in the decades after independence.

The Indian press in general was going through profound confusion soon after independence about its role *vis-à-vis* the state and society. Since the nationalist press had played a prominent role during the freedom struggle by aligning with the Indian nationalist leadership and fighting against colonial rule, the nationalist newspapers could not suddenly detach themselves from this role once colonial rule ended. Rather than critically examining the programmes and policies of the Indian government designed to advance economic and social progress, the nationalist press started supporting the policies and programmes of the Nehru government, at least in its initial years. This support was also due to the lack of any strong opposition in Parliament against Nehru.

The relationship between the media and the state is often mediated by oppositional politics. On occasion, the media alone has been successful in bringing various issues to public scrutiny. But in order to successfully pursue an issue, the media relies on support from oppositional politics, which often feeds and keeps the issue alive by issuing statements. This was not the case in the initial years of the Nehru government because of the media's fixation with Nehru's stature, which led Inder Malhotra (2008) to describe this period as the 'age of consensus'. However, in reality the 1950s was far from the age of consensus, particularly after the mid-50s, as there were several critical voices. Even the newspaper with the largest circulation, the *Times of India*, in 1951 was 'trying to shape itself as an opposition paper to the Nehru administration'

(Mani, 1954, ix).[1] Some small newspapers also sought to project an image of themselves as opposition papers, such as the *Blitz* of Bombay, a bi-weekly, and the *Statesman* of Calcutta. Mani (1954) argues that on occasion the Indian press 'has been extremely critical of the Government, and it has been responsible for exposing a number of scandals in internal administration' (xvi). The relationship between the Hindi press and the English press in independent India needs to be understood within the larger political context as well as within the relationship of Hindi with other vernacular languages.

There were sharp divisions between the English and vernacular media in terms of power, prestige and influence. This division was directly related to differing perceptions about English and Hindi in the public sphere, a legacy of colonialism, which helped the English media dominate the political power structure and other aspects of life. English was viewed as the language of the modern and modernity. It thus commanded 'cultural authority' over vernacular languages, including Hindi. Such cultural authority ensued from its dominance in institutions such as the bureaucracy, the market, the press and the education system.[2] The Hindi language failed to establish its authority in the market, which was concomitant with its failure to widen its social base beyond the north Indian region in independent India.

At one level the dominance of English in the public sphere in India might appear as a legacy of colonialism and prevalent global trends. But it was also the failure of Hindi to widen its social constituency and emerge as a vehicle of communication that privileged English over the Indian languages. The use of Sanskritised Hindi, which started in the late nineteenth century and later came to be associated with Brahmin domination, further hampered the growth and

---

1   The critical approach of the *Times of India* towards the Nehru government could be attributed to the strained relationship between the owner of the *Times of India*, Ramkrishna Dalmia and Jawaharlal Nehru. In 1955, Ramkrishna Dalmia sold the controlling share of Bennet, Coleman and Co. (BCCL), publisher of the *Times of India* to his son-in-law, Shanti Prasad Jain under controversial circumstances. Ramkrishna Dalmia was arrested in 1955 for fraudulant transactions by the Dalmia Group, but was released on bail soon. The issue was raised in Parliament that led to the setting up of a commission of inquiry. Dalmia was found guilty by the court and jailed for two year in 1962. After Dalmia was released from jail in May 1964, he tried to regain the control of the *Times of India*, but Shanti Prasad Jain refuse to sell it back. For details, see Malhan (2013, 8–18).

2   Elder (1971) has pointed out the continuities in the colonial education system in India after the departure of colonial power. Though he admits that India has shown impressive success in decolonising the educational system, still 'the Indian textbooks transmit to their students an awareness of a West that is still technologically superior, still to be blamed, still to be emulated, and still to be sought for approval' (295). Krishna Kumar (2005) in his seminal work on the Indian education system has also clearly shown the link between the education system under colonial rule and one after India achieved independence.

adoption of Hindi by a larger population. Even within the north Indian region, Hindi 'became the chosen vehicle for an upper caste literati's self image' (Kumar, K., 2005, 149), which kept lower caste groups and Muslims from adopting Hindi.[3] Therefore, the contestation in postcolonial India was not only between English versus Hindi, but also between Hindi versus the Dravidian languages. In this contest, English in postcolonial India emerged over Hindi what I have termed the 'secular middle', which was acceptable to people across different regions in India, particularly in South India.

English not only became the language of modernity in India but it also came to be recognised as the language of science, business, press and literature. While looking at the decline of Latin in Europe, Anderson (1991) aptly remarks that 'Language-of-state it [Latin] might be, but it could not, in the nineteenth century be the language of business, of the sciences, of the press, or of literature, especially in a world in which these languages continuously interpenetrated one another' (78). In the Indian context, we observe that Hindi, though aligned with the national liberation movement, could not exert its influence on the market. Further, the insularity of the Hindi literary class and its inability to acknowledge the overlap with other languages such as Urdu had a detrimental impact on the ability of Hindi to expand its social base.

During the colonial period, the vernacular realm had been very important and its activities subsequently provided an important impetus and form for the development of Indian nationalism. Freitag (1996) shows how alternative arena activities such as the Cow Protection Campaign, which was not part of a narrowly defined nationalist movement, still laid the important foundation for how nationalism might find very different kinds of appeals that worked at a popular level. This vernacular realm has become important with the rise of regionalism and regional elites since the late 1960s, which paved the way for the Hindi press to play a new and proactive role along with the English press. But it was not until the 1980s when the Ayodhya movement reappeared that the resurgence of the Hindi press was recognised in the national mainstream. Although this recognition established the image of the Hindi press as communal and reactionary, it also contributed to its massive expansion and laid the foundation for challenging the perception of the English press as the so-called

---

3   Similarly, Dalmia (1997) points out that in its claim to national status in British India, 'Hindi as the language of Hindus not only shut out Muslim participation, but in its increasing Sanskritisation, unwittingly, as it were, also achieved polarisation with the Dravidian languages of the South. The territory it could be said to cover was thus automatically reduced. It was to have a long and chequered career in its aspirations to be recognised as the national language of India' (221).

national press. The Hindi media provided a platform for emerging political leaders of northern India to raise their individual and collective voices in the public arena that further helped in the consolidation of Indian democracy.

Indeed, a complex relationship existed between an ostensibly modern English language press and the Hindi press vernacular realm, and I explore this relationship further in this chapter with empirical data. I discuss the link between formal politics and media, drawing upon voter turnout data in Hindi-speaking states and its relationship with the growth in the circulation of Hindi newspapers. I provide evidence that the resurgence of Hindi newspapers in the 1980s and 1990s challenged the dominance of English newspapers in the social, cultural and political spheres, if not in the economic sphere.

High expectations, low performance: 1947–77

'The Hindi language newspaper will take the place of the English language newspaper after fifteen years, when Hindi becomes a national language and the language of the administration' (xvi), remarked A. D. Mani, chief editor of the *Hitavada*, in 1954. As we will see later, his hope remained just that – a hope – because of several unforeseen developments. After India achieved independence in 1947, in the decades that followed the media landscape was largely dominated by the English language press. Politicians and bureaucrats at the national level hardly bothered about news published in Hindi and other Indian language newspapers. The domination of the English press was noted in 1954 by the First Press Commission (1954) while analysing the state of the press in India after independence. In 1952, the English press had the highest circulation of 6,97,000 copies with 41 dailies, and the 76 Hindi dailies had the second highest figure of 3,79,000 copies (15). This domination of the English press continued until 1979 when the combined share of English daily newspapers in circulation came down to 22.5 per cent compared to 27.6 per cent in 1952, while the Hindi press for the first time moved ahead of its English counterpart with a 23 per cent share as opposed to 15 per cent in 1952 (Second Press Commission, 1982, 11).

Very few Hindi newspapers survived for long after independence simply because most of them had been started by people who wanted to serve their country by fighting the British. Once the British left the country, they had neither a common enemy nor the ideological motivation. Yet, after independence several new Hindi newspapers were set up from different parts of India and included *Nai Duniya* from Indore (1947), *Amar Ujala* from Agra (1948), *Rajasthan*

Patrika from Jaipur (1956), *Dainik Bhaskar* from Bhopal (1958), *Deshbandhu* from Bhopal (1959) and *Punjab Kesari* from Jalandhar (1965).

This period from 1947 to 1977 in the history of Hindi newspapers can be characterised as one of high expectations. Editors and owners of Hindi newspapers thought that with independence the dominance of English language newspapers would disappear and Hindi newspapers would emerge victorious. Far from disappearing, however, the English language and English newspapers entrenched themselves further in the public sphere and English continued its image as the language of 'modernity'.[4] The notion of English being 'modern' and the indigenous languages being 'non-modern' or 'traditional' was the legacy of colonialism and its education system, which privileged English over indigenous languages. However, one would not have expected the domination of English to continue after the departure of the British from India. English continued to hold a superior position *vis-à-vis* Hindi and was nurtured by the Indian elite, who benefitted both economically and politically because of their knowledge of English. Moreover, the political elite at the national level found it difficult to dismantle the existing educational, administrative and market structures that were already institutionalised. There was great demand from various quarters to make Hindi the 'national language' immediately after independence and throw out English altogether as English was a symbol of the British Empire and its domination over Indians. Nehru declared Hindi as the official language in 1950; however, he allowed English to be used for official purposes until 1965 after which Hindi would replace English (though it should be noted that this did not emerge as planned).[5]

Even though there were many powerful voices raised in protest against the continued hegemony of English, the significance of English and its usage continued in public life. People like Dr Rajendra Prasad and Ram Manohar Lohia were ardent supporters of Hindi as the national language over English. While delivering a speech at the foundation stone laying ceremony of Rashtra Bhasha Prachar Samiti in 1956, Dr Prasad hoped that 'it is not difficult to make Hindi our national language' because people in the South understand more Hindi than English' (176). Similarly, in his speech at Banaras Hindu University in 1956, Lohia remarked,

---

4   Despite the fact that they were serving two different constituencies, the English press commanded greater respect and was consulted by the Government of India and Indian policymakers to stay informed about events.

5   For a detailed discussion on the language controversy, see King (1997).

the importation of the English language under the guise of an all-India character will no longer be tolerated and that the continued use of this feudal language to India results in characterlessness, although it may achieve a superficial all-India shine (196).

Yet, in the contest between Hindi and English, it was the latter that emerged victorious and dominated the discourse in the public arena.

During this period Hindi newspapers were not only marginalised from the national mainstream debates, but also suffered from a credibility gap that was a reflection of the larger image of the Hindi language in the public sphere. Below I discuss eight significant reasons for the secondary position of Hindi newspapers compared to English newspapers.

First, in contrast to the image of Hindi as the language of the masses, English became the language of the elite. Thus, the dominance of English in public life was the result of the hegemony of the English-educated national elite to whom power was transferred after India attained independence in 1947 and who set the norms and decided the procedures through which India's vision of development and modernisation would be articulated. Since the power structure at the national level was largely dominated by the English-educated elite, they projected the argument that retaining English was in the national interest and thrived on this argument because it provided them with the means to hold on to power. In this context, Ram Gopal (1966) remarks, 'many officers kept up the superiority complex with the aid of English even after Hindi was lawfully adopted as the official language' (198). Thus, the English-speaking elite assumed the role of the saviour, taking India ahead to the next stage of development.

Second, the ideological dominance of English in the national discourse was far greater than that of Hindi or any other Indian language. Almost all national policy papers and reports were prepared in English. Even government press releases were issued in the English language, the translation of which took time. At the same time, there were no Hindi news agencies until 1982. United News of India (UNI) and the Press Trust of India (PTI), the two major Indian news agencies, launched their Hindi news services in 1982 (UNI Varta) and 1986 (PTI Bhasha), respectively.

Third, English was perceived as an instrument of social mobility, a view that continues to inform contemporary Indian society. The job market for people who are educated in English is larger than that for people who are educated in Hindi or other regional languages (Nayyar, 1969). Moreover, there are hardly any colleges or universities in India that can provide quality degrees in engineering, medicine, information technology, fine arts, etc. in Hindi. People educated in Hindi-medium schools had limited career avenues and could mainly be employed in teaching jobs, as journalists or in low-paid jobs. This made it difficult, if not impossible, to attain social mobility. Although the Kothari Commission on Education in 1966 recommended English as the third language, higher education and competitive exams are heavily skewed towards English. Until the 1970s, even the prestigious Indian Administrative Service (IAS) exams were exclusively conducted in English. So, in high-profile white-collar jobs, the English-educated elite dominated. India's major indigenous corporations, such as those owned by the widely respected Tata and Birla families, were also led by men who spoke both English and Hindi. However, the booming Hindi media industry since the mid-1990s gave relief to those being educated in Hindi-medium schools and boosted their confidence, which I discuss later in this section. Nevertheless, one cannot overlook the continuing importance of English in entering the high-end labour market in India or in aspiring for a global career.

Fourth, the Hindi-speaking intelligentsia had high expectations after independence that their position would change and 'they would eventually replace the English-speaking intelligentsia and thus attain a higher status within the Indian society' (Malik, 1977, 575). But Hindi-speaking intellectuals and the intelligentsia did not play a significant role in raising consciousness among Hindi media users. This was because the Hindi intellectual tradition is not as well developed as the language; it is a new construct and is devoid of a major literary history (Stahlberg, 2002a). In contrast to the Hindi language, other Indian languages such as Bengali, Tamil, Telugu and Marathi are better placed in this respect with their rich classical literatures.

Fifth, the people living in the Hindi-speaking states, otherwise known colloquially as the 'Hindi belt' and comprising the six states of Uttar Pradesh, Bihar, Madhya Pradesh, Rajasthan, Haryana and Himachal Pradesh, were not only largely illiterate, but also economically backward. The majority of population in the Hindi belt were not only unable to read newspapers, but also lacked the purchasing power to buy newspapers. However, some scholars have held the English press responsible for the dismal performance of the Hindi press in postcolonial India (Jain, 1970). As most of the English newspapers were associated with power before independence and were mostly owned by the British, they were able to commercialise themselves after the British left India. Even a nationalist English newspaper such as the *Hindustan Times* was owned by a large Indian business house, which made it easier to sustain publication without major interruption. Similarly, ownership of the *Times of India*, another important English daily, passed to the famous industrial family of the Dalmiyas, which was later taken over by Sahu Shanti Prasad Jain, a leading industrialist. In contrast, most Hindi newspapers had been started to propagate the cause of the independence struggle and depended on donations for their survival. Owners of Hindi newspapers had been imbued with 'missionary zeal' to liberate the country from the clutches of the colonial masters and had not bothered about other qualities of a newspaper, such as design, layout and presentation, focusing instead on ideological content and propaganda. Not surprisingly, most of the Hindi newspapers that had been popular during the freedom struggle could not survive long after independence (Jain, 1970). The Hindi press did not realise that in order to survive in independent India they needed a different objective and a different mission, because in the new context 'political slogan-mongering and living on bold words has no meaning and relevance' (Jain, 1970). Operating under the garb of idealism without adopting new technology and professionalism, Hindi newspapers remained secondary and the dominant market position was retained by English newspapers.

Sixth, Hindi newspapers lacked the credibility of English newspapers. Most of the Hindi newspapers borrowed news from English language newspapers. Thus, Hindi newspapers made themselves a mere 'satellite press' without attempting to carve a separate domain of operation where they could have an independent identity outside the shadow of English newspapers. The image of the Hindi newspaper as a carbon copy of its English counterpart acted as a major handicap. News published in Hindi newspapers was always looked upon with suspicion, unless the news had been provided by news agencies such as the PTI or UNI (Chaturvedi, 1970). According to A. K. Jain (1970), a prominent Hindi journalist and editor of *Navbharat Times*,

> the Hindi press fought for the country's freedom ... It was free when the country was not, but I am pained to point out that in a free India it is compelled to be a camp follower of its English brother (63–64).

Thus, in their zeal to emulate English newspapers, Hindi newspapers lost their critical dispensation and originality, which hampered their credibility. Instead of looking at the reality of the Hindi public sphere and catering to the needs of the Hindi readership, the Hindi press simply copied the English press. The Hindi press could have done better if it had tried to reach out to the semi-urban and rural areas of the 'Hindi belt' or 'Hindi heartland', where most of the Hindi readers lived. But they confined themselves to the urban areas and could not voice the grievances of the vast majority of the population living in rural areas. The Second Press Commission (1982) also reports the urban bias of newspapers.[6] In sum, English-educated people in urban areas relied on the English press, rather than subscribing to Hindi newspapers, which were suffering from a 'credibility deficiency'. For this reason the combined circulation figure of the Hindi dailies fell far below those of English dailies, despite the Hindi press having the highest number of dailies. In 1968, for example, the combined circulation of English newspapers was 17,52,000 copies for 61 dailies, while Hindi newspapers had a combined circulation of 9,55,000 despite publishing 174 dailies (Press in India, 1996).

Seventh, the owners of the major English language newspapers also published Hindi newspapers after independence, which made it difficult for indigenous Hindi newspapers to sustain themselves. There were already some Hindi newspapers owned by English language dailies, such as *Hindustan*, published by the *Hindustan Times* which had started in 1936, and *Swatantra Bharat* and *Navjivan*, owned by *Pioneer* and *National Herald*, respectively, started in the year of independence in 1947. The *Times of India* started *Navbharat Times* in 1950. *Aaj*, started in 1920, was the only major Hindi language newspaper that was able to survive after independence.[7] Put simply, the Hindi language newspaper market was captured by English newspaper publication houses that had a comparative advantage in the market soon after independence. English newspapers were professionally organised and had better news gathering operations. Having consolidated their position and credibility in the English newspaper market because of the latest technology and the image of English as the medium of the elite, these newspaper houses were able to establish their brand. Through their brand, they were able to get advertising for their Hindi publications, so they could simultaneously reach both the English-speaking elite as well as vernacular audiences.

---

6   In 1979, 76.6 per cent of all newspapers were published from larger cities with as many as 30.3 per cent of newspapers of all periodicities published from the four metropolitan cities of Mumbai, Kolkata, Delhi and Chennai. Only 23.4 per cent of the total number of newspapers was published from towns and other places with a population up to 1,00,000. See *Report of the Second Press Commission*, 1982 (10).

7   *Aaj* was the only Hindi newspaper that managed to obtain better foreign coverage through letters from London, Rangoon, Singapore, Moscow and Peking. Moreover, *Aaj* was the only Hindi newspaper besides *Nai Duniya* of Indore that was connected to a Hindi teleprinter service from the state capital. For details, see Chaturvedi (1970). I have not included *Dainik Jagran* here since it was not a major newspaper during colonial times.

Finally, the rise of linguistic consciousness, which resulted in the reorganisation of Indian states along linguistic lines, hampered the emergence of Hindi as a national language. The formation of linguistic states such as Andhra Pradesh out of Madras Presidency and Maharashtra and Gujarat out of Bombay Presidency while helping in the development of regional languages and literatures, affected national language planning. There were large-scale protests in Andhra Pradesh and Tamil Nadu against the imposition of Hindi, which was seen as the domination of north Indian culture over the rest of India. In the wake of rising linguistic consciousness, even supporters of Hindi changed their stance. Thus, at the All-India Language Conference on 8 March 1958, C. Rajagopalachari declared, 'Hindi is as much foreign to the non-Hindi speaking people as English to the protagonists of Hindi' (quoted in Gupta, 1970, 192). Ironically, C. Rajagopalachari was responsible for introducing Hindi in the school curriculum of Madras Presidency in 1937 (Dua, 1993). The protests against Hindi intensified on the eve of the expiry of the 15-year deadline in 1965, especially in Madras. However, the outbreak of war with Pakistan in 1965 made the language rivalry dormant for a brief period and people from all over India rallied to support the government. The language issue resurfaced after the 1967 general election in which Congress lost power in nine states. This made the Indira Gandhi-led Congress government realise the potential of regional forces in shaping national politics. In December 1967, the Indian Parliament passed the Official Language (Amendment) Bill that legalised the continuance of the use of English, in addition to Hindi, for all official purposes.

Though the passing of the Bill helped resolve the language issue, this divide actually helped English occupy a privileged position over Hindi. English emerged as the link language for communication between the states. With the growing importance of state politics after the 1967 general election, regional languages started gaining greater importance. The bases of the political elites begun to diversify with the coming of a significant number of politicians from rural backgrounds, though the bureaucracy and civil services still remained dominated by the English-speaking class. Such a development did not affect the importance of English in the non-Hindi belt, but it hampered the growth of Hindi. To achieve upward mobility and to get decent employment, people in the non-Hindi belt started learning the regional languages and English, while Hindi was considered less significant for upward mobility in these states. It also accelerated the development of regional languages, the press, theatre and cinema. The same elites who opposed Hindi embraced English, because they did not want to lose the social privileges that came with knowledge of English.

The cumulative effect of these factors played a prominent role in marginalising Hindi newspapers in the public sphere during the first three decades after independence in 1947. However, in the late 1970s, Hindi newspapers started asserting themselves by contesting the dominance of English newspapers. Such assertions became possible because of several important social, political and economic transformations during the late 1970s and 1980s. Importantly, political developments during this period provided an important impetus to the ways in which the relationship between the media and politics subsequently evolved. From 1951 to 1967, Indian politics was dominated by one party, namely, the Indian National Congress, which Kothari (1964, 1974) termed the 'Congress system'. The weakening of the 'Congress system' after the 1967 general election resulted in a parallel rise in regional consciousness in which the regional and vernacular press played an important role. Opposition parties, who were sharply divided among themselves, were unable to create a viable alternative to the ruling party and acted instead as pressure groups outside it. Further, the Congress party was quick to co-opt the programmes of the opposition and absorb their leadership into its fold, which limited the growth of opposition parties. The regional press began to align with regional political classes to provide support to regional causes.

The 'Congress system' operated in power successfully for more than one-and-a-half decades, but it failed to accommodate the increasing regional aspirations that needed different institutions to articulate themselves not only at the regional level, but also in the national mainstream. The English press, as the supposedly national press, also failed to provide adequate representation for regional and local voices. This regional and local space, which was inadequately represented by the English press, was captured by the regional press, which began to play a proactive role in the unfolding political developments. But this rise in regional consciousness was mainly confined to south India, in particular, the states of Tamil Nadu and Kerala.

Kerala and Tamil Nadu, in the 1960s, were the most politically mobilised states in India and witnessed the mobilisation of lower caste groups that resulted in state power being captured by lower caste political parties. Varshney (2000) argues, 'If the Hindu-Muslim cleavage has been a "master narrative" of politics in North India for much of the twentieth century, caste divisions have had the same status in Southern India' (3). Kerala was the first Indian state to challenge the dominance of the Congress party in national politics when the Communist party captured state power in 1957; the Communist party in Kerala largely drew its support from the Ezhava community, a low-caste group engaged in producing indigenous liquor. Tamil Nadu witnessed the rise of the Dravida Munnetra Kazhagam (DMK), an anti-Brahmin party in the 1960s. This was the period when both Kerala and Tamil Nadu had the highest newspaper penetration rates compared to north Indian states (Table 3.2). When newspaper penetration started to rise in northern India, there was a parallel rise in political mobilisation. In making this point, I am not trying to establish a causal relationship between the rise of media and the increase in political mobilisation. Rather, I am highlighting the close linkage between media and political mobilisation and how the vernacular media has played a key role in this mobilisation.

Rudolph and Rudolph (1987) have argued that since 1965 there has been a rise in demand politics where voters' sovereignty is paramount, which is 'expressed through elections and through the demands of organised interests and classes, political parties, social movements and agitational politics' (89). They argue that the reasons for the rise of demand politics were partly exogenous, such as military failure in wars with China (1962) and Pakistan (1965), the deaths of two Prime Ministers (Nehru in May 1964 and Shastri in January 1966) and the food crisis in1965–66 when food production plummeted and prices soared. They further attribute the rise in demand politics after 1965 to an increase in electoral participation, riots, strikes, student 'indiscipline' and agrarian unrest.

What Rudolph and Rudolph (1987) ignore in their analysis is the role played by the spread of information through the regional press in mobilisation and the rise in demand politics especially in the 1970s.[8] News play a very important role in mobilising people and shaping public opinion. The power of the vernacular press in mobilising public opinion becomes evident when we look at its history: it aligned with nationalist forces to fight the British during the colonial period as shown in the previous chapter. Therefore, it can be argued that the serious challenge to the dominance of the Congress party did not come from the English press; rather, it was the regional and the vernacular press that contributed significantly to the rise in demand politics. Some of the important mass mobilisations such as the JP Movement (named after its leader Jayaprakash Narayan) – a Gandhian-inspired protest aimed at removing corruption – were

---

8   The nature of demand politics changed in the 1980s and 1990s with the greater participation of marginalised groups in the political arena (See Rudolph and Rudolph, 1987).

largely a northern Indian phenomenon. Similarly, the Emergency greatly affected political and social life in northern, rather than in southern, India. This suggests a huge gap in the existing knowledge on political mobilisation that requires one to explore the role of Hindi newspapers in the entire mass mobilisation starting from the 1970s or to explore how Hindi newspapers contributed to the rise in demand politics. Such a linkage becomes clear when we analyse the working of the press during the Emergency.

Indira Gandhi proclaimed a National Emergency on 25 June 1975 at midnight. The Allahabad High Court had found Indira Gandhi guilty of violating electoral laws by using official machinery and spending more money than was allowed in her campaigns (Guha, 2008). This resulted in Jayaprakash Narayan, popularly known as JP or Lok Nayak (translated as the people's hero) asking Indira Gandhi as well as other Congress chief ministers to resign, as their continuing in office was now unconstitutional. JP even went to the extent of urging police and military to disobey any order from Gandhi since she had lost both legal and moral sanctity to govern because of the Allahabad High Court nullifying her election. This resulted in Gandhi declaring a National Emergency.

During the Emergency, in addition to censorship, several restrictions were imposed on the press. Indira Gandhi held the press responsible for her declaring the Emergency since 'it was the newspapers which were inciting the people and creating a terrible situation … and had exaggerated rumours' (Shah Commission Report, 1978, 33). She went on to say, 'the agitation was only in the newspapers and once the newspapers were placed under censorship there was no agitation' (Shah Commission Report, 1978). A set of guidelines was issued to the press and the editors were required to submit the materials, deemed to be critical of the government, for approval before it could be published. This resentment against the newspapers clearly reflects the threat that the press as an institution was posing to the authoritarian regime of Indira Gandhi.

All newspapers were categorised as A, B, or C based on their response to the Emergency: 'A' was for friendly newspapers, 'B' denoted hostile press and 'C' meant neutral reporting by newspapers. The categorisation was not only used to release government advertisements through the Directorate of Advertisement and Visual Publicity (DAVP), sole advertisement agency for the government, but also to clamp down on hostile press. Three key Hindi newspapers – *Swadesh*, *Vir Prataap* and *Pradeep* – were placed in the hostile category. While the *Indian Express* is known for registering its dissent against the imposition of the Emergency by leaving the editorial page blank. The first blank editorial of the

Indian Express appeared on 28 June 1975 (Paul, 2017). However, *Nai Duniya*, a noted Hindi daily published from Indore in Madhya Pradesh left its editorial page blank on 26 June 1975 in response to the imposition of the Emergency (See Figure 3.1). Interestingly, two Hindi newspapers were placed in the friendly category. One of them, *Hindustan*, is published by the Hindustan Times group, which also publishes the leading English daily, the *Hindustan Times*, while the other, *Naveen Duniya*, was a small newspaper from Madhya Pradesh. In contrast, the large national English dailies such as the *Hindu*, the *Times of India* and the *Hindustan Times* were

Figure 3.1: The blank editorial published in *Nai Duniya* on 27 June 1975

classified as friendly. The duality of this response to the Emergency by the Hindi and English newspapers demonstrates that Hindi newspapers were able to defy the government's authority, whereas the major English dailies fell in line with the dictates of the government.

Contesting the subordination: 1977–90

From 1975 to 1977 when the Emergency was imposed and India was under the authoritarian regime of Prime Minister Indira Gandhi, the press as an institution failed to put up resistance. Several repressive laws were imposed on the press and there was censorship, which further impacted press freedom.[9] On 8 December 1975, three ordinances were issued that banned the publication of 'objectionable matter', abolished the Press Council of India and removed the freedom of the press to report the proceedings of Parliament. The ordinance relating to publication of objectionable matter was made law on 28 January 1976.[10] Under such circumstances, the press was not able to put up strong resistance.

---

9   For a detailed analysis of the repression of the press during the Emergency, see Shah Commission of Inquiry, *Interim Report I* (11 March 1978, 33–47) and *Interim Report II* (26 April 1978, 1–9).

10   For a detailed discussion of the muzzling of the press during the Emergency, see Government of India (1977), White Paper on the Misuse of Mass Media during the Internal Emergency (1977); Shah Commission of Inquiry (1978); and Singh (1980).

After the Emergency was lifted in 1977, the Indian media landscape started to change. Indian language newspapers began growing at a faster rate. People wanted to know what had happened during the Emergency and they wanted to know it in their own language. The growing interest of the public in political developments following the dramatic events during and after the Emergency helped Hindi newspapers as well as other Indian language newspapers increase their circulation and readers among the masses. The Janata Party-led government of 1977 to 1979, which was elected as a result of both the Emergency and excessive centralisation of power under Prime Minister Indira Gandhi, 'exposed the state to the ongoing and dramatic democratic forces that had been working throughout society' (Hewitt, 2008, 9). The regional and vernacular forces were being galvanised, which was paving the way for regional and Hindi newspapers to play a new and proactive role in the shifting political space.

Spearheaded by Hindi-language newspapers, this growth was largely driven by an increase in the levels of literacy, an increase in purchasing power, growing political awareness, the spread of technology and offset presses and the use of marketing strategies by newspapers to reach out to readers. In 1961, there was a large gap between the circulation of Hindi and English daily newspapers, but in 1979 Hindi dailies overtook English dailies in terms of circulation (3 million versus 2.97 million). The circulation of Hindi and English dailies remained almost even in 1981, but Hindi newspapers began to grow faster from the mid-1980s and the gap continued to widen over the late 1980s and 1990s (Figure 3.2).

Figure 3.2: Percentage share of Hindi and English dailies in total dailies circulation, 1961–2016

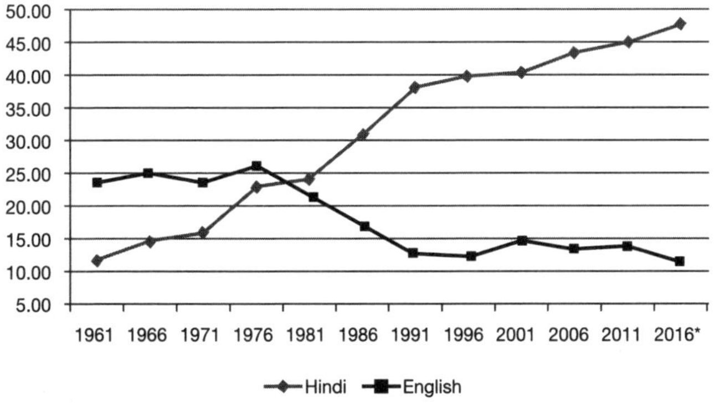

Source: Press in India (relevant years).

Note: Figure for 2016 is based on 2015 data.

According to the latest circulation figures for 2015, Hindi dailies lead with 141 million copies or 47.7 per cent of the total claimed circulation, while English dailies stand at a distant second with 33 million copies, claiming 11.4 per cent of total circulation (Press in India, 2015).

Besides taking to technology, Hindi newspapers also took advantage of the social transformation that was going on in India. The rise of grassroots movements and popular mobilisation from the 1980s, in which new social groups, who needed new ways of expressing their political aspirations, began entering the political arena (Hasan, 2000; Kohli, 1990), found expression in vernacular newspapers. In this development, the Hindi media helped these social groups by providing them not only the language but also the institution, and contributed to presenting an alternative discourse of democratic participation that was more inclusive since it provided a voice to those who were marginally present in the mainstream English press. By offering such an alternative, the Hindi press, since the 1980s, has challenged the dominance of the 'national' elite in the public sphere who depended more on the English media. To access the vernacular public sphere, the national elite needed the help of the vernacular media, which were becoming more robust and proactive in providing an alternative approach to development. Since the 1980s, there has been greater mobilisation of the masses in north India. Lower caste groups and rural populations started participating in the political process more actively (Yadav, 2000).

After 1977, the emergence of important political figures in northern India, such as Charan Singh, Devi Lal, Mulayam Singh Yadav, Kanshi Ram, Lalu Prasad Yadav, Atal Bihari Vajpayee and Mayawati, helped the Hindi media emerge from its political slumber and claim an equal, although not a dominant, share of the public arena. In fact, these vernacular elites had started emerging since the 1960s, but attained ascendency in the 1980s and 1990s. In the colonial period, a similar trend was witnessed when the emergence of leaders from the Hindi-speaking states in the early twentieth century resulted in the increasing focus in the Hindi press on political issues and the nationalist cause. The close linkage between media and politics cannot be overlooked. It is important here to identify the characteristics of the vernacular elites who began to challenge the dominant discourse in the public sphere since they did receive space in the Hindi media. Unlike the national elites who were mostly English-educated and had an urban background, vernacular elites came from rural backgrounds and for them English was not so important (Sheth, 1995). For them, local and regional issues were as important as national issues. In other words, the rise of vernacular elites displaced the binary discourse of national versus regional/local, urban versus rural, elites versus masses and English versus vernacular. Such a redefinition of the dominant discourse also contributed to questioning the ostensibly national elites' paramount position in national politics and showed that vernacular elites are as important for national development as national elites.

The rise of the Hindi media provided a platform to the emerging vernacular elites of northern India to raise their voice in the public arena. Compared with English newspapers, which have an urban concentration, Hindi newspapers in 1981 had a larger presence in small towns and rural areas – 32.7 per cent versus 5.3 per cent (Table 3.1). Around this time, Hindi newspapers started consolidating their presence in state capitals, which became the centre of political activities after the regionalisation of politics in the 1980s. From a 13.4 per cent presence in state capitals in 1981, the concentration of Hindi newspapers rose to 19.2 per cent in 1991 and reached 24.5 per cent in 2016. As we know, state capitals are important for political activities. The increasing presence of Hindi newspapers in state capitals shows the close linkage between the media and regional politics. In this context, Stahlberg (2002a), argues that 'politics in India has to a great extent shifted its focus from New Delhi to the regional centres during the same period that the vernacular press has grown in strength' (3).

Table 3.1: Concentration of English and Hindi newspapers (%), 1981–2016

Year	Metropolitan cities		State capitals		Big cities (population over 1,00,000)		Small towns (population below 1,00,000)	
	Hindi	English	Hindi	English	Hindi	English	Hindi	English
1981	17.1	62.4	13.4	14.1	36.1	15.1	32.7	5.3
1986	16.8	62.0	16.3	14.9	33.1	14.3	33.2	5.6
1991	16.2	62.5	19.2	15.1	34.5	14.1	29.5	5.5
1996	15.3	62.8	19.7	15.2	35.3	13.9	29.2	5.4
2001	16.3	61.3	19.9	15.3	37.2	15.5	26.2	4.8
2006	17.4	60.1	22.1	15.5	39.0	17.8	21.0	3.9
2011	18.31	56.2	24.3	17.3	39.1	20	17.1	3.2
2016*	19.3	53.6	24.5	19	37.1	20	12.9	3

Source: RNI (relevant years), Press in India (relevant years).

Note: Figure for 2016 is based on 2015 data. Union Territories have not been included here and hence the total percentage would not add up to 100 per cent.

In the early 1980s, no one predicted that the political discourse for the coming decade would be new, identity-based political movements largely emanating from northern India, nor that it would lead to an invigoration of the political and cultural significance of the Hindi media. This process was the result of two major political movements that emerged in the north Indian 'heartland' and changed the overall course of Indian politics: the Ram Janmabhumi–Babri mosque controversy, which propelled the right-wing 'Hindutva' forces to national significance, and 'Mandal' politics that allowed marginalised groups, especially the lower castes, to assert their rights in the public sphere.

These two northern Indian movements that started in the 1980s dominated national politics for more than a decade. However, the biased role played by Hindi newspapers in reporting and documenting the Ram Janmabhumi–Babri mosque controversy damaged the reputation of these newspapers. Several studies show clear links between the Hindi press and its role in producing and sustaining communal discourse that likely led to greater violence.[11] Engineer (1991) has analysed the role of four Hindi dailies – *Aaj, Dainik Jagran, Swatantra Chetna,* and *Swatantra Bharat* –that engaged in biased reporting during the Ayodhya events and by their inflammatory writings incited communal conflicts. His analysis confirms the findings of the Press Council of India (1991) that these newspapers had shown 'gross irresponsibility and impropriety, offending the canons of journalistic ethics, in covering the events relating to the mandir–masjid issue on and around October 30, 1990' (338).

Rajagopal (2001) shows the difference in reporting by the English and Hindi media in covering the Ram Janmabhumi controversy. While the Hindi newspapers were more rhetorical and biased in reporting events, the English press was largely 'objective and rational' in its approach. The variation in reporting events, he further argues, can largely be attributed to the different patterns of functioning of English and Hindi newspapers. The English press gives greater emphasis to objectivity and the truth value of the news because their audiences are largely a 'critical-rational public'. In contrast, the Hindi press is more rhetorical and less objective and caters to audiences with a different outlook. Although one cannot completely disagree with Rajagopal's arguments given the considerable evidence to that effect, several Hindi

---

11 Some important studies on the subject are Engineer (1990, 1991); and Nandy (1995). For details of the dubious role of Hindi newspapers, see Hasan (1998); Rajagopal (2001); and Srivastava (2000).

newspapers have also played a vibrant and objective role in highlighting social issues. One example is *Dainik Bhaskar*, the second largest Hindi newspaper, whose critical approach following the Bhopal gas tragedy of 1984 invoked the wrath of the state government and it lost substantial advertising revenue. Instead of supporting the government, *Dainik Bhaskar* aligned with the people with the stated aim of obtaining justice.[12] Similarly, in the wake of communal riots that broke out in Bhopal following the demolition of the Babri Mosque on 6 December 1992, *Dainik Bhaskar* through its editorial appealed to people to maintain communal harmony.[13] Rajagopal's argument that the English press is serving a 'critical-rational public' (152) is questionable, because it is based on the assumption that the Hindi-speaking public lacks critical-rational thinking.

Politics and the Hindi media in post-1991 India

The decade of the 1990s is the most important phase in the development of Hindi newspapers. Not only have they been able to overcome their earlier reputation of being a 'communal' press that has induced communal violence since the 1980s, or in an earlier stage a 'satellite press' that reprinted the agendas of the national English newspapers, they have also challenged the long-held hegemony of English newspapers in the national discourse. No doubt this began in the 1980s when we noted that they provided support to grassroots movements. They found it difficult, however, to suddenly challenge the reputation developed over a long period given that they largely reprinted news from English sources. The terms of discourse in the public sphere had largely been set by the English language media. Despite the dramatic expansion of the Hindi media in the 1980s, they could not seriously challenge the ideological dominance of the English language media at that time, which was already entrenched in the public sphere.

This period saw the dramatic rise of *Dainik Bhaskar* and *Dainik Jagran*, the two most widely read Hindi newspapers today that also changed the image of Hindi newspapers. Many other Hindi newspapers also rose during this period:

---

12   Interview with Ramesh Chandra Agarwal, Chairman of the Dainik Bhaskar Group, 29 November 2006, Bhopal.

13   On 10 December 1992, *Dainik Bhaskar* published an article titled '*Tum Nahiṃ Jante, Tum Kiya Kar Rahe Ho*' (You Don't Know, What You Are Doing). This article appealed to the people of Bhopal to maintain the communal harmony and blamed the government for being unable to stop the communal riots in the city.

Rajasthan Patrika, published from Jaipur, *Amar Ujala* based in Agra, *Punjab Kesari* from Jalandhar and *Prabhat Khabar* from Ranchi.[14]

Several scholars view the rise of Hindi newspapers as part of the rise of communal and identity politics in India and, hence, are sceptical about the role of the Hindi press as a vehicle of democratisation (Hasan, 1998; Rajagopal, 2001). However, I would argue that part of the role of the Hindi press has furthered democracy in three ways. First, one cannot ignore the voice provided by the Hindi media to hitherto marginalised groups such as people in small towns and rural areas where English newspapers are almost absent. Second, in order to access the vernacular public sphere in north India or the happenings beyond urban metropolitan cities, the national political elite needed the help of the Hindi media, which was becoming more robust and proactive in providing an alternative approach to development. Third, the Hindi press has provided a space for civic discourse since their recent growth, especially since the mid-1990s, has not been fuelled by major communal events such as the Ayodhya movement of the late 1980s and early 1990s. Rather, the growth of Hindi newspapers is due to several factors including the rise in levels of literacy in Hindi-speaking states, aggressive marketing strategies by businesses via the Hindi press to the rising numbers of Hindi-speaking middle class consumers, better transport infrastructure, use of computer technology and the internet, the rising political significance of the Hindi public and an awareness among the masses that they are able to actively participate in the political process.

The character and nature of the growth in participation has been the subject of research. For example, Yadav (2000) notes the growing participation of marginalised groups and while looking at voter turnout at the national level, remarks:

> Although overall turnout figures have not increased dramatically, the social composition of those who vote and take part in political activities has undergone a major change. There is a participatory upsurge among the socially underprivileged, whether seen in terms of caste hierarchy, economic class, gender distinction or the rural-urban divide (120).

Commenting on the changing pattern of political participation in north India, Hasan (2000) argues:

---

14 I have intentionally not included Hindi newspapers published by English newspaper groups since the aim of this chapter is to show the growth of Hindi newspapers or newspaper businesses that started with the publication of a Hindi rather than an English daily. The political economy of the Hindi press is dealt with in Chapter 5.

What is new is the heightened political awakening among the lower castes and Dalits, a process hastened by the fragmentation of the old Congress coalition into constituent groups of upper castes, Muslims and Dalits. What is new is the formation of local and regional parties that represent marginal groups hitherto under the Congress umbrella (152–53).

Between Yadav (2000) and Hasan (2000) we see consensus among scholars about the increasing participation by previously marginalised groups of society in the political process, which has contributed to the further consolidation of Indian democracy. However, among these scholars and others writing on the topic, there is a conspicuous silence on the role of the media in fostering or facilitating such an upsurge in participation by aligning with local forces, which propelled them to challenge the dominance of the existing national political elite.

When the mobilisation of lower caste groups was underway in southern India, both Kerala and Tamil Nadu had the highest newspaper penetration; in 1961, Kerala had 40 newspapers and Tamil Nadu had 27 newspapers per 1,000 people (Table 3.2). This is in contrast to Madhya Pradesh and Uttar Pradesh in the Hindi heartland that had five and four newspapers per 1,000 people, respectively. Northern India began to witness the mobilisation of lower caste groups from the 1980s. In 1991, newspaper penetration in Madhya Pradesh and Uttar Pradesh went up to 28 and 29, respectively, per 1,000 people. This was the period when groups based on identity politics were becoming mobilised and actively participating in political developments. The mobilisation intensified in the decade of the 1990s, which Yadav (2000) has termed 'the second democratic upsurge'. Not surprisingly, in 2001 Madhya Pradesh and Uttar Pradesh had 76 and 56 newspapers, respectively, per 1,000 people. This suggests that there may be a link between fostering democratic participation among formerly marginalised Hindi-speaking groups and the growth of the Hindi language press.

Table 3.2: Literacy rates (%) and number of daily newspapers (per 1,000 people), 1961–2011

	Northern India				Southern India			
	Madhya Pradesh		Uttar Pradesh		Kerala		Tamil Nadu	
Year	Literacy rate	No. of dailies	Literacy rate	No. of dailies	Literacy rate	No. of dailies	Literacy rate	No. of dailies
1961	21.4	5	20.9	4	55.1	40	36.4	27
1971	27.3	8	24	6	69.8	52	45.4	30
1981	38.6	10	32.7	12	78.9	57	54.4	31
1991	44.7	28	40.7	29	89.8	72	62.7	30
2001	63.7	76	56.3	56	90.9	99	73.5	48
2011	70.6	217	64.3	187	93.9	199	80.3	104

Source: Census of India (relevant years) and Press in India (relevant years).

One might claim that newspaper circulation was rising because of the increase in literacy rates, but the growth of literacy alone cannot be the crucial factor: the percentage growth of newspaper circulation is higher than the growth of literacy.[15] This is reflected in Figure 3.2: no doubt, from the 1950s until the 1980s, the growth rate of literacy virtually matched the growth rate of daily circulation figures for newspapers. However, the decade of the 1990s witnessed phenomenal growth in the circulation of daily newspapers, which is more than double the growth rate of literacy (Figure 3.2). While the growth rate of literates was 59 per cent, the percentage growth of daily circulation was 134 per cent. Similarly, the first decade of the twenty first century saw further

---

15 I have used circulation data here to assess the growth of newspapers in India. Circulation data is based on the Annual Statement submitted by registered newspapers to the Registrar of Newspapers for India (RNI), published as *Press in India Report*, which publishes a circulation report every year. Some newspapers do not submit their annual report and, hence, are not counted in the final circulation figures released by the RNI. In 2015, the total number of registered newspapers in India was 1,05,443, whereas the Annual Statement was submitted by only 23,394 newspapers. Thus, the circulation figures must be higher than what are reported. The Annual Statement submitted by the registered newspapers is also verified by the RNI before preparing the final circulation figure, as some newspapers submit inflated figures. Another method is to look at the readership figures, but these figures are always disputed because several people read one newspaper and there is no agreement on the number of people reading one newspaper. Also, systematic readership data is available only from 2001 onwards. In order to make any meaningful analysis of the rise of newspapers and its impact on political mobilisation, one has to depend on circulation figures that are available from 1954.

massive growth of daily circulation. Interestingly, this is the period in which daily newspaper circulation has seen more significant growth than at any other period in the past. Thus, to get a comprehensive picture, one needs to investigate factors beyond literacy.

Figure 3.3: Growth rate of population, daily newspaper circulation and number of literates (%), 1951–61 to 2001–11

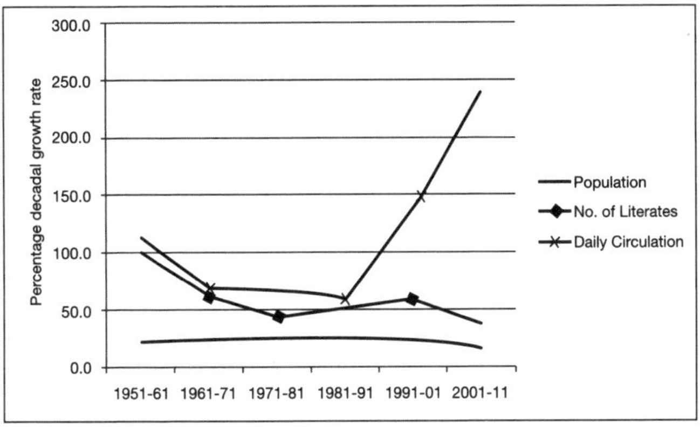

Source: Census of India (relevant years) and Press in India (relevant years).

There is no correlation between the percentage of literates and newspaper circulation as shown in Table 3.2. When Kerala had 55 per cent literacy, it had 40 dailies per 1,000 people, whereas when Tamil Nadu reached 54 per cent literacy it had just 31 dailies. Uttar Pradesh, which has a substantially higher population of nearly 200 million, had 56 dailies with 56 per cent literacy. Similarly, Madhya Pradesh reached 76 dailies per 1,000 people with just 64 per cent literacy, while Kerala had 72 dailies per 1,000 population with 90 per cent literacy. This highlights the need to look beyond literacy to understand the newspaper revolution in India.

Besides literacy, other factors have been responsible for the unprecedented growth of newspapers in India. One important factor is the improvement in purchasing power. With the growth of the Indian economy since 1991, purchasing power has increased; this has benefitted newspapers as people now subscribe to more than one newspaper. Even readers who exclusively used to read English newspapers have begun to subscribe to Hindi newspapers to get news about local happenings (Ninan, 2007; Ranganathan and Rodrigues, 2010).

Has the packaging of news to suit the changing orientation of readers contributed to the growth in daily circulation? The 1990s witnessed the opening up of the Indian economy to permit some foreign direct investment and movement of currency out of the country in 1991 for Indians to invest abroad, as well as the start of the consolidation of the communications revolution at the end of the twentieth century. There was also a simultaneous improvement in road transport, and many villages are now well connected to towns and cities. Pradhan Mantri Gram Sadak Yojana (PMGSY), launched in 2000, contributed a great deal to expanding rural road networks.[16] Earlier, people in villages could not read newspapers because of inaccessibility, illiteracy, or both. Now, most Indian language newspapers have opened regional and local offices even in remote areas to ensure that newspapers reach an interior village early in the morning. Newspapers have also customised news and content to suit specific audiences in different geographic locations through the process of localisation; this theme is explored in Chapter 4. Not surprisingly, *Dainik Bhaskar* and *Dainik Jagran* publish more than 200 sub-editions of the newspaper on a daily basis.

Table 3.3: Voter turnout in state assembly elections and number of daily newspapers per 1,000 in four Hindi-speaking states

Bi-party states					
Madhya Pradesh			Rajasthan		
Election year	Voter turnout	No. of dailies per 1,000	Election year	Voter turnout	No. of dailies per 1,000
1990	54.2	22	1990	57.1	27
1993	60.5	38	1993	60.6	37
1998	60.2	63	1998	63.4	70
2003	67.3	117	2003	67.2	98
2008	69.7	146	2008	66.3	134
2013	72.1	227	2013	75.0	206

Multi-party states					
Bihar			Uttar Pradesh		
Election year	Voter turnout	No. of dailies per 1,000	Election year	Voter turnout	No. of dailies per 1,000
1990	62.0	19	1991	48.5	29
1995	61.8	28	1993	57.1	31
2000	62.6	77	1996	55.7	42

16 For details, see Government of India (2011), Basic Road Statistics.

Multi-party states					
Bihar			Uttar Pradesh		
Election year	Voter turnout	No. of dailies per 1,000	Election year	Voter turnout	No. of dailies per 1,000
2005(Feb)	46.5	102	2002	53.8	56
2010	52.7	119	2007	46.0	82
2015	56.8	133	2011	59.4	187
			2017	61.0	

Source: Election Commission of India (relevant years) and Press in India (relevant years).

Returning to the role of Hindi newspapers in political mobilisation in north India, the pattern may be different in states with two-party systems versus multi-party systems. A two-party system is defined here as one in which the vast majority of the votes cast in an election in the state are for two parties. A multi-party system is defined here as one in which the vast majority of votes cast in elections are spread across more than two political parties in the state. I briefly explore developments in electoral turnout, which can be seen as an ultimate indicator of political mobilisation, and in the press since 1990, in four states in the Hindi-speaking heartland. Two of the states can be described as two-party systems and two can be described as multi-party systems.

Madhya Pradesh and Rajasthan are examples of states with two-party systems. The vast majority of voters in these two large Hindi-speaking states, with current populations of 72.59 and 68.5 million respectively, have shown over the past several elections a preference for one of two political parties. Turnout in these two states has for the most part increased over the past six elections. In Madhya Pradesh, from 54.2 per cent in 1990, voter turnout went up to 60.5 per cent in 1993 and remained stable in 1998 at 60.2 per cent before it rose in 2003 to 67.3 per cent. Voter turnout rose again in 2008 to 69.7 per cent before reaching the highest level in the state's history to 72.1 per cent in 2013. We see a similar upward trend in turnout in Rajasthan. From 1990 to 2003, voter turnout has seen a linear rise; 57.1 per cent in 1990 to 60.6 per cent in 1993, voter turnout rose to 63.4 per cent in 1998 and again 67.2 per cent in 2003. It stabilised in 2008 state election with 66.3 per cent turnout to rise again in 2013 to reach to a historic level of 75 per cent in 2013.

Bihar and Uttar Pradesh (UP) are examples of states with multi-party systems. The vast majority of voters in these two north Indian states, with current populations of 103.8 in Bihar and 199.6 million in UP, over the past several elections have shown a preference in voting for three or more political parties since 1990. Voter turnout in Uttar Pradesh was 48.5 per cent in 1991, which went up to 57.1 per cent in 1993 before it started to decline. Voter turnout declined slightly to 55.7 per cent in 1996 and came down further to 53.8 per cent in 2002 and then dropped to 46 per cent in 2007. Voter turnout rose dramatically in the 2012 state assembly election reaching to 59.4 per cent and went up slightly to 61 per cent in 2017. Voter turnout in Bihar remained stable with highest turnout throughout the decade of 1990s before it declined massively in 2005. In 1991, voter turnout was 62 per cent, the 1995 election recorded voter turnout of 61.8 per cent, while the 2000 assembly election saw voter turnout at 62.6 per cent. Voter turnout declined to 45.9 per cent in the 2005 assembly election before it rose again to 52.7 per cent in 2010 and 56.8 per cent in 2015.

Figure 3.4: Voter turnout (as a percentage of the eligible electorate) in Hindi-speaking states

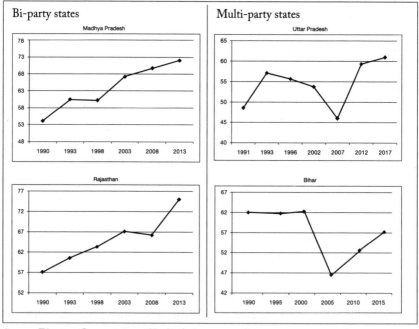

Source: Election Commission of India (relevant years).

Mayawati, a Dalit and former Chief Minister of Uttar Pradesh who was ousted from office in the 2012 state election, detested the mainstream media and accused them of an 'upper caste' bias (Bose, 2008). Mayawati's view of mainstream media suggests that her party, the Bahujan Samaj Party (BSP), which was founded by Kanshi Ram in 1984 and attracted support from lower caste groups, particularly Dalits, used means other than the mainstream press to garner public support and mobilise voters successfully until 2012. Both UP and Bihar have seen the mobilisation of people from the lower castes and lower class, who now have a significant voice in the political arena. The same sort of mobilisation has not been seen on a large scale in Madhya Pradesh and Rajasthan where upper caste groups are still powerful in politics.

In both two-party and multi-party states, the number of daily newspapers per 1,000 people increased from one election to the next as can be seen from the last column in Table 3.3, but at different rates of increase overall. In Uttar Pradesh, the number of dailies per 1,000 people increased more than six-fold from 29 in 1990 to 187 in 2015, compared with a seven-fold increase in Bihar from 19 in 1990 to 133 in 2015. In Madhya Pradesh, the number of dailies per 1,000 people increased more than ten-fold from 22 in 1990 to 227 in 2013. And in Rajasthan, the number of dailies increased more than seven-fold from 27 in 1990 to 206 in 2013.

An interesting project for future research would be to investigate the ways in which the growing number of daily newspapers may have helped or hindered political mobilisation in the form of electoral turnout in these states. Such a project could have three foci: first on turnout and party support based on aggregate voting data at the district level in each state at each election; second on party strategies at the district and state levels to foster political mobilisation, turnout and party support; and a third on how newspaper content may have fostered political engagement.

Conclusion

Hindi newspapers have traversed a long path in independent India and have come to occupy an important place in a globalising India judging from the record increases in Hindi newspaper numbers since 2000. The English media, which were mostly confined to the urban and English-educated sections of society, could not play an effective role in the grassroots mobilisation that started in the 1980s. The fragmentation of the national political system in the 1980s also saw the rise of the regional press alongside regional parties. The rise of vernacular political elites who were spearheading subaltern politics proved instrumental in the increasing role of the Hindi media in regional and national politics. The Hindi media provided a platform to the emerging political leaders of northern India to raise their voices in the public arena.

I have argued that the growing numbers of Hindi newspapers circulation in northern India has paralleled a trend of increasing mobilisation of marginalised groups since the 1980s. I have not attempted to disentangle which came first as that is the subject of a different volume. At the same time, I have noted how Hindi newspapers have strategically increased their concentration in state capitals since the mid-1980s, a period that witnessed the regionalisation of Indian politics. In the absence of sufficient data, one cannot assert that political participation in terms of voter turnout has been precipitated mainly by growth in the number of newspaper outlets.

Given the unequal contest between the English and Hindi media in independent India, few realised that Hindi would begin to triumph by the end of the twentieth century at least in the political, cultural and social spheres. Such is the effect of the rise of the Hindi news media that perhaps for the first time the English news media has had to seriously consider the challenges posed to its longstanding dominance over the social, cultural and political spheres in a globalising India. Thus, one needs to question the binary construction of domination and subordination, which are conceptual opposites that have long been used to simplify the discussion of colonial and post-independence India. In contemporary India, the situation is more complex: Hindi newspapers now are increasingly influencing political decision-making. However, Hindi newspapers still do not occupy the status that is commanded by English, the language of a growing Indian middle class.

4

Localisation, Grassroots Mobilisation
and Hindi News Media

Mobilisation is an important indicator of citizens' participation. With globalisation, the transformation in the nature of party politics and the increasing importance of non-party politics has facilitated the emergence of the new space for mobilisation. This new space is often visible in mediated grassroots mobilisation[1] that is marked by the participation of multiple actors trying to communicate and influence public opinion while pitching their own demands. India has witnessed rising grassroots mobilisation since the 1980s along with an explosion of identities – caste, regional and religious. The decades-long political control of the national political party, the Congress, at the centre and various states started to decline. Scholars writing on Indian politics began to pay great attention to these disruptive transformations particularly caste-based mobilisation (Chandra, 2004; Hasan, 2000; Jaffrelot and Kumar, 2009; Varshney, 2000; Yadav 2000), the rise of Hindu nationalism (Hansen, 1999; Hansen and Jaffrelot, 1998; Jaffrelot, 1993; Rajagopal, 2001; Thachil, 2014; Varshney, 1993) and regionalism (Baruah, 1999; Singh, 2000; Subramanian, 1999). These scholarly analyses certainly expanded our understanding of chaotic transformations. Yet, with the exception of Rajagopal (2001), most of these studies largely ignored the role played by the media in these transformations.[2]

Writing on India, Rajagopal (2001) has demonstrated how Hindutva politics took advantage of television to expand its mass base. Other studies in the Indian context, though not focusing on media alone, have found that newspapers can deliberately misinform citizens and actually serve to instigate conflicts among communities.[3] Hallin and Mancini (2004) show that in the West too, the newspapers play many different roles, often beyond just the 'liberal' function of providing neutral information. In some Western media systems, newspapers represent organised social groups or serve as tools for intervention by the elite.

This chapter analyses the role of localisation of Hindi newspapers in

---

1   Elsewhere this space has been termed as the vernacular public arena (See Neyazi and Tanabe, 2014).
2   The study by Rajagopal (2001) is an exception.
3   For example, Engineer (1991); Hasan (1998); and Nandy, Trivedy, Mayaram and Yagnik (1995).

grassroots mobilisation that provided an opportunity to vast numbers of the heterogeneous Hindi-speaking public from big and small towns, and rural areas to connect with each other and the world outside. By providing appealing, customised news to local societies, Hindi newspapers expanded their reach into the hinterland, and simultaneously created a space for marginalised groups to raise their grievances in the public arena. Interestingly, the study of localisation also shows the manifestation of three dominant forces in Indian politics – Hindutva, regionalism and caste politics – in more nuanced and complex ways.[4] At the same time, localisation has also helped in mobilising beyond the locality, particularly after the arrival of the internet. The empirical evidence from my fieldwork reflects the simultaneous trivialisation and sensationalisation of news as well as a concern for marginalised groups, which can be seen in the focus on the politics of the livelihood of its own public. This hybrid character of localisation mediated by Hindi newspapers is examined in this chapter. The burgeoning Hindi newspapers have not only affected politics and society at the local level, but have also changed the way people look at the Hindi media.

For example, in her study of the growth of newspapers in the Hindi-speaking states of India, Ninan (2007) tried to grasp the changing contours of Hindi journalism and its growing impact on local administration and politics. The localisation of news was followed by a process of delocalisation to cleanse the system. Newspaper management initiated the process of delocalisation to 'restore their credibility':

> … basic news ethics was revived, planted stories were eliminated, and circulation, reporting and advertising functions separated. … They became watchful of whom they appointed as stringers, and began to insist on basic reporting ethics being adhered to (139).

However, unlike Ninan (2007) who asserts that the process of localisation has been overtaken by delocalisation, I would argue that localisation is an ongoing process that has not been completed. Further, localisation has provided a space to diverse social groups in the vernacular to raise their grievances and demand basic livelihoods from the state. At the same time, the vernacular and the Hindi media have become important conduits of the process of globalisation, taking the workings of governance and the market deep into grassroots everyday life.

---

4   In an interesting study on local riots in a Uttar Pradesh town, Basu (1997) shows how various actors, including journalists and the press, play an important role in fomenting tensions and conflicts.

This chapter shows that through localisation, which is an offshoot of the process of globalisation, there has been politicisation of much larger spheres, which has helped previously marginalised groups raise their demands for better living standards and livelihoods in the public arena. To buttress my argument, I draw on examples from my fieldwork in Madhya Pradesh.

Localisation in the Hindi press

Localisation helped Indian language newspapers retain their advertising revenue in the face of competition from television news channels and new media. Until the 1970s, Hindi newspapers were produced like English newspapers, mostly from urban centres where most of the English-speaking readers lived. It took more than three decades for Hindi proprietors to go looking for readers in the smaller towns and rural areas. Hindi newspapers started to localise in the 1980s and were greatly facilitated by the communications revolution. There was also simultaneous improvement in road transport and many villages are now well connected to towns and cities. Localisation not only provided appealing, customised news to local societies, but also helped Hindi newspapers compete with television, which was eating away at the advertising revenues of newspapers.[5]

The process of localisation by Hindi newspapers involved decentralising production, distribution and consumption. This was made possible by the new technology and the information and communications revolution in the mid-1980s. Rajiv Gandhi, who became Prime Minister in 1984, looked favourably on the development of modern technology and 'promoted indigenous business in semi-conductors, telecommunications, computers and computer software' (Singhal and Rogers, 1989, 155).[6] With the introduction of economic reforms and the rapid globalisation of the Indian economy in the 1990s, the process of localisation accelerated. Jeffrey (1993, 2000) has illustrated the success of *Eenadu*, the Telugu newspaper with the largest circulation, launched in 1974, in localising the newspaper and creating a new base for local advertising from

---

5   Since 1991 when satellite channels started coming to India, the share of newspapers in the total advertising revenue has been sliding, while the share of television is continuously increasing. The share of newspapers in total advertisement revenues fell from 73 per cent in 1990 to 46 per cent in 2005, whereas during the same period, the share of television in total advertising revenues increased from 23 per cent to 44 per cent. However, this decline in advertising revenue for newspapers is not in absolute number. For details, see Kohli (2006, 20–21).

6   From 1984 to 1988, the number of computers increased ten-fold, the computer industry's revenues increased four-fold and computer software exports increased five-fold. This shows the increasing use of technology during this period (Singhal and Rogers, 1989, 155).

retailers, small businesses and sometimes from unexpected sources such as those mourning the death of prized pets and working farm animals.

The localisation of production involves decentralising newspaper production units. Newspapers used to be produced from a single centre and then distributed to different places, which was expensive and time-consuming. However, as multiple production centres were set up, newspapers could be printed simultaneously from different places. The development of offset printing technology and the advent of computers and the internet helped newspaper proprietors decentralise production and often provide even more local focus on specific pages of the newspaper in the locale where they were printed.

The localisation of distribution has multiplied the number of distribution centres and located them in previously remote areas to ensure that people in the hinterlands get their newspaper early in the morning.

Localisation of consumption involves taking news to the grassroots by including local happenings, such as local crimes, marriages, inauguration ceremonies and obituaries. Thus, *Dainik Jagran* and *Dainik Bhaskar*, the two leading Hindi newspapers, employ large numbers of local stringers, who need not be specialists in journalism, to send news from small towns and villages to be published in pages tailored for particular districts and towns.

Dainik Bhaskar, the Hindi newspaper with the second largest circulation, has 37 editions published across 12 states of India. The 37 editions are divided into sub-editions or satellite editions; one edition usually has a minimum of five and a maximum of nine sub-editions.[7] Currently, *Dainik Bhaskar* publishes more than 200 sub-editions on a daily basis. Each edition is different and only about 40 to 50 per cent of the stories are common across all editions, while the rest of the content is customised for the local area and the region. This helps the newspaper not only connect with the national, but also highlight regional aspirations and local sensibilities.

Localisation of newspaper production

The process of printing and distributing an edition is fairly complicated. This is illustrated below using the example of the interactions between the head office at Bhopal and the bureaus of *Dainik Bhaskar*. The interactions between the Bhopal office and Itarsi bureau are more or less similar across all editions.

---

7   The sub-edition is also known as the *dak* edition or satellite edition. These terms have been used interchangeably in this chapter.

Itarsi is a small town with a population of around 114,000 located 93 kilometres south of Bhopal. It is in Hoshangabad district and is a commercial centre for agricultural goods. *Dainik Bhaskar* established an office at Itarsi in 1989, but a sub-edition of four pages was launched only in 1996. This means that until 1996 there was no separate sub-edition for Itarsi; instead, the Bhopal edition of *Dainik Bhaskar* was distributed there, which would contain no more than a few stories on Itarsi. With the launch of the Itarsi sub-edition, four pages were created to carry stories exclusive to Itarsi. To showcase the paper as local, one or two stories in the Itarsi sub-edition are printed on the front page.

In 2007, eight satellite editions and one main edition were printed from Bhopal (Figure 4.1). Interestingly, Bharat Heavy Electricals Ltd (BHEL), an industrial town within Bhopal city, and Bairagarh, a suburb of Bhopal, have separate sub-editions; this reflects the extent of localisation that is practised by Hindi newspapers.

Figure 4.1: Sub-editions from Bhopal

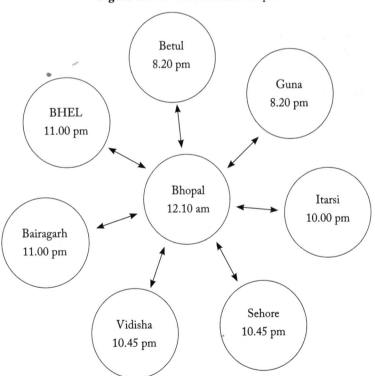

The release of the nine different editions depends on the distance from the city; the further the place is from the city, the sooner the pages are released from the editorial office. Thus, the pages for the first sub-edition of Betul, a town located about 151 kilometers from Bhopal, are released by 8.20 pm, while the pages for the main Bhopal edition are released only after midnight. Pages from editorial offices are transmitted through the internet to the printing centre. The printing technology installed in Bhopal can print around 32,000 pages an hour which was subsequently upgraded in 2010. Once printing starts at 9.00 pm, it prints various editions until 2.30 or 3.00 am. After the required number of copies of an edition is printed, the circulation department takes over and is responsible for selling and delivering newspapers to readers. Copies are stacked in different bundles and dispatched to the distribution centre by car or van. The first *dak* edition, that is Betul, is dispatched by 10.30 pm, while the final edition of Bhopal/BHEL city is dispatched between 2.30 and 3.00 am.[8] Bundles of the paper are dropped at roadside outlets, which are small outlets at road corners that have been set up by circulation agents. From there, hawkers collect their copies for distribution to readers. The transportation and delivery of the paper is the most important aspect in the process of newspaper production, as a delay in delivering the newspaper early in the morning would affect circulation. The circulation department organises and operates the distribution system to ensure that newspapers are delivered on time.[9] Figure 4.1 shows that there are two-way interactions between the head office and local bureaus. This is because the content of the pages from local bureaus is transmitted to the head office via the internet around 7.00 pm. The decision on the final product or what goes into the four-page pullout in each sub-edition is made at the head office. This also reflects the paradox of localisation; on the one hand, the news gathering process has been decentralised, but on the other hand, what people read at the local levels is decided at the head office. But in most cases, stories sent by the local bureaus are published unless they are sensitive or controversial.

There has been further diversification in the process of localisation of news production with the establishment of new printing centre at Hoshangabad in 2010. With the establishment of a new printing centre, two editions (Betul

---

8   The Bhopal and BHEL editions are dispatched at the same time, because BHEL is an industrial town located within Bhopal city. Although the BHEL edition has separate four-page pullouts called *BHEL Bhaskar*, the content in the main pages is nearly identical.

9   A detailed description of the functioning of the circulation department is given in Chapter 5 on advertising.

and Itarsi) have been separated from Bhopal. The new printing centre was established to ensure that late night news could be printed in the main pages of the newspapers. The latest printing technology has been installed in big cities including Bhopal which could print up to 85,000 copies per hour compared with 35,000 copies previously. With this new printing technology, newspapers begin printing at 11.00 pm instead of 8.00 pm, which often resulted in missing some important events. Together, new printing centre and high speed printing technology have further enabled the newspaper to cover late night happenings including sports events.

Localisation and expansion

To widen their readership, *Dainik Bhaskar* introduced *Upcountry City Bhaskar*, a four-page weekly pullout on lifestyle and local happenings that is targeted at youth and women. This is along the lines of *City Bhaskar*, a four-page pullout carrying soft news about happenings in and around Bhopal city, but targeted at rural areas. This concept has not yet been tried by any other Hindi newspaper, because 'upcountry' is considered less desirable for consumer-oriented lifestyles. Mukul Gupta, in charge of *Upcountry City Bhaskar*, said:

> Usually in the local pullouts, we publish routine news and provide information to the readers, rather than giving something for entertainment. Keeping in view the changing expectations of the readers from a newspaper, we have come out with the idea of providing them stuff that would not only inform them, but also entertain them. In those four pages we are not going to talk about *garibi* (poverty), *netā* (politicians) and *khetī* (agriculture). The content would exclusively be positive, directed to create feel-good among the readers with inspirational stories about local heroes who have moved forward in life with struggle, rather than corruption.[10]

This statement reveals that highlighting aspirational values is the main focus of *Upcountry City Bhaskar*. Keeping in view the 'conservative' lifestyles practised in the countryside compared to the city, *Dainik Bhaskar* is careful and moves slowly, rather than making a radical move that might alienate readers. Mukul Gupta said, 'We are not going against the *saṃskriti* (culture), but focusing on urban *saṃskriti.*' This demonstrates that *Dainik Bhaskar* emphasises local specificities, while trying to introduce new ways to attract readers.

---

10 Interviewed on 12 December 2007, Bhopal.

Dainik Bhaskar has also been successful in creating a new constituency of readership that has helped them multiply their circulation. It is commonly believed that the younger generation is largely apathetic towards newspapers. The trend of declining readership among young people with the rise of television was also observed in the US (Donovan and Scherer, 1992, 305). However, *Dainik Bhaskar* has successfully captured young readers. Through its coverage of cultural programmes in the schools and colleges, *Dainik Bhaskar* has gained popularity among the younger generation and other newspapers subsequently followed the format. The advantage of newspapers over television is their ability to capture the moment through still photos that readers can clip and save. By using this feature effectively, *Dainik Bhaskar* has been able to reach younger readers, who have a different orientation from older readers. Through regular and photographic coverage of such events, *Dainik Bhaskar* has changed the media landscape not only in Bhopal but also in other parts of India where it has editions.

Dainik Bhaskar has also been able to attract women readers through regular features on issues relating to women and coverage of events organised by women groups in the city. According to National Readership Survey (NRS) 2006 data, 66 per cent of women readers in Madhya Pradesh read *Dainik Bhaskar*. Events covered by *Dainik Bhaskar* include fashion shows, beauty contests and health workshops and it also publishes regular features on women's health and wellness, safety, etc. To provide exclusive coverage on issues pertaining to women, *Women Bhaskar* was started in December 2007 as one page in the four-page *City Bhaskar* pullout.[11] The main aim of *Women Bhaskar* is to highlight the achievements of local women and publish inspirational stories about women.[12]

Localisation has, thus, helped Hindi newspapers target different audiences more effectively. This enabled them to cash in on the local market and businesses for advertising. Since the principal outlook of television is national, the regional and local spaces have largely remained unoccupied and are now being

---

11 *Women Bhaskar* was first launched from Indore. It is the first daily pullout designed exclusively for women, distributed along with the main edition of *Dainik Bhaskar*. Its success in Indore prompted the Bhaskar Group to launch an edition in Bhopal as well in December 2007. However, it is only one page combined with *City Bhaskar* because the group wanted to see the response of readers before launching a full four-page pullout. Despite being a success, Women Bhaskar as a separate page was discontinued and was integrated in City Bhaskar in 2014.

12 Personal interview with Bhoomika Kalam, central desk, in charge of *Women Bhaskar*, 12 December 2007, Bhopal.

appropriated by Indian language newspapers.[13] A similar process was noted in the US in the 1970s when major newspapers started 'zoning, the provision for special sections within a newspaper that are addressed to only one area of a city or suburb' (Smith, 1980, 143). This helped them offer their advertisers opportunities to reach their audiences at a lower cost and more effectively than was possible in rival media. In India, however, the fight for regional markets has already begun with the coming of regional satellite channels, such as Sahara TV and ETV.

Hindi newspapers have begun to emphasise special reporting over routine news. The initial apprehension that television would sound the death knell for newspapers has died down. The early years of television expansion sent alarm signals across newspapers circles, but newspapers are now reconciled to the fact that television has usurped the monopoly of breaking news, which was once the domain of newspapers. Since routine news is usually shown on television early in the morning before it is published in the newspapers, the need to provide news that has not already been broadcast on television has become paramount. *Dainik Bhaskar* has several special correspondents who travel regularly to develop special and exclusive stories.

Localisation has required newspapers to spread their reach into the hinterlands and move beyond the headlines of television. On occasion, special stories covered by newspapers are picked up by television. Ganesh Sakalle, special correspondent at *Dainik Bhaskar*'s Bhopal office, observed that often his stories are taken up by television channels and this point is validated by other television journalists.[14]

News channels continuously monitor the stories printed in newspapers, since they might come across stories from remote areas or even from big cities that have human interest or commercial value. 'We have to admit that newspapers have a strong network in remote areas and if we come across some stories which

---

13 It must be noted that city-based cable channels are already present in several big cities including Bhopal. There were two cable channels in Bhopal: *BTV*, owned by the Dainik Bhaskar Group and *Raj TV*, owned by the Raj Express Group. There was sharp rivalry between the two over their share in the limited available advertisement revenue. They could get only retail or educational advertisements because of their limited reach. However, along with digitisation that has already been completed in Tier 1 cities and will soon be implemented all over India, cable networks have to either convert to satellite broadcast or close down.

14 For example, Deshdeep Saxena, Special Correspondent, Star News, Bhopal, explained, 'As newspapers have wider networks of reporters and stringers than television channels, it is possible for them to reach areas where the television crew cannot go. However, once a story is published in the newspaper and is worthy of being covered by our channel, we immediately ask our local stringer to get that story.' Personal interview on 1 January 2008, Bhopal.

we find important, we have to follow it then', explains Amit Jain, Principal Correspondent, TV Today Network Limited, Bhopal. Ajit Wadnerkar, a news editor of *Dainik Bhaskar* in Bhopal office, told me that on several occasions television journalists would call them to get details about a particular story published in the paper so that they could cover it.[15]

This discussion shows how through localisation Hindi press has started to provide more customised news to its readers and a more specialised audience to the advertisers. The discussion also brings out the interaction between newspapers and television at the local level, in which the latter has been able to exploit the vast resources of the newspapers for its own benefit to select stories to cover. Yet, this interaction between newspapers and television should also be viewed as a process that helps in bringing local issues to the larger public.

Hindi newspapers and marginalised groups

Most of the people working at the *Dainik Bhaskar* editorial office were local middle class or lower middle class residents of Bhopal. There were a few people who had migrated from a small town to Bhopal in search of the better work opportunities that large cities offer. There was a small minority that was more ambitious and wanted to move to a larger city, such as Delhi, for the career advancement that the political capital could offer. However, they felt handicapped because they did not know English.

Despite the middle class background of the reporters, they belonged to the Hindu upper caste. Despite Hindu being the majority group in India constituting 79.8 per cent of total population according to the 2011 census, they are divided along caste lines. The caste structure in which upper caste Hindus occupy a privileged position marginalising Dalits and tribals recognised as Scheduled Castes and Scheduled Tribes in the Constitution, constitute nearly 16.6 per cent and 8.6 per cent, respectively, within Hindu group. The other religious groups such as Muslims constitutue 14.2 per cent of India's total population (Census of India, 2011c). In India, along with class in terms of economic status, caste is an important determinant of one's status in society. For instance, a person might belong to the upper class of society, but if he/ she belongs a lower caste group, class does not help much in commanding

---

15 Interviewed on 26 December 2007, Bhopal.

respect.[16] Hindi newspapers are largely dominated by upper caste professionals who come from the middle or lower middle class. This is in contrast to English newspapers, which have mainly been dominated by upper castes from the upper middle class of society. Such class and caste combinations of domination in India were reflected in the structure of *Dainik Bhaskar*, as there was not a single Dalit reporter working for the newspaper and only one Muslim reporter, Alim Bazmi, who had been associated with *Dainik Bhaskar* since 1980. One might ask why in a city with a population that was nearly 40 per cent Muslim there was such a conspicuous absence of Muslims from the newsroom. Yet, the overall representation of Muslims in the Bhopal news media is better than that of Dalits and tribals. There are several Muslim journalists working for national and international news media, such as New Delhi Television Limited (NDTV) and British Broadcasting Corporation (BBC). What surprises one most is the almost negligible presence of Dalits and tribals in the news media in Bhopal. Such upper caste domination has had a strong impact upon the process of reporting and happenings related to the lower caste and gender that are discussed later in this chapter.

An institution that is incapable of representing social diversity in its structure and functioning cannot claim to be democratic and progressive. No doubt, the Indian media has played a reasonably important role in reflecting social problems in the public sphere and is admired as a role model for other third world countries. Yet, when looking at the composition and structure of the Indian media, it was and continues to be dominated by the upper caste, without giving adequate representation to people belonging to Scheduled Castes/Scheduled Tribes and other minority groups. In a 2006 survey, Yogendra Yadav highlighted the unrepresentative nature of the Indian national media, noting the dominance of upper caste Hindus who constitute 71 per cent of the key decision-makers in the national media. Similarly, in his study of Indian language newspapers, Robin Jeffrey (2000) writes:

… in more than ten years studying Indian language newspapers, including twenty weeks of travel in which I stayed in twenty towns, visited dozens of newspapers and interviewed more than 250 people, I did not – so far as I know – meet a Dalit journalist working for a mainstream publication, much less a Dalit editor or proprietor (160).

---

16   There is plenty of literature that examines the institution of caste in India. Some of the important literature is Srinivas (1962); Beteillé (1965, 1969); Dumont (1970); and Gupta (2000).

Such a trend is also evident in Hindi newspapers. During my fieldwork in Bhopal and Itarsi, I was able to find only a few journalists from a Scheduled Caste or Scheduled Tribe background. *Dainik Bhaskar*, the second widest-read newspaper in India with multiple editions, did not have a single Dalit journalist among its staff at its Bhopal and Itarsi offices. Similarly, there was not a single Dalit in the management or marketing department.

Based on the 2011 census, the population of Dalits or Scheduled Castes in India is 20.14 crore or over 200 million people. The Dalit population grew 20.8 per cent since the 2001 census compared to India's population as a whole that incresed 17.7 per cent during the same period (Sivakumari, 2013). Given the size of the Dalit population, what factors are responsible for the absence of Dalits in the institution of media? Their absence might be attributed to the lack of competent professionals among Dalits and other minority groups suited to work as media professionals. Sunil Salve, a Dalit reporter in *Free Press*, a local English daily, believes that 'many Dalits are not aware of the opportunities existing outside the government sector which is largely responsible for their absence from the media.'[17] N. K. Singh, the resident editor of *Dainik Bhaskar* in Bhopal from 2000 to 2004, told me that when he was the editor he tried to recruit people from the lower caste, but he could not find any applications from them.[18]

For educated Dalits, the profession of journalism indeed may be one to which they least aspire because of potential obstacles to their career advancement in the industry, and given the perceived higher risk of taking a job in the private sector when they would be able to advance in a public sector job. Thus, educated Dalits prefer more secure jobs in the government sector, where they obtain positions because of the reservation policy, which makes it relatively easier for them to advance in their career.[19] Such a perception ignores structural limitations that keep certain groups from aspiring to particular professions. It is a fact that upper caste groups own all the large media groups in India. This creates a perception among Dalits, who have been both socially discriminated against and economically exploited by some upper caste groups, that they would not be welcome in the media industry even if they obtained the necessary skills. Such structural limitations might not be visible in the public arena, but are internalised by marginalised groups who feel that certain occupations and jobs are beyond their reach.

---

17 Interviewed on 4 January 2008, Bhopal.

18 Interviewed on 8 January 2008, Ahmedabad.

19 As observed by Sunil Salve, a Dalit journalist. Interviewed on 4 january 2008, Bhopal.

Another reason for the invisibility of Dalits might be the reluctance of Dalit reporters to reveal their identity, since this might expose them to further discrimination. P. P. Karadey, a noted Dalit journalist in Bhopal, felt that there must be a few Dalit journalists in Bhopal, but they might not want to reveal their caste for fear of being marginalised.[20] Such social and structural constraints that force certain groups to hide their identity cannot be considered good for a healthy democracy. A society that does not allow people to live freely with their inherent identity forces the group to assimilate, willingly or unwillingly, to the dominant culture.

Karadey, who started his career in journalism in 1962 with *Hitvada*, an English daily, described the difficulties that he confronted whenever he wanted to highlight Dalit issues. But he also praised A. D. Mani, the editor of *Hitvada* and a noted journalist, for his support and encouragement, which allowed Karadey to write about Dalits' problems.[21]

Whatever the reasons behind the marginalisation of Dalits from one of the important institutions of democracy, the outcome is obvious. Invariably, the Dalit agenda has been marginalised and has received inadequate coverage in the national press. Atrocities inflicted on Dalits rarely find adequate coverage in the national media. In the absence of adequate representation of Dalits in the institution of media, issues pertaining to Dalits, if not totally effaced from the public sphere, are left at the mercy of those manning the media organisations. Babu Lal, a reporter at *Dainik Jagran*, Bhopal told me that news pertaining to Dalits gets space in the paper even though marginally. But when he wants to do special stories on problems related to Dalits, he cannot get anyone interested in publishing the stories.[22] Similarly, Stahlberg (2002b) in his study of a Hindi language daily has noted biased reporting by *Dainik Jagran* against the Bahujan Samaj Party (BSP) chief, Ms. Mayawati, who is a Dalit. The newspaper not only claimed that Ms Mayawati had a 12 year old illegitimate daughter, but also went to the extent of using the derogatory word 'chamarin' for her.[23] According to her biographer, Bose (2008), the hostile relationship of Mayawati with the

---

20 Interviewed on 4 January 2008, Bhopal.

21 P. P. Karadey used to write about the issues related to *Majhi* or fishing community to which he belonged.

22 Interviewed on 29 December 2007, Bhopal.

23 In December 1995, *Dainik Jagran* published a story based on an interview with a former Uttar Pradesh state minister, who claimed that Mayawati, the former chief minister of UP, had a 12 year old illegitimate daughter. For details, see Stahlberg (2002).

mainstream media was one of main reasons that they ignored the rising political graph of the BSP. Not surprisingly, Mayawati, who won the assembly election in Uttar Pradesh in 2007, preferred to work at the grassroots level to reach out to voters rather than using the mainstream media – print and television, which she described as biased *manuwadi* (upper caste) media. In this context, Loynd (2008) argues that BSP and Mayawati by disengaging with mainstream media and using local myths, icons and oral histories to mobilise support have been able to create a counter-public sphere.[24]

While Dalits were able to achieve political empowerment in northern India by forming their own political parties and contesting elections, they are yet to achieve adequate representation in one of the important institutions of modern democracy. Political agency might be an important milestone in achieving self-respect for groups who have remained marginalised for decades, but to achieve overall development and progress it is equally important for marginalised groups to get adequate representation in all democratic institutions. Otherwise, political agency might be used for limited gain as happened in Bihar during the Rashtriya Janata Dal (RJD) rule. When the chief of the RJD, Lalu Prasad Yadav, realised that upper caste influence are dominant in state institutions, he started to weaken them, which affected policy-oriented governance during RJD rule (see Witsoe, 2011). To escape this eventuality, all democratic institutions need to provide at least adequate, if not proportional, representation to all minority groups.

Do Dalits need to establish their own media in order to reflect their problems in the public arena? Or can media organisations be asked to devise policies and make efforts to recruit Dalits and other minority groups in the newsroom in their own interests? One needs to be reminded of the race riots in the 1960s in the US when most mainstream news media did not have any African-American reporters who could go to the riot-affected areas to report on the violence. In the wake of the violence, all media organisations realised the importance of recruiting African-Americans in their newsroom and made conscious efforts to create newsroom diversity.[25] This offers an important lesson for Indian media on how to make their newsroom more diverse and democratic by taking special measures to recruit Dalits and other minority groups.

---

24 Narayan (2011) in his painstaking work shows how by using local symbols, iconography, oral histories and popular Dalit booklets – *choti kitabein*, Dalits have been able to form a Dalit public sphere in northern India that has worked for Dalits' empowerment.

25 For details, see Donovan and Scherer (1992).

Despite the absence of Dalits from the news room, stories about Dalits do find a space in the newspaper. Such stories are often presented as human interest stories instead of being highlighted as a consequence of the caste issue. This is a recent development in the Hindi newspaper-mediated public arena. By creating a discourse based on common human values, Hindi newspapers have been able to attract wider attention and forged a new vernacular identity that cuts across caste, class and region. Yet, the Indian media in general report Dalit issues within two dominant frames – either as victims or privileged. The victim frame is used for stories related to atrocities and oppression of Dalits while the privileged frame is used to attack the reservation policy for Dalits in government jobs. Such framing can lead to oversimplification of more complex issues ignoring Dalits' perspectives and perpetuates existing bias against the community.

Gender and the Hindi newspapers

Another gap in the structure of Hindi newspapers is the limited presence of women journalists. There were only a handful of women journalists working at *Dainik Bhaskar's* Bhopal office during my early fieldwork in 2006. Of the 27 journalists, only five were women in *Dainik Bhaskar*, including two in *City Bhaskar*. There were no women journalists at the Itarsi office until 2006. The situation had improved by my second round of fieldwork in 2008; three new women joined *Women Bhaskar* and one woman was appointed to work at Itarsi for a new supplement of *Dainik Bhaskar* called *Upcountry City Bhaskar*, a publication aimed at youth and the aspiring middle class. When I returned for another round of fieldwork in December 2012 to January 2013, there were still only about the same number of women journalists as in 2008.

Women journalists were usually assigned beats where they did not need to run to different places. Popular beats among women journalists were health, education, and women and child-centric issues. Now, political reporting is also assigned to women journalists. While commenting on women journalists' preference for certain beats, Jayshree Pingle, a special correspondent in *Dainik Bhaskar*, commented, 'It's also a matter of personal choice. Many women do not prefer doing political or crime beats, as it requires travelling to different places.'[26] She further stated that she has been doing political reporting for the

---

26 Interviewed on 12 December 2007, Bhopal.

past decade and her editor always encouraged her to continue with it. Similarly, Bhoomika Kalam worked as a crime reporter with *Dainik Bhaskar* in Indore before shifting to Bhopal to head the *Women Bhaskar* team.

While in some cases it was a matter of personal choice, the decision to work on a particular beat is also related to women's position in Indian society. In addition to work, Indian, women also need to look after household chores and take care of children, or hire a maid, or count on family for support, as Indian men are largely exempt from these household responsibilities which leaves men free to work until late at night. Neelam Sharma, a senior reporter, told me that it was always difficult for her to manage the home as well as her job. 'You need family support in order to survive in the profession of journalism as sometimes you need to work late in the night.'[27] The personal preference of women for certain beats is both structurally embedded and influenced by personal and family considerations, rather than the nature of the beats.

However, the marginal presence of women journalists in Hindi newspapers is in sharp contrast to English newspapers where women journalists have a significant presence, and even outnumber male journalists. N. K. Singh remarked that when he was working with *Dainik Bhaskar*, he would see hardly any women after 9.00 pm. However, after he joined the *Indian Express* as a resident editor in Ahmedabad, he hardly noticed male journalists working in the office at night, instead there were women.[28]

N. K. Singh's remarks reveal how English journalism has been occupied by women journalists, whereas Hindi journalism is still not chosen by Indian women. Stahlberg (2002a), in his study of a Hindi language Lucknow daily explained the reasons for the absence of women from Hindi journalism, which he attributes to the different perceptions of Hindi and English journalism in Indian society. English journalism is perceived as concerning the elite, which deals with issues of national concern. Thus, educated Indian women looking for respected jobs find English journalism attractive, whereas Hindi journalism is viewed as a less desirable profession.

When I began my second round of fieldwork, I observed more women in the editorial staff of *Dainik Bhaskar*, although their numbers were still lower than the number of male journalists. Unlike English journalism, women are new to the field of Hindi journalism, which has traditionally been dominated by men. Jayshree Pingle mentioned that she was the only woman journalist when

---

27 Interviewed on 12 December 2007, Bhopal.
28 Interviewed on 8 January 2008, Ahmedabad.

she started working in Indore in 1991, but now there are at least eight women journalists in the Indore office.[29] Hindi newspapers did not feel the need to recruit women until the late 1990s when they realised that women were also among their readers because they were also becoming major consumers. This generated the move to recruit more women who could provide better insights into issues of interest to women.

Further, most English newspapers are published from metropolitan areas and large cities where women have greater freedom and access to better education, whereas Hindi newspapers are largely published from small towns and cities in northern India where female literacy is still far lower than the male literacy rate. The change in perception towards women is slower in small towns than in metropolitan areas. Not surprisingly, the percentage of women is abysmally low in Hindi newspapers compared to English newspapers.

The rapid transformation of Indian society since the 1990s accompanied by the change in outlook towards Hindi journalism has contributed to an increase in the number of women in the field of Hindi journalism. Jayshree Pingle told me that working with *Dainik Bhaskar* was a matter of choice for her, rather than a compulsion.[34] She also praised the concern of the Bhaskar Group towards women journalists. In 2006, *Dainik Bhaskar* held a conference in Bhopal that brought together all their women journalists working on different editions of the newspaper. The aim of the conference was to create a better working environment for women journalists and understand their concerns and special needs, as well as their perceptions of the management, explained Shravan Garg, Group Editor, *Dainik Bhaskar*, Bhopal.[30]

Despite these efforts to become more diverse at *Dainik Bhaskar*, women journalists still remain at the margins of Hindi journalism. The inadequate presence of women journalists in *Dainik Bhaskar* was sometimes reflected in the way stories related to women were reported and presented. For example, on 26 December 2006, a story was published on the front page with the headline, *Abhī bebas hī rahenge patnī pīḍhit pati* (The wife-tormented husband will remain helpless for now). The publication of such a sexist headline, according to Rakesh Dewan, special correspondent, was directly related to the lack of women editorial staff who could go over the story, before it was approved for printing.[31]

---

29 Interviewed on 12 December 2007, Bhopal.

30 Interviewed on 1 November 2006, Bhopal.

31 Interviewed on 17 December 2006, Bhopal.

With the launch of *Women Bhaskar*, the total number of women on the editorial staff increased. Three new women were recruited to write features on women-related issues. Similarly, the launch of *Upcountry City Bhaskar*, targeted at young people, created the need to recruit more women to interact with younger teenage girls and write stories on issues of interest to women. One can question this approach of Hindi newspapers towards women, which appears to consider them competent only in the area of women-related issues which is not the case in the English press where one finds many more women journalists. This is contrary to the fact that women have excelled in other fields such as business, politics, sports, creative writing, and have a significant presence in the field of English journalism.

Localisation and grassroots mobilisation

Localisation has spurred significant debates and discussions and helped in mediating the issues and problems of the diverse groups and individuals in the public arena. One important theoretical concern of the present research is to examine democratic consolidation not only at the macro-level, but to examine how diverse social groups in local arenas are being mobilised through Hindi newspapers. While looking at the development of the public sphere in the colonial period, Freitag (1989) argues that alternative-arena activities played an important role in mobilising the masses and constituted an important alternative to political institutions created by an imperial state. In western Europe, private individuals came together to support the public cause through the exercise of public opinion. However, in the alternative realm of the public arena, communities and collective activities played a vital role. The continuity discernible in public arena activities in contemporary India is the use and existence of collective activities to apply pressure on the state in order to achieve a particular goal. However, in the absence of state intervention, private individuals also come together to take up development issues on their own.

Newspapers play a central role in informing, and potentially shaping, public opinion. Newspapers can also serve as an important channel for raising public grievances and can put pressure on the state to act in a more responsible manner. Looking at the dramatic growth of Hindi newspapers over the past two decades, one cannot ignore the power and potential of the Hindi press to influence the implementation of state policies. As people have become more aware of their rights, there has been increasing pressure on local administrative authorities and government bodies to deliver. When I visited the Municipal Corporation Office at Itarsi, the Chief Municipal Officer (CMO) told me:

> There has been a collaborative approach between the authority and the newspapers. Issues are brought to our notice through the newspaper and then we take action accordingly…Two years ago we used to go through 100 files in a day, but today we deal with around 400 files everyday.

He further said, 'We take action on most of the issues highlighted through different newspapers, but the probability of quick action is high if news is aired in *Dainik Bhaskar*.' His statement shows that the localisation of newspapers has reinvigorated local authorities to take action on issues of public concern raised through newspapers. Instead of a confrontational approach, local media and the local administration have adopted a collaborative approach to resolve local issues and problems.

However, the dominant position that a large newspaper has come to occupy in the local discourse of power is also evident. The bargaining power of a large newspaper in relation to the local administrative authority is inevitable, but is also a major cause of corruption. During my fieldwork I observed the prevalence of corruption among journalists. According to one of my informants at Itarsi:

> Most of the journalists make money by hiding real problems from the people. They only publish stories that are non-controversial and not going to adversely affect the local administration and powerful people in the town. If there are some honest journalists who are bold enough to highlight the issues of corruption going on at a higher level or who write against the local criminals, they are soon transferred to another place.[32]

He pointed out that the former head of *Dainik Bhaskar*'s local bureau at Itarsi was threatened by local criminals when he exposed their illegal activities in the town and their nexus with the local administration. He was asked to move to another bureau and was replaced by a new bureau head. One could question how far the localisation of newspapers has encouraged meaningful debates and discussions at the local level. Has it revealed genuine problems in the public arena or has it become an instrument of manipulation in the hands of local journalists, criminals and officials who collaborate in their own self-interest? Before answering these questions, I want to highlight some evidence from my

---

32 I have not used his real name to maintain his anonymity.

fieldwork that reflect the complexities of the process of localisation that could not be settled in an either/or paradigm. The Hindi media-enabled grassroots mobilisation is not only directed against the government and to demand rights, but is also facilitating the development of alternative-arena activities or a space of community feelings where there is no shared community moral or norm but collective engagement with matters of common interest (Tanabe, 2007).

The first case comes from Itarsi, where the government was forced to respond by the local media and citizens. The evidence comes from a *qasba*[33] called Sohagpur,[34] which is 46 kilometres east of Itarsi. The area was affected by floods in August and September of 2006. News about the flood and the people affected by it was regularly covered by Abhinay Soni, a stringer for *Dainik Bhaskar*. The headline on the story, which appeared on 3 September2006, was *Jalastar utrā, khatra ṭalā* (The level of flood water receded, danger averted). In the same story, he mentioned a man named Dhanraj, who had taken shelter from August 14 in a makeshift camp in the compound of a government school. Dhanraj was running a fever and his condition was deteriorating.

The story appeared on the front page of the four-page pullout for Itarsi with a photograph of Dhanraj. The text warned local administrators and asked them to provide immediate help or Dhanraj might die. When the story was published, the administration went into action and Dhanraj was asked to go to the *tehsil* office for help. Since Dhanraj was unwell, his wife Anita went to the *tehsil* office on 4 September, but when she arrived, she was told that her husband had passed away. The next day, Abhinay Soni had another by-line on the front page with the headline *Antataḥ mar gayā Dhanraj* (At last: Dhanraj died). The story was flashed along with a micro-copy of the previous story that had warned the administration. The story highlighted the administration's lacklustre attitude that had resulted in Dhanraj's death, pointing out that instead of asking Dhanraj to come to the *tehsil* office for help, the administration should have sent someone to meet him. These were the questions raised in the story. The next day people blocked the main road to protest the administration's mishandling of the situation. Later, Dhanraj's wife and five-year-old daughter received Rs. 20,000 as compensation; she was also given a clerical job in a local government office.

---

33 A *qasba* is a place between a small town and a village.

34 Sohagpur is 125 kilometres from Bhopal. It has a population of 25,040 and the literacy rate is nearly 84.5 per cent. See Census (20011).

This incident highlights the impact of the localisation of newspapers. It was only through the publication of the story in the local edition that the administration came to know about Dhanraj's condition and tried to help him. While the delay in providing help may have resulted in his death, it provoked people to protest against the administration and to apply pressure to help the family of the deceased. It can be argued therefore that without localisation it would have been nearly impossible for the issue to get such wide attention and Anita would not have been given a payout nor a secure job. Since the news published in the local pullout goes to the district collector as well as the local Member of Legislative Assembly (MLA) and Member of Parliament (MP), and is widely read within the district and nearby towns, the administration was pressured to take action.

This case could be compared with another case in which mobilisation through localisation received global attention because of the internet.

Localisation after the internet

> I am Shilpy Sharma, calling from California. I read the news about Tulsabai in the internet edition of *Dainik Bhaskar*. I want to help her, please let me know the way.

This call was received after *Dainik Bhaskar* published a story about Tulsabai on 12 October 2006.[35] The title of the story was *Pati keśav ko lāvāris choḍ jāegī Tulsa* (Tulsa will have to abandon her husband's body). The window of the news story mentioned that *Antīm saṃskār ke liye Rāmcandra kī lāś ko Betul le jāne ke liye patnī Tulsa ke pās paise nahiṃ hai* (The wife Tulsa does not have the money to take the body of her husband back to Betul for the final rites).

The story was about a wife whose husband was electrocuted while going to the fields for work. They were residents of a village called Chirapatla in Betul district, which is around 95 kilometres from Bhopal. The only good hospital in the region was in Bhopal. With great difficulty and the meagre support of INR 500 provided by the local police station, Tulsabai took her husband to Bhopal and admitted him in a local government hospital called Hameedia. However, her husband Ramchander died the next day on 11 October 2006. The

---

35   It was covered by Sunit Saxena, a crime reporter in *Dainik Bhaskar*.

publication of the news story resulted in an unexpected call from a woman in California who offered to give Tulsabai money to take her husband's body back to her village for the final rites. In Bhopal, after reading the story published in *Dainik Bhaskar*, many people gathered at Hameedia hospital in the morning to help Tulsabai.

Two days later on 13 October the newspaper published a story on the front page with the caption, 'Bhaskar Impact'. It read, *Bhopāl se Kailīphorniā tak uṭhe madad ko hāth* (From Bhopal to California, people raised their hands to help). The story had a line stating, '*Pati kī lāś ko lāvāris choḍ jāegī Tulsa' khabar chapne se jāgī mānvie sanvednāe'* (People's consciousness rose after the publication of the story that 'Tulsa will have to abandon her husband's body'). The story highlighted the concerns of the people who kept calling the *Dainik Bhaskar* office to find out how to help Tulsabai. Further, many people rushed to the Hameedia hospital to personally help. By the time the body was handed over to Tulsabai after the post-mortem, she had received a collection of INR 30,000. Before leaving for her village, she expressed her gratitude to the local people and told them that there is not one Tulsabai, but many who visit the hospital and need financial assistance.

The impact of the story can be judged from the way people came forward to help Tulsabai. It also resulted in vigorous debates about setting up an emergency fund to help needy people. Instead of approaching the government, people decided to set up an alternative way of dealing with such issues. The story was followed upon the next day, 14 October with the title *Tāki nahiṃ dekhnā paṛe sarkār kā mūṃh* (So that we don't need to beg from the government).

This story also highlights the increasing connection between offline and online media, a subject discussed in greater detail in Chapters 6 and 7. The help received from California might not have been possible in the pre-internet era and shows the potential of transnational mobilisation in the post-broadcast era. At the same time, the story shows that alternative-arena activities are being used to deal with development issues. After the story was published, it was not the government that came forward to help the victim; rather, common citizens were mobilised. On 14 October, the local MLA, Uma Shankar Gupta, wrote a letter, which was published in *Dainik Bhaskar*, that it would be good for society to come forward to help such needy people and the government would provide some assistance. The reason for encouraging society to take up such issues on its own was to avoid the misuse of development organisations by different political parties that had a vested interest. It is apparent that the government is willing to provide indirect support to such organisations, but without direct intervention.

Although in both cases the victims belonged to the Dalit community, the issue was not framed in parochial terms to make it a caste issue. Rather, it was framed as a general problem that might be experienced by common people. By framing an issue in particular ways, the media might facilitate political and civic engagement. By reporting people's experiences and linking them to the experiences of others, people interpret their personal experiences as part of a larger societal trend (Semetko, 2004). The research on framing has shown that the issue and the event are not important in themselves, but the way they are defined and presented by the media plays an important role in affecting public opinion and shaping people's perception towards the issue and the event.[36] Frames help journalists to emphasise and present the issues in particular ways, and decide what the audience needs to know about the issues and the events (Gitlin, 1980). The collective action taken in the examples discussed above was the result of people feeling confronted by a similar situation, either real or imaginary.

It would be naïve to undervalue the potential influence resulting from the localisation of newspapers. Localisation has helped create awareness at the local level among citizens and enabled them to mobilise public opinion on issues pertaining to their immediate surroundings. The issue highlighted in the newspaper because of localisation is related to the everyday livelihood issues of local citizens. This might appear to be trivialisation of content by the newspaper, but it helped people relate the issues in the newspaper to their own lives. It is not about awareness of high politics, but something that people feel is related to their everyday lives and reflects a more nuanced transformation going on in the Hindi media-mediated public arena.

Complexities of localisation

A third example I want to discuss is also from Sohagpur. On 2 December 2006, a protest march organised by a local doctor, Gopal Narayan Authay, a Dalit, to

---

36 Research on framing effects in non-election contexts has shown that it may increase the likelihood of individuals interpreting the world around them through the lens of the frame (De Vreese, 2004; Haider-Markel and Joslyn, 2001; Kiihberger, 1998; Kinder and Sanders, 1990; Schuck and De Vreese, 2006; Valkenburg, Semetko and De Vreese, 1999). There are several widely cited studies on framing, for example, Chong and Druckman, 2007; De Vreese, 2005; Druckman, 2001; Entman, 1993; Gamson and Modigliani, 1987; Gitlin, 1980; Goffman, 1974; Iyengar, 1991; and Semetko and Valkenburg, 2000.

object to an accusatory news story about him written by stringer Abhinay Soni of *Dainik Bhaskar* in Sohagpur. The story was published in the local pullout of *Dainik Bhaskar* on 23 November 2006 under the headline *Zindagī ko taras rahā māsūm* (Child fighting for his life). The story described how the doctor, Gopal Authay, mishandled a child's treatment and resulted in the child's condition becoming critical. The story accused Gopal Authay of bribing the mother with INR 12,000 when she threatened to go to the police. When Dr Authay was contacted by the reporter Abhinay Soni, he denied that he tried to bribe the child's mother and claimed that the accusation was baseless.

Dr Authay managed to get around 80 to 90 people from a rally of Dalits en route to Delhi on 2 December 2006, and organised a protest march in Sohagpur with placards reading *Dainik Bhāskar saṃvāddātā murdābād, Dalit virodhī murdābād* (Down with *Dainik Bhaskar* correspondents, down with the enemies of Dalits). Since none of the local newspapers agreed to cover the protest march, he sent a photograph to the *Dainik Bhaskar* office in Bhopal.

Dr Authay complained to the *Dainik Bhaskar* management that Abhinay Soni was biased against him. The incident created apprehension among the management in the Bhopal office since it could affect the reputation and sales of the newspaper and Abhinay Soni was asked to visit Bhopal. When Abhilash Khandekar, the resident editor of *Dainik Bhaskar* in Bhopal, came to know that I had visited Sohagpur and met Abhinay Soni, he asked me about him. He told me that he was trying to cleanse *Dainik Bhaskar* of all crooks (*Sāre badmaśoṃ ko nikālnā hai Bhāskar se*).

Abhinay Soni told me that initially he was unhappy with the attitude of the management and felt that he underwent a kind of 'court martial' alluding to a harsh treatment at the hands of the people responsible in Bhopal. However, after he provided evidence of his innocence, they came out in his support. When asked if there were any differences between him and Gopal Authay before this incident, he explained:[37]

> Since, Gopal Authay had been running an NGO he wanted publicity for it. Thus, on occasion, he would send me a press note about a social event organised by his organisation in the area. But I did not get them published and instead asked him if his organisations organised an event why he didn't invite me, so that I could provide detailed coverage? After a few days, I got

---

37 Interviewed on 23 December 2006 in Sohagpur.

an invitation from Gopal Authay and went to attend the function. To my surprise, the event was organised to discuss 'why journalists did not publish news on Dalits.'

According to Abhinay Soni, the event was organised to humiliate and pressure him into publishing press notes about social events without questioning whether such events had taken place. The other party labelled Abhinay Soni as biased against Dalits.

This incident brings to light the contested domain of influence in the public arena between the media and various parties with vested interests. Such contestations have not yet been resolved, and no amount of democratisation at the local level will be complete without giving marginalised groups access to institutions of democracy including the media.

Conclusion

Localisation has played a very important role in the growth and expansion of Hindi newspapers. The politics emerging from the localisation of newspapers has certainly facilitated grassroots mobilisation in which the diverse mass of the public consisting of people in rural areas and small towns, farmers, women, Dalits and the middle class are participating. By mobilising the diverse public and by connecting the local arena with the regional, national and global arena, Hindi media helped them gain a voice that contributes to the consolidation of Indian democracy. These vernacular voices, which are largely absent in the national mainstream media, are beginning to challenge the dominant discourse of participation hegemonised by the English-speaking metropolitan middle class. Despite significant progress in facilitating grassroots mobilisation, Hindi newspapers have failed to adequately highlight the grievances of substantial numbers of marginalised groups, particularly the Dalits, which has made critics question the ability of the media to carry out its role as the Fourth Estate. This duality of inclusion and exclusion of marginalised voices reflects the ongoing contestation in the rapidly transforming media landscape of India.

It would be inappropriate to conclude that the localisation of newspapers has not generated any meaningful transformation in the public arena. The examples and discussion show that the localisation of newspapers has mobilised local citizens, made them aware of their rights and allowed them to assert them when needed. It has also activated the administration to address local issues.

What appears as trivialisation of news for the so-called national English media does in fact bring previously marginalised groups into a network of dialogue and negotiation with each other and with the representatives of the state by highlighting their everyday experiences in the public arena. The reporting of everyday experiences of the Hindi-speaking public has politicised their issue of livelihood. Basic necessities now have to be addressed by the state and local administration in order to sustain their legitimacy.

The visibility of women in the Hindi media-mediated arena has become more pronounced, which is evident from both the increasing number of women readers of a Hindi newspaper as well as the growing number of women working in the Hindi media. At the same time, Dalits, who constitute a significant proportion of the local population, have not found adequate representation in Hindi newspapers. The absence of Dalits from the newsroom has not resulted in the complete marginalisation of Dalit issues in the Hindi newspaper-mediated public arena, but it has affected how the issues of Dalits are framed in the press. Issues of caste discrimination are often framed as poverty and development issues. The repackaging of the Dalit and caste issue in a new form making it a common problem affecting poor people amid the growing affluence in a globalising India might help widen the support base and forge a new alliance based on certain common interests, but it fails to address the issue of caste discrimination that still informs social relations at various levels. This also shows how a very complex and nuanced transformation is underway in the Hindi media-mediated public arena, one that should not be captured by a simple either/or dichotomy, but can be best thought of as a scenario in which marginalisation and empowerment can go hand-in-hand.

5

Political Economy
of the Hindi Press

There have been growing debates about the increasing influence of markets and governments on the role of the fourth estate. A number of studies have analysed the ramifications of the corporatisation of the media and ownership concentration in the context of mature western democracies (Bagdikian, 1983, 2004; Bennett, 2004; Doyle, 2002; McChesney, 2007, 2008; McChesney and Schiller, 2003; Thussu, 2006b; Winseck, 2008). These and other studies have highlighted corporate influence and the ways political elites have inhibited news diversity and undermined the potential of the media to offer diverse perspectives on issues (Bennett, 2007; Entman, 2010; Hamilton, 2004; Waisbord, 2010). Younger and economically developing democracies have been witnessing a different, yet serious, challenge to the way the media system is evolving. Studies have shown increasing commercialisation along with globalisation (Thussu, 2007), opaque media ownership (Chakraborty and Rao, 2014; McCargo, 2011) as well as a cosy relationship between the government, the media and the top corporations (Bromley and Romano, 2005; Jakubowitz, 2007). Despite the diversity in the focus and contexts of these studies, they all question whether privately-owned corporate-run media is compatible with democratic values. India's public service broadcaster *Doordarshan* lost its monopoly decades ago, when most media scholars in India were critical of that monopoly's voice. Now with a cacophony of media outlets, almost all privately owned, most media scholars remain critical (Thakurta and Chaturvedi, 2012; Thakurta, 2014a; Thomas, 2014). While offering a critical perspective may be the role of the scholar in India, more research is needed to understand the contribution of media to democracy at this time of rapid digitalisation. While acknowledging the important contribution of these studies to understanding the political economy of the media, I also show the ways in which privately-owned corporate media has facilitated the rise of political activism in India and brought previously marginalised groups into the public sphere. I demonstrate that the relationship between privately-owned news media and editorial independence is not a zero-sum game, where one of more necessarily means less of other and instead argue that both can coexist in a complementary and competitive way.

The efflorescence of Indian language newspapers in the 1980s and 1990s was partly facilitated by government subsidies and the rise of consumerism that facilitated the parallel growth of the advertising industry during the same period. The rapid expansion of Hindi newspapers, particularly since the late 1980s, not only shattered the long-held monopoly of English newspapers over advertising revenues, but also helped create an alternative discourse of participation by providing a platform for marginalised groups such as people living in rural areas and small towns, and farmers to raise their demands in the political arena. This duality of growing consumerism that emerged with the rising advertising industry and promoted the growth of the Hindi press on the one hand, while also enabling the possibility of political activism on the other, has not gone unnoticed by scholars. Jeffrey (2000), for example, mentioned this development and drew on the example of the role of Indian language newspapers in the creation of the public sphere.

Table 5.1: Ad spend on TV and print, 1991–2015 (INR billion)*

	TV	Print	Total
1991	3.9	10.6	**16.9**
1995	13.4	27.3	**46.2**
2000	44.3	43.1	**96.1**
2005	67.4	79.2	**162.6**
2010	103.0	126.0	**266.0**
2015	181.3	189.3	**475.0**

Source: Vanita Kohli (2006) and FICCI-KPMG (2016).

Note: * Figures for 2010 and 2015 are from FICC-KPMG. I have not included radio, cinema, outdoor and the internet; hence, the total is more than the sum of TV and print.

The growth of Hindi newspapers in the late 1980s with booming advertising revenues, however, was soon threatened by the rise of satellite television in the 1990s. The arrival of private satellite channels was direct competition for press advertising revenue, evident from Table 5.1. Television quickly became the place for providing breaking news and the arrival of 24X7 satellite and cable news not only changed television news but also traditional print journalism. It was even more difficult for Hindi newspapers, which had just embarked upon the phase of expansion and consolidation. In order to compete with television for advertising revenue, the entire focus of newspapers underwent a major transformation. Through localisation, Hindi newspapers started creating a niche for themselves and were able to survive the onslaught of television by retaining and expanding their advertising revenues. Two important Hindi newspapers – *Dainik Bhaskar* and *Dainik Jagran* – came from quite modest beginnings and went on to become India's most widely read newspapers. They are still among the most widely read newspapers in the world with some 16 million readers of *Dainik Bhaskar* and 18 million readers of *Dainik Jagran*. Starting out in one city where they remained for over 30 years, they have different ownership patterns and growth stories in comparison with the largest English newspapers including the *Times of India* and the *Hindustan Times* that are controlled by large corporate houses.

In this chapter, I analyse both the ownership pattern and the process of advertising in Hindi newspapers. I show how the process of economic liberalisation in India that made the private sector an important player in the Indian economy led to a spurt in advertising markets, making the middle class the nucleus of its growth and benefitting the newspaper industry. I then delineate the process of advertising as it operates in *Dainik Bhaskar* by focusing on the head office in Bhopal and the local bureau in Itarsi. While unravelling the linkages between the head office and the local bureau, I explain the various facets of advertising and the strategies adopted by newspapers to attract advertising from different sources and create a niche for themselves in light of the threat from television.

Ownership, interests and ideology

The issue of ownership is central to research on the political economy of the media. Concentration of ownership is considered detrimental to democratic values because it would affect diversity of opinion. The concentration of ownership in the Indian media market has not yet reached the level of western democracies such as the US where a handful of media houses control the majority of the media business with a strong presence of media conglomerates.[1] Media scholars in India have expressed concern over the recent buyout by Reliance Industries of Network 18 and ETV groups (Thakurta 2014a; Thakurta and Chaturvedi, 2012). With this acquisition, Reliance Industries has a presence in several language media markets such as English, Hindi, Urdu, Bengali, Kannada,

---

1   In the US, for example, the Big Six (General Electric, Walt Disney Co., News Corporation, Time Warner, Viacom and CBCS Corporation) controls the majority of the shares in different media outlets. See http://www.freepress.net/ownership/chart. Also, see Pickard (2014) for a historical account of the evolution of the concentration of media ownership by a few corporations.

Marathi, Odiya, Telugu and Gujarati. The acquisition causes concern because Reliance Industries is India's largest corporate house whose main interest is not the media business. At the same time, India does not yet have restrictions on cross-media ownership in which media conglomerates can have a presence across print, broadcasting and digital platforms as well as own distribution channels. However, voices demanding restrictions on cross-media ownership to protect both free expression and free media have been raised (TRAI, 2014). This is in contrast to more mature democracies of the US, UK and Canada that have certain restrictions on cross-media ownership in place. The revelation of a growing nexus between journalists, politicians and corporations in India has cast further doubt on the nature of journalism and whether it can be a fourth estate and protect the public interest (Bhusan, 2013; Saeed, 2015; Thakurta, 2014a). The entry of established business groups into the media business, which is financially less lucrative, also makes one question the economic logic of such a decision. Despite financial losses, the media business offers disproportionate political gain (Mehta, 2015). McMillan and Zoido (2004) demonstrated that the media grants the strongest form of a shield against political abuse. Therefore, the media business cannot be understood in the way conventional businesses operate (McCargo, 2011).

Commenting on the state of Hindi newspapers in the 1990s, Jeffrey (2000) mentions that most of these newspapers are 'family-owned and not listed on the stock market' (112). Most Hindi newspapers are still family-owned and embedded in particular social and political contexts. At the same time, most of the Hindi newspapers with the highest circulation in 1991 belonged to large media houses such as the Times of India Group and the Hindustan Times Group. Looking at the state of the Hindi press in 2015, we notice a remarkable change. Of the top five Hindi newspapers in 2015 in terms of readership, four belong to owners who started their businesses from Hindi newspapers and subsequently ventured into the non-Hindi media business. The Dainik Bhaskar Group was listed on the National Stock Exchange (NSE) in Mumbai under the name of DB Corporation on 6 January 2010. Shares of the DB Corporation have performed well since then and displayed more or less average vulnerability compared to the major drop in the index in August 2015. Its main competitor, the Jagran Prakashan Group, which publishes *Dainik Jagran*, was already listed in 2006 and its share price has more than tripled since its launch. This shows the ever-growing market of Hindi news media and their growing popularity. The most striking part of the success story of these two Hindi newspapers is their unconventional growth trajectory compared to that of the established media houses. Two of the most successful English newspapers, *Hindustan Times* and the *Times of India*, are owned by large corporate houses; the *Hindustan Times* is owned by the noted industrialist group, the Birla family, and Bennett, Coleman and Company Limited own the *Times of India*.

Importantly, both *Dainik Bhaskar* and *Dainik Jagran* began expanding from the 1980s, yet those expansions were confined to their respective states. The real success of both these newspapers began in the mid-1990s when they started expanding to other states. From its inception in 1958 until 1995, *Dainik Bhaskar* was confined to Madhya Pradesh. The first expansion in 1996 was the launch of the Jaipur edition in Rajasthan. This was the first time that a Hindi media group ventured outside its home state to launch editions from a different state. Today, *Dainik Bhaskar* has a presence in four different language markets, including English. Similarly, *Dainik Jagran,* though it was established in 1942, expanded out of Uttar Pradesh only in 1990 with the launch of its Delhi edition.[2] The real expansion of *Dainik Jagran* began from 1999 with the launch of the Jalandhar edition in Punjab.

Dainik Jagran now has a presence in four language markets – Hindi, Urdu, English and Gujarati. In 2010, the group acquired *Mid-Day*, which publishes newspapers in English, Gujarati and Urdu (the Urdu version is called *Inquilab*) from Mumbai and Pune. The most interesting aspect of the Dainik Jagran group's expansion is the buyout of *Nai Duniya* in 2012. *Nai Duniya*, published from Indore, was the most important Hindi newspaper in Madhya Pradesh before the rise of *Dainik Bhaskar*. Several important Hindi journalists were associated with *Nai Duniya*. When *Dainik Bhaskar* and *Dainik Jagran*, after establishing their dominance in their respective states, began to expand beyond their state borders in the mid-1990s, they had a tacit understanding that they would not encroach on each other's territory. This meant that *Dainik Bhaskar* did not launch an edition from Uttar Pradesh, Bihar or Jharkhand, which was the main base of the Jagran group. Similarly, *Dainik Jagran* did not make any serious attempt to launch editions from Madhya Pradesh or Chhattisgarh. *Dainik Jagran* was the first to break the truce by launching an edition from

---

2 The Delhi edition of *Dainik Jagran* was not very successful and it was meant only to have a presence in the national capital. On the other hand, *Dainik Bhaskar*'s venture beyond Madhya Pradesh was intended to capture a new market to expand and grow its media business.

Indore in 2006. However, *Dainik Jagran* did not do well since it had to compete with both *Dainik Bhaskar* and *Nai Duniya*. This was followed by *Dainik Bhaskar* launching editions from Ranchi and Jamshedpur in 2010 and from Dhanbad in 2012 where *Dainik Jagran* had been present since 2003. The acquisition by the Jagran Group of *Nai Duniya* should be seen within this larger context, since it allowed the Jagran group to have a meaningful presence in Madhya Pradesh. *Dainik Bhaskar* launched another edition from Patna, a city where *Dainik Jagran* had a presence from 2000, in January 2014, which was just months before the Indian national election. By 2017, *Dainik Bhaskar* had 44 editions with a presence in 12 states, whereas *Dainik Jagran* had 37 editions and a presence in 11 states, with direct competition between these two Hindi newspapers in five states and nine cities.

The most striking feature of their expansion is their diversification into non-media sectors. Dainik Bhaskar Corporation has invested in sectors such as real estate, solvent extraction, oil refineries and hydrogenated vegetable oils. Jagran Prakashan's other commercial interests include real estate, electronics, sugar and textiles. A different kind of media conglomerate has emerged that after successfully establishing its presence in the media business has started to diversify into non-media business sectors.

In contrast to *Dainik Bhaskar* which has no permanent attachment to a political party, *Dainik Jagran* has on occasion supported the cause of the right wing Hindutva forces, and biased reporting during communal conflicts, particularly during the Ayodhya movement, is also associated with the newspaper (Stahlberg, 2013). The chief editor of the paper, Narendra Mohan, was elected to the Rajya Sabha, which is the upper house of the Indian Parliament, representing the BJP. During the 1998 Kargil War between India and Pakistan, BJP Prime Minister Atal Bihari Vajpayee gave an exclusive interview to *Dainik Jagran*, which was copied by the English press and circulated widely. Though the exclusive interview to *Dainik Jagran* can also be interpreted as the growing importance of Hindi language newspapers, one cannot deny signs of favouritism by the ruling party to a politically loyal newspaper.

This strategy of supporting a political party is often found in a partisan media system and is more evident in a two-party system such as the US or UK.[3] In a multi-party system, media groups in general are reluctant to have permanent

3	For a study of the media system, see Hallin and Mancini (2004).

political loyalty and might give importance to business over ideological interests. This is why even though *Dainik Jagran* has soft political leanings towards the BJP it has never admitted it openly. Both *Dainik Jagran* and *Dainik Bhaskar* claim to be neutral in their political orientation. The newspapers' varied interests result in supporting one political party in one state, while providing support to another political party in another state. Even within a state, the support shown to a political party is not permanent and can change depending on exigencies. Interestingly, one also finds contradictory political support in different editions of the newspaper within a state that is contingent on the political preference and interests of the resident editor. From the perspective of this writer, this is an important and exciting indicator of political pluralism in the media system. McCargo (2011) in his study of the media in Thailand and Indonesia has shown a similar pattern where media outfits speak in multiple and contradictory voices, and hence, challenge any settled information order. The most important aspect of the Hindi newspaper business, also found in other language media sectors, is the prevalence of multiple interests, with economic logic being one of them.

Dainik Bhaskar and *Dainik Jagran* were two of the newspapers named in a report on paid news submitted by the Press Council of India (PCI) in April 2010. Paid news is defined as occurring when media outlets unethically and illegally produce content on behalf of others – often politicians, celebrities and companies – that is passed off as actual news rather than advertising. The problem of paid news came into the limelight in the 2009 national election and subsequent state elections. The Andhra Pradesh Union of Working Journalists (APUWJ) brought the issue into the public sphere by organising a seminar in Hyderabad on the issue of paid news after the 2009 national election.[4] This public discussion of the issue contributed to a detailed report on paid news by the PCI in 2010. Initially, the PCI was unwilling to publish the report, based on a vote in which nine of the 30 members voted against it. The report was subsequently leaked and then made available through the legal alternative of the Right to Information Act (RTI). Paid news not only violates journalistic ethics, but also violates the rights of citizens to fair and balanced information so as to make informed decisions. Despite the existence of circumstantial evidence on the phenomena of paid news and the denial of its existence by most of the media companies except in isolated cases, there

---

4   See APUWJ (2010). Memorandum submitted to the Press Council of India on paid news, Hyderabad. Available at: http://www.apuwj.org/Magzine/report%20on%20paid%20news2.pdf.

are strong grounds to believe that the phenomena might be widespread (Sainath, 2013; see also Standing Committee on Information Technology, 2013). In a personal interview with the state editor, Abhilash Khandekar, of *Dainik Bhaskar* in Bhopal, admitted that the newspaper was involved in paid news. At the same time, he contended that the management has taken a firm decision to ensure that under no circumstances would paid news be permitted in the future.[5] The existence of paid news casts a long shadow over India's independent journalism.

Amartya Sen (1981) has shown how a free press in combination with an electoral democracy can act as an effective watchdog during crises. Sen compares the loss of life in India's famine of 1943 (estimated at 3 million) with the Chinese famine of 1958–61 that resulted in the deaths of some 16.5 million to 29.5 million people. Given no major differences in agricultural growth rates and the food grain supply in both countries, Sen attributes the huge difference in mortality rates to the lack of freedom of the press and the absence of an opposition in China. The Chinese press could not warn the government in advance, which resulted in a delay in rectifying the situation. Sen argues that the positive role played by a relatively free media and the active role played by opposition leaders and the imperative of electoral democracy, where the elected representatives have to be accountable to their electorate every five years in post-independence India, averted a famine with the death toll of similar proportions.

The effectiveness of a free press in democracies cannot be overlooked. The recent evidence of the existence of the phenomena of paid news raises questions about the existence and efficacy of freedom of the press in India.

Advertising, market reform and consumerism

The presence of advertising in the media is now well accepted. The post-war discourse of advertising where it was regarded as sinister propaganda because of its power of mass manipulation[6] has been replaced by a market discourse that legitimises the placement of advertising by emphasising its social role.[7] It has been argued that advertisers exert an influence on the media's content. There might not be evidence of strong control on the media by advertisers, yet it is

---

5   Personal interview in Bhopal, 16 September 2011.

6   For an excellent account of such a genre, see Packard (1957).

7   For a detailed analysis, see Wilmshurst and Mackay (1999).

possible to observe the existence of pressure. Before the 1990s, the Indian state used its advertising muscle to promote its agenda since there were few avenues for private advertising. The global literature has shown how the presence of a large private advertising market can help reduce bias in the media by reducing government influence (Gehlbach and Sonin, 2008). In study in the context of the US, Petrova (2009) demonstrated that multiplying the sources of advertising revenues could lead to a more independent press. What happens if the bias is coming from the market?

Media capture, which is closely related to the issue of media ownership, has been the focus of the literature on political economy. The work on media capture analyses two kinds of threats of capture: one from the government and the other from corporations. Economists have demonstrated that government advertising in a newspaper is associated with the appearance of news on government corruption on the front page in Argentina, for example (Di Tella and Franceschelli, 2009). State control of the media also increases political longevity (Besley and Prat, 2006). In the context of Italy, Gambaro and Puglisi (2009) showed the use of advertising by corporations to capture media and prevent the media from reporting on corruption. Despite the strong evidence of media capture by government and corporations in specific contexts, there is no conclusive literature that shows its effects on policy outcomes. In the context of India, most of the studies on advertising have tried to understand the relationship with consumerism against the backdrop of economic liberalisation (Fernandes, 2000; Mankekar, 1999; Mazzarella, 2003a). There is little detailed analysis of the ways advertising works at the local level and its potential in affecting the content of the newspapers.

In terms of advertising expenditure, India stands fifth among emerging markets with an annual expenditure of $5,860 million in 2013 after China ($40,951), Brazil ($16,380), Russia ($10,212) and Indonesia ($7,510) (World Press Trends, 2014). However, it is important to look at the decade of the 1980s when Hindi newspapers started growing rapidly with support from advertising. The rise of consumerism began in the mid-1980s partly because of the state policy of liberalisation and because foreign firms started entering the Indian market.[8] With deregulation and the pro-business policies of the government led

---

8   The tendencies towards liberalisation of the Indian economy can be traced to the beginning of 1980s, but the paradigm shift in the development policy occurred in 1991 when P. V. Narasimha Rao was the Prime Minister of India. For details, see Kohli (2006a, 2006b).

by Prime Minster Rajiv Gandhi, private businesses started flourishing during this period.[9] In order to sell their products they needed to advertise them, which provided an opportunity for advertising agencies to expand and the advertising industry started growing rapidly from the mid-1980s. Though there is no clear agreement about the precise figures of the growth of the advertising industry, a rough estimate of its growth between 1980 and 2000 is astonishing. According to Karlekar (1986), the advertising industry in India doubled from 200 rupees ($232.5 million) in 1981 to 400 crore rupees ($317.5 million) in 1986.[10] Lintas India, a leading advertising company, estimated that advertising billing jumped from about $177 million in 1980 to $784 million in 1987 (Hazarika, 1988). Similarly, capitalised billing of the advertising industry grew from INR 930.9 crore ($423 million) in 1990–91 to INR 5,331 crore ($1.4 billion) in 1997–98 (Jeffrey, 2000, 58).[11]

The real boost to advertising and consumerism started with the hosting of the Asian Games (Asiad) in 1982 in Delhi.[12] It was broadcast internationally, which led to the popularity of television across urban India and subsequent years witnessed the massive growth of television sets in India. The Nehruvian notion of development was slowly being replaced by a consumerist agenda that emphasised modern lifestyles built around the idea of comfort. A detailed study of the advertising flow in *Dainik Bhaskar* shows that advertising of more expensive consumer goods started in 1984. The late 1980s saw advertisements for luxury products and the means for personal gratification appearing in *Dainik Bhaskar*. Still, the larger perception of the Hindi-speaking public as 'consumers' was not yet recognised by advertisers. Such recognition came only in the late 1990s when *Dainik Bhaskar* and *Dainik Jagran* started expanding beyond their homeland to other states and into the hinterlands with multiple editions. With their expansion came aggressive marketing, a tool so far used largely by English

---

9   Rahul Mukherji (2007) has delineated the various phases of reforms carried out by different governments and the obstacles that came along with policy changes. While talking about the pro-business policies of the Rajiv Gandhi government, Mukherji shows how big business was redefined with the modification of the Monopoly and Restrictive Trade Policies (MRTP) Act in 1985; this allowed the easing of regulations since only businesses worth more than INR 1 billion came under the MRTP's regulatory sway compared to the earlier limit of INR 200 million. This process of deregulation freed many firms, which made it easier for capacity expansion (12–13).

10   Quoted in Mazzarella (2003a, 292).

11   Figures were adjusted in US dollar by Mazzarella (2003a).

12   Asiad was an opportunity for the Indian state to showcase, 'its image as a modern nation capable of hosting and organising an international event, not just to the rest of the world but also to its own citizens' (Mankekar, 1999, 56).

dailies. Private businesses and advertising agencies began to rethink the image of the Hindi public and their propensity to become potential consumers who could buy their products and services. At the same time, Hindi newspapers also became aware that they had a niche market of 'captive consumers', who could neither be reached effectively by English newspapers nor by television. These captive consumers were exclusively Hindi readers as well as people located in rural areas with limited access to cable and satellite television.

The liberalisation of the Indian economy in the early 1990s further buttressed the private sector. To manage the fiscal crisis in agreement with the IMF, the government implemented a programme of macro-economic stabilisation in 1991. It also announced a Structural Adjustment Programme (SAP) to improve the competitive strength of the economy in the long term. The structural measures included a broad series of reforms in trade policy, industrial policy and licensing, public sector, financial sector, foreign investment and technology.[13] If the earlier attempts at liberalisation had altered only certain aspects of the policy regime, the 1991 statement fundamentally changed the overall framework (Mukherji, 2007). With complete deregulation, the private sector became a significant part of the Indian economy and started operating various businesses. To sell their products, they started targeting the rising Indian middle class, which opened further avenues for the rise of consumerism.

The debates about the exploding 'middle class' of India, said to be close to 250 to 300 million, was taken to new heights and celebrated as a nucleus to attract multinationals (MNCs) into India.[14] In this context, Bijapurkar (2007) remarks:

> The truth is that the Great Indian Middle Class was a seductive idea that was conceived, packaged and sold to the world by India as part of its sales pitch for foreign direct investment (FDI) in the early to mid-1990s … The story put out was that there was a sleeping beauty called Middle Class India, comprising 250–300 million people, who had money and a burning desire to consume, but nothing decent to buy (84).

It was soon discovered that the figure was bloated and the real figure might be as low as 150 million, which is by no means small when one considers the per

---

13 For an analysis of the key reforms undertaken by the Indian state, see Jenkins (1999) and Frankel (2005).

14 There is no clear agreement about the real size of the Indian middle class. The hype of a 250 to 300 million middle class, created when India started liberalising its economy in the early 1990s, was soon discovered to be a myth (Bijapurkar, 2007, 84–89). For updates on consumption data of the Indian middle class, see Sridharan (2008).

capita size of the middle classes in less populated wealthier countries that could provide FDI in India. The National Council of Applied Economic Research (NCAER), which classifies the Indian middle class based on consumption patterns, revised its estimate to 160 million in 2011.[15] This figure is based on a definition of middle class households that have an annual income of INR 3.4 lakh to 17 lakh ($5,862 to $29,310) based on 2009–10 prices.[16] Whatever the number, the middle class became the nucleus of India's new economic policies, and MNCs and private Indian companies tried to reach them through the best possible means. The sudden outpouring of consumer goods with economic liberalisation in 1991 also created profound confusion for the Indian middle class, which was unable to enjoy it because of the poor infrastructure.[17] The late 1990s and early 2000s witnessed the further consolidation of a middle class aspiring to be part of global modernity.

The rise of a rural middle class has been a very important development in the past decade. The Census (2011d) enumerated over 246 million households, of which 168 million (or 68 per cent) were in rural areas, while 78 million (32 per cent) were in urban India. The Indian rural market, with its vast size and demand base, offers a huge opportunity that MNCs cannot afford to ignore. With 168 million households, the rural population is more than double that of the urban. It is the great potential of rural India, which has nearly two-third of India's population, which has been attracting foreign and private firms to market their products in rural India.

Rural India is moving beyond agriculture and diversifying into non-

---

15 While critiquing the definition of middle class on the basis of consumption patterns, Fernandes (2006) argues, 'While income-based definitions of middle class provide important parameters for assessing and qualifying purely discursive approaches to studying the middle classes, they cannot be used as a singular foundational measure for a deeper understanding of the politics of middle class identity. Such income-based definitions neglect both the dynamic and contested processes of group formation, as well as the ways in which the politics of measurement are an intrinsic part of such processes' (34).

16 The total number of middle class households was 31.4 million. See *The Economic Times*, 6 February 2011.

17 Mazzarella (2003b) has identified the contradiction that was witnessed in the first phase of liberalisation of the Indian economy, which made possible the sudden availability of shiny new consumer goods, but there existed miserable conditions of much basic infrastructure. 'Microwave ovens were becoming available to some, but it was almost comically difficult to procure a reliable supply of cooking gas. Cable television and mobile telephony were readily available (the former, in particular, for relatively little money), but getting a basic terrestrial telephone connection required an exasperating amount of bribery and months of tireless effort. Fancy imported cars gleamed in shop windows, but roads were so poorly maintained and so overcrowded that attempting to drive was often hardly worth the aggravation' (57).

agriculture activities by reducing its dependence on farming and hence, one needs to question the association of rural with agriculture (Sharma, 2015). According to a report by India Ratings and Research, only about 33 per cent of rural income is generated by agriculture (Tayagi, 2015). A different kind of rural market is emerging. The NCAER occupation data shows a decline in cultivators and there is enough evidence of dual-sector households.[18] Besides, through increasing exposure to the mass media, especially to the top end of rural society through television and cable, the rural market is becoming closer in its mindset to the urban market.

The importance of the rural market for marketers of some fast-moving consumer goods (FMCGs) and durable goods is underlined by the fact that the rural market accounts for close to 38 per cent of all two-wheelers purchased and half the total market for TV sets, fans, pressure cookers, bicycles, washing soap, razor blades, tea, salt and toothpowder (Balakrishna and Sidharth, 2004). Large MNCs have realised the potential of the Indian rural market and started investing in advertising to capture consumers. Companies need to participate in village and community festivals, which are often sponsored by media groups. Not surprisingly, Hindi newspapers that have a greater presence in the rural areas have been able to attract advertisements, not only from MNCs but also from local sources. Products that were earlier available exclusively to urban consumers are now gradually reaching the rural and semi-urban population. Hindi newspapers have become important channels for private companies to tap new markets in order to expand their profit margins. The growing advertising revenues of *Dainik Bhasakar* from small towns, which we will see subsequently, and the multiplying local editions to capture new territory for a possible increase in advertising income is testimony to the fact that the hinterlands are important for the growth strategy of the Hindi press.

Besides the market potential of rural India that attracted MNCs and private Indian companies, one needs to understand the mobilisation of rural farmers in the wake of economic reforms that also proved beneficial for the expansion of Hindi newspapers. Economic reforms resulted in the withdrawal of subsidies and reduction in farm loans and prices on farm products. The growing discontent among farmers started to be tapped by farmers' movements such as the Bharatiya Kisan Union (BKU) in the late 1980s. The mobilisation of farmers through the non-party political process created a challenge for the

---

18 For details, see NCAER (2002, 21–23).

state to push the agenda of economic reforms given the electoral importance of rural constituencies (Varshney, 1998). The mobilisation of farmers also helped Hindi newspapers grow and expand their readership and political importance. The poor networks of English newspapers in rural areas meant that they had to depend on Hindi journalists and newspapers to get information about happenings in the countryside. The economic reforms proved beneficial to Hindi newspapers, both economically and politically.

The process of advertising

Dainik Bhaskar had a well-organised marketing department that is further divided into advertising and circulation. There is a very strong relationship between advertising and circulation, since an increase in circulation also increases the cost of newsprint, ink and transportation. Increased costs of production of newspaper must be backed by a proportionate increase in advertising revenue to maintain a healthy profit ratio. It costs around INR 7 to produce a 20-page newspaper, while the cover price of the newspaper is only INR 2.[19] INR 5, which is nearly 70 per cent of the total cost of production, has to be recovered from advertising just to break even, as there is no other legitimate source of revenue for the newspaper business. The importance of advertising revenues is, thus, central to the survival of the newspaper.

The advertising division in Bhopal receives a yearly revenue target by the central management that they are expected to achieve by the end of the financial year. This target was divided into segments by the local marketing manager based on the demands of the local market. Keeping in mind the conditions of the local market, the advertising division in Bhopal was divided into various segments such as automobiles, education, banking, pharmaceuticals, electronics, real estate and classifieds. Each segment or sometimes a combination of segments was placed under a local market executive, who was responsible for meeting the targets within the stipulated time. The annual target for advertising revenue was divided into quarterly and monthly targets. A segment-wise division of the yearly target was decided based on the performance of a segment during the previous financial year. The marketing department also kept track of business development in the

---

19 This estimate is for the year 2007–08. In 2017, the cover price of a newspaper has gone up to INR 5, but there is also a parallel increase in the cost of production. However, many major newspapers are still priced at INR 3. For example, *Dainik Bhaskar's* Bhopal edition is priced at INR 5, while its Patna edition is priced at INR 3. The differential price is also used to capture a new market or if the market is competitive.

region before deciding the target for a particular unit. The concept of 'Key Result Areas' (KRAs), which investigated the performance of particular segments over the years, was used to allot targets for each segment. KRAs were also decided by studying trends in a particular market over a particular period. For example, if a company was going to establish a new automobile industry in the region, the target for automobile segment would be increased for that region. Though the advertising division was demarcated segment-wise, the bulk of the revenue was generated largely through a few segments. For example, *Dainik Bhaskar*'s Bhopal division generated the majority of its revenue through the education, automobiles, real estate and pharmaceutical segments.[20]

There was constant fluctuation in the monthly volume of advertising at *Dainik Bhaskar*. During the festive season, advertising revenues far exceeded the regular flow. Keeping in view the fluctuating conditions of the market, the executive in charge of a particular segment divided the target based on various criteria. Thus, during the festive season or major local events, the respective department tried to meet a large share of the target revenue.[21] The increased earnings during festive seasons compensated for revenue lost during the slack seasons.[22] If the respective executive was able to draw advertising beyond the target, he was rewarded by management. When asked if he faced any problem in meeting the targets for advertising revenue, Atul Dixit, who had been working for over nine years with *Dainik Bhaskar* in Bhopal, replied:

> Before 1997 we faced difficulty in meeting the target as *Nav Bharat* was the number one newspaper in terms of readership in Bhopal. But since 1998 we have been able to achieve our target without much problem, and often we exceed our target.[23]

---

20 Mudid Gulati, General Manager, said that nearly 42 to 50 per cent of the revenue in Bhopal is generated through the education and automobile sectors.

21 According to S. K. Jha, Manager of Regional Marketing, advertising in the automobile sector goes up during Dushera, while electronic sector advertisements occupy more space during Deepawali, which are two important festivals in India. Another important festive season in India is Eid-ul-Fitr, celebrated by Muslims. Besides national festive seasons, there are many local festive seasons and events, which also increase the flow of newspaper advertisements. When the volume of advertising increases in the newspaper, the casualty is the coverage of news items. In order to ensure that most of the important news items get space in the newspaper, news is shortened. Interview with Pankaj Srivastava, the city desk in charge and the sub-editor, 30 October 2006.

22 According to S. K. Jha, the slack seasons are normally the months of February and March, which is just before the end of the financial year. During this period, most companies are busy preparing and analysing their annual financial results.

23 Atul Dixit was Manager, Marketing. Interviewed on 3 November 2006, Bhopal.

However, Vijay Gupta, who was Assistant Manager Marketing with *Dainik Bhaskar* in Bhopal, said that excess revenue would 'never exceed 10 per cent of the actual target as the Bhopal market is not lucrative compared to Indore.'[24]

Advertising in Bhopal was largely channelled through advertising agencies. These agencies collected advertisements from different companies and distributed them to newspapers according to the clients' requirements. When asked about the possibility of advertising directly in the newspaper, Mudid Gulati, General Manager, Bhopal, told me, 'We don't encourage clients to advertise directly. Even if we are in direct touch with the clients, we try to channel it through advertising agencies.'[25] He added:

> through an advertising agency, the client can get some tariff facility in terms of discount and a grace period for payment. But if the client tries to advertise directly with us, it is on a cash-and-carry basis. The client has to immediately deposit the money. Second, the client also gets a service benefit, as the advertising agency helps design the advertisement for clients.

However, the main reason to channel the advertisements through advertising agencies was to relieve the newspaper of the hassle of dealing directly with the clients, as explained by S. K. Jha, Manager of Regional Marketing.

Advertising agencies also helped clients figure out their target audiences. If the target audience was from a particular locality, advertising agencies only advertised in the local pullout of the newspaper. This helped the advertisers not only save money, but also reach the target consumers more effectively. When multiple editions were not present, advertisers were compelled to advertise in regional newspapers even though the target consumers were located somewhere in the hinterlands. This was not only expensive, but was also not effective in reaching the target audience. In this context, Mudid Gulati explained: 'By launching various new sub-editions such as *Kolar Bhaskar*, *BHEL Bhaskar* and *Belagarh Bhaskar*, we provide the right platform and the right rate to our clients.'[26] Multiple editions with local pullouts have enabled advertisers to effectively advertise their products and reach the target consumers without bothering non-intended recipients.

---

24 Interviewed on 2 November 2006, Bhopal.

25 Interviewed on 18 December 2007, Bhopal.

26 Kolar, BHEL, and Belagarh are suburbs of Bhopal. This shows the extent of localisation by Hindi newspapers. Details of the production process in the Bhopal edition and its sub-editions are given in Chapter 4.

Dainik Bhaskar also received combined or national advertising targeted at all the readers of the newspaper. Combined advertising for all editions was usually collected by people based at the Mumbai marketing office. However, people in charge of the marketing department in the regional and local offices also attempted to grab those clients so that they could achieve their annual target. Surendra Singh Rajput, who was Assistant Manager, Marketing with *Dainik Bhaskar* in Itarsi, told me, 'Though we have been asked to focus on the local advertising market, we also attempt to get national advertising in order to achieve our yearly target quickly and thus get extra perks on the surplus revenue.'[27] Combined advertising usually came from large national firms and MNCs, as well as several educational institutes.

Another important method invented by *Dainik Bhaskar* to increase their advertising revenues was through organising events. Mudid Gulati explained, 'We make efforts in terms of creating more opportunities to advertise, such as organising events where companies can meet their customers.' *Dainik Bhaskar* organised an auto loan *mela* on 17 December 2007 in Bhopal to attract more advertising. On this, Mudid Gulati said:

> We gave a platform to all major car dealers, and also helped the State Bank of India (SBI) in getting around 1,000 + inquiries. Through this, inquiries-level values booked by the SBI were about 30 crores+($ 46.6 million); whatever matured was different, but they were confident that they had a good lead of 30 crore. This came just at the low cost of organising a *mela*.

Through these attempts *Dainik Bhaskar* had been able to attract more advertising revenues. At the same time, it also reflects the growing competition in the market and how newspapers had been devising new strategies to expand their advertising revenues.

Deciding the advertising rate

Newspapers fix their advertising rate based on cost per thousand (CPT). However, the circulation figure provided by the Audit Bureau of Circulation, as well as surveys conducted by research organisations, plays an important role in fixing the cost of buying space or advertising in a newspaper. A small

---

27 Interviewed on 13 December 2006.

newspaper with a meagre reach cannot charge advertising rates based on the CPT and must instead be content with the rate decided by the market, based on its share in the total circulation and readership in the market. Thus, there might be a great difference between the card rate of a small newspaper and the actual rate charged from advertisers. One assistant manager in charge of marketing in *Dainik Bhaskar* said:

> The difference between the card rate and the actual rate of a small newspaper in Bhopal is nearly 70 per cent. He had an argument with one of his loyal advertisers who started advertising in a small newspaper because the difference in their advertising rate was far greater ... Advertising in small newspaper cannot give you proper returns, as the expectation of the advertisers to reach certain target consumers cannot be channelled through a small newspaper, which is sometimes not understood by advertising agencies. Thus, they waste their client's money in order to make a larger profit.[28]

Dainik Bhaskar gave a maximum of 15 per cent discount on the card rate to its loyal clients. A big newspaper with a greater market share in terms of circulation, readership and reach to a higher social stratum can also dictate terms to potential advertisers. The social class of readers is important in deciding the advertising rate for a newspaper, which requires not only adding more readers, but also adding readers into a profile that can be considered 'saleable' to advertisers. Not surprisingly, the advertising rate of the *Times of India*, an English daily, is higher than that of *Dainik Bhaskar*, despite the fact that the latter's readership is much higher.[29] During my fieldwork, editors and managers repeatedly told me that *Dainik Bhaskar*'s target group was the upper and middle class. No doubt, they were successful in attracting them, as the advertising rate in *Dainik Bhaskar* was the highest among all the Hindi newspapers.[30]

---

28   Interview on 12 December 2006, Bhopal.

29   A full-page colour advertisement in the *Times of India* costs INR 3,952,000 as against INR 2,808,000 for *Dainik Bhaskar*. *Dainik Jagran*, another leading Hindi newspaper, also has a much lower rate of advertising, which stood at INR 1,760,000 rupees in 2002 (World Association of Newspapers and News Publishers, 2006).

30   For details, see ibid.

Figure 5.1: Advertising revenue for English, Hindi and vernacular print media in percentage, 2010–15

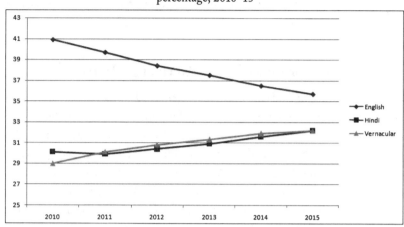

Source: FICCI-KPMG (2016).

But later they realised that it was naïve to desire readers from the upper strata of the society, who were largely educated in English and read English newspapers. A new set of policy guidelines was issued in 2005 by the management of *Dainik Bhaskar* asking the editorial department to design the content of the paper to target the middle class, which was a major source of the consumer boom in India.[31]

At the national level, Hindi newspapers continue to lag behind English newspapers in terms of their share in total advertising revenues (Figure 5.1). This is surprising when we look at the national readership statistics in which five Hindi newspapers figured in the top 10, whereas there was only one English newspaper in the list (Indian Readership Survey, 2014). However, Hindi newspapers are rapidly catching up and the gap in advertising revenues between English and Hindi newspapers is narrowing. In 2014, the share of English newspapers in the total advertising revenue came down to 36.5 per cent, while it increased for Hindi and other vernacular language newspapers to 31.6 per cent and 31.9 per cent, respectively.

The political influence of Hindi newspapers is disproportionate to their economic and market value. This is an intriguing aspect of the political economy of the media business in India and one cannot understand it by applying the simple market logic of profit maximisation. The associated

---

31 Telephone interview with Pankaj Srivastava, city desk in-charge and sub-editor with *Dainik Bhaskar*, on 14 April 2007, who informed me about recent policy changes.

political benefits and the involvement of murky capital, for example in the form of paid news that is often unreported in companies'balance sheets, need to be taken into account.

The process of local advertising – Itarsi

In Itarsi, the marketing and editorial departments of *Dainik Bhaskar* were in the same location. There were three people working in the marketing department of the Itarsi office. Surendra Singh Rajput, Assistant Manager, Marketing, moved to Itarsi in July 2004 and was responsible for advertising and circulation (Sales and Marketing Division or SMD) at Itarsi. He was assisted by Sanjeev Dubey, Marketing Executive, and Niraj Pagare, SMD Executive. Local or retail advertising was the major source of revenue for *Dainik Bhaskar*. Local display advertising was usually placed by local businesses, organisations, individuals or local politicians and the local unit of political parties. Since Itarsi is a small town, Sanjeev Dubey directly approached clients to advertise in the newspaper. Clients were largely local retailers, shops and banks. Once the clients confirmed that they would advertise, it was channelled through local advertising agencies to facilitate payment.

There were two local advertising agencies: Kohli-Ad Agency and AB News Agency. Kohli-Ad Agency was opened by the Bhaskar Group in the name of Navneet Kohli in 2003. Navneet Kohli was a B.Com graduate, who started his career as a reporter in 1988. He moved to marketing in 1998 after joining *Dainik Bhaskar*. Being satisfied with his performance in drawing advertisements for the newspaper, the Bhaskar Group opened an advertising agency for him. Thus, the Kohli-Ad Agency was functioning more as a marketing wing of *Dainik Bhaskar* than as an independent advertising agency. AB News Agency was managed by Bharat Bhusan Gandhi and acted as the sole newspaper agent for *Dainik Bhaskar*. However, in August 2006 the Bhaskar Group asked Bharat Bhusan Gandhi to collect advertisements as well. Bharat Bhusan Gandhi was not happy about this and said:

> Two advertising agencies cannot survive in a small town like Itarsi. Further, delving into the advertising market would spoil my friendship with Navneet Kohli. As Bhaskar people are mainly concerned about profit, they cannot understand the complexities in a small town.[32]

---

32 Interviewed on 12 December 2006, Itarsi.

So, Bharat Bhusan Gandhi did not make any serious attempt to collect advertisements for *Dainik Bhaskar*.

Advertisements in small towns and rural areas where *Dainik Bhaskar* did not have its bureau office were largely collected by local reporters or stringers in those towns. This was to cut down the cost, as it would be unprofitable to appoint separate advertising sales personnel for small towns and rural areas where business activities were not developed. Those stringers got a 15 per cent commission for bringing in advertising. Thus, stringers in small towns earned a little extra money by collecting advertisements for the newspaper. Some people raised objections about mixing the news and marketing teams at the local level. Sachin Jain, journalist and Director of Vikas Samvad, a people-centred advocacy organisation, complained, 'Media is marginalising their development role by emphasising marketing'. However, he admitted that the system of hawkers sending news had now been discontinued. Similarly, newspapers have separated the news/editorial and marketing function at the local level since 2006.[33] A similar point is made by Ninan (2007), who argues that the process of localisation has been taken over by the process of delocalisation, which has resulted in the revival of basic news ethics and the separation of the circulation, reporting and advertising functions.

It is important to recognise that localisation and delocalisation will continue in parallel and until the Indian media landscape stabilises. This is not to deny that newspapers have become more conscious about appointing local stringers as I show in Chapter 4. However, the evidence from this case study of *Dainik Bhaskar* shows that the marketing and newsgathering operations at the local level still get mixed up.

In Bhopal, advertising agencies prepared the advertisements and then forwarded them to the newspaper, but in small towns newspapers had to design the advertisement for their clients. For instance, *Dainik Bhaskar* in Itarsi had personnel who created appropriate artwork and prepared display advertisements for clients. Once the advertisements were designed, customers reviewed it before it was published. However, classified advertisements did not require artwork and were directly typed into the computer.

One important development in the nature of local advertising was the increase over the years in political advertising beyond the election period. When an important political event took place or important political dignitaries visited

---

33 Interviewed on 2 January 2008, Bhopal.

Itarsi, local politicians advertised in newspapers to welcome them. Surendra Singh Rajput told me:

> Though commercial advertising is an important component in our total advertising revenues, political advertising beyond election time constitutes an important source of revenue from small towns, which has been continuously expanding. For the past two years, political advertising has ranked top among different advertising categories in Itarsi.

Political advertising outside of election campaigns did not exist before 2003. It started due to the concerted efforts of local marketing executives, who went to individual political leaders to convince them about the benefits of advertising. Now it has come to occupy a significant source of revenue at the local level or for sub-editions. On the birthday of local MLAs or MPs, supporters of the candidate or local-level politicians advertise in the paper. Such advertisements usually consist of the photo of the candidate along with the photos of supporters who want to greet the candidate on the occasion (Figure 5.2).

Figure 5.2: Advertisement on the birthday celebration of the local MLA

Though there is a close connection between local businessmen and politicians because they donate funds to local candidates during campaigns, most local businessmen were reluctant to overtly associate themselves with a particular candidate and did not directly advertise in the paper on birthdays or political events. This was in view of the fluctuating nature of Indian politics and uncertainty about whether or not a candidate would continue in office beyond a five-year term. Surendra Singh Rajput told me that when they approached businessmen to advertise for a political event, they would request us to take money instead of placing an advertisement in their names.[34] However, other businessmen were openly associated with a political party and would advertise in the newspaper when their party held a political event.

Figure 5.3: Special page on the birthday celebration of the local MLA

This special supplement was created to celebrate the birthday of a local MLA, Kamal Patel, who was also a minister. This idea was created by the staff of *Dainik Bhaskar* marketing department at Itarsi. They were able to convince local politicians as well as local business people to celebrate the birthday in this fashion to show their loyalty to the minister.

Another strategy adopted by local businessmen to minimise the consequences of unforeseen developments in the political arena was to provide donations across different political parties. Thus, if there were two members in the family, one supported the ruling party while the other supported the opposition to avoid any drastic fallout from political events. Surendra Singh Rajput mentioned that he received advertisements from two members of the same family for two different political parties.

---

34 Interviewed on 13 December 2006, Itarsi.

This shows that political advertising beyond the election period constituted a significant aspect of revenue generation at the local level. To what extent has political advertising had an impact on the content of the newspaper? In other words, did local politicians get favourable reporting in exchange for advertisements in the paper? Whatever governs the decision of businessmen also determines the decision of the newspaper and the editor. We have already noted how in a multi-party system a media group tries to maintain a neutral position among competing political interests and often treads middle-of-the-road position without trying to meddle in political controversy. It is even more difficult at the local level where media actors are embedded within the social and political milieu and where informal networks are more prevalent than formal rules. A big newspaper cannot afford to openly support a political party at the local level, because it might jeopardise advertising revenues from other political parties. One of the policy guidelines in *Dainik Bhaskar* was to check the source before publishing anything controversial that might affect the credibility of the newspaper. Shailesh Jain, reporter at Itarsi, remarked, 'We are never discouraged from writing against political happenings, as long as we have evidence to support the story.'[35] At the same time, *Dainik Bhaskar* had a greater focus on development stories that can interest a wide audience than on political reporting. Such a policy was also supported by a survey conducted by the Poorest Areas Civil Society (PACS) programme, which found that *Dainik Bhaskar* ranked first among all the newspapers in Madhya Pradesh because it devoted the highest number of columns as well as published the highest number of news items related to development in 2005–06.[36] There has been a self-conscious attempt by *Dainik Bhaskar* to promote development stories that are appreciated by a wider range of readers.

35	Interviewed on 15 December 2006, Itarsi.

36	The newspapers covered were the *Times of India, Hindustan Times, Nav Bharat, Central Chronicle, Dainik Bhaskar, Dainik Jagran* and *Raj Express*. The highest number of columns devoted to development news was by *Dainik Bhaskar*, (1,332 columns), followed by *Dainik Jagran* (1,315) and *Nav Bharat* (1,088). The English press had relatively fewer columns devoted to development news: *Central Chronicle* had 928, *Hindustan Times* 307 and the *Times of India* 137 columns. The highest number of news items devoted to development news was by *Dainik Bhaskar* (667 news items) followed by *Dainik Jagran* (640) and *Raj Express* (548). *Central Chronicle* had 368, *Hindustan Times* 149 and the *Times of India* 70 columns. For details, see *PACS Media Audit: Madhya Pradesh and Chhattisgarh, 2005–06*, available at: http://www.empowerpoor.org/downloads/Copy%20of%20 Media%20audit%20PACS.pdf.

Local advertising as a source of revenue

A notable feature of the local advertising market was the expanding nature of advertising sources. Surendra Singh Rajput mentioned that in 2004 when the Itarsi bureau had an annual target of INR 24 lakh ($37,265), it was difficult to meet that target. But in 2005, they were given a target of INR 44 lakh ($ 68,320) and managed to generate INR 45 lakh ($69,873) from advertisements in that financial year. Since then, the Itarsi bureau has never faced difficulties in achieving its annual advertising revenue targets. The target for 2006 of INR 54.26 lakh ($84,253) was fulfilled successfully and the advertising revenues for fiscal year 2007 exceeded the target of INR 78 lakh ($121,116). The target for the 2008–09 financial year was increased by 40 per cent to 1.19 crore ($184,773),[37] but Surendra Singh Rajput was optimistic about achieving it although it would be difficult.[38] This shows that the local advertising market has become more lucrative for Hindi newspapers and has come to occupy an important place in their share of the total advertising revenue. However, it is difficult to get advertising at the local level, as people are not 'advertising conscious'. While explaining the difference between a local market (Itarsi) and a regional market (Bhopal), Abhay Ashok Sarwate, Senior Manager of Regional Marketing, said: 'At the local level we have to create the clients, while at Bhopal advertisers come to us on their own.'[39]

Another important development in the local market was the beginning of *Upcountry City Bhaskar*, which was a weekly four-page supplement targeted at teenagers and the middle class.[40] The aim of the supplement was to celebrate the achievement of local 'heroes', who rose through hard work rather than corruption. It also featured events organised in the town or nearby areas. Looking at the role of local newspapers in the US, Peterson (1981), points out that:

> Although in larger cities the news media will seek to sell papers and exert influence by discovering a local 'scandal,' in moderately sized cities newspapers seem to concentrate more on local successes: scholarships local students have won, athletic victories won in the city's name, the unveiling of new public facilities, and any hint of economic expansion (124).

---

37 Figures were converted to US dollar based on 2017 exchange rate of 1 USD = 64.4 INR.

38 Telephone interview with Surendra Singh Rajput on 17 June 2007. This helped get the figures for 2007.

39 Interviewed on 14 December 2007, Bhopal.

40 More details about *Upcountry City Bhaskar* are provided in Chapter 4.

We notice a similar trend in *Dainik Bhaskar*, in which the local pullouts were largely filled with stories of successes achieved by local citizens. However, Surendra Singh Rajput said that with the launch of *Upcountry City Bhaskar* there was greater pressure on them to create content for it by organising events such as quiz competitions and career fairs. Such events had rarely taken place earlier in small towns.

> In order to create consciousness among local people about the content of the supplement, we have to do the initial groundwork. Once people become aware of the content, they start organising such functions. We also tried to organise kitty parties at various places where we launched *Upcountry City Bhaskar*.[41]

The launch of *Upcountry City Bhaskar* has boosted advertising revenues, which was also a reason to increase the target for advertising revenues to 40 per cent for the year 2008–09. At the same time, it reflects how newspapers are making concerted efforts by using various techniques to create the content. This raises questions about the commercialisation and dumbing down of the content with localisation, even though it has increased awareness among marginalised sections of society that are not reached by the elite English press.

Circulation or readership?

Besides advertising, newspapers generate limited revenue through circulation. *Dainik Bhaskar* followed a distribution system by which copies of the newspaper were delivered to agents who sold it to hawkers who then distributed it to readers. Under this system, agents had to deposit a certain amount of security money with the *Dainik Bhaskar* circulation department to avoid default of payment. Agents usually received a commission of 35 per cent per copy and the agents gave hawkers a commission of 28 to 30 per cent per copy. *Dainik Bhaskar* also had a policy of taking back five unsold copies out of 1,000 copies per day from the agent. To increase newspaper circulation, which would concomitantly help in getting more advertising, *Dainik Bhaskar* provided extra incentives to agents and hawkers, besides providing various incentives to readers.

The cap on the commission ratio of 35 per cent per copy existed only on paper and on occasion might exceed 50 per cent. According to the Audit

---

41   Local Reporter, interviewed on 27 December 2007, Bhopal.

Bureau of Circulation (ABC)[42] rules, if a newspaper gives more than 35 per cent commission to agents/hawkers, that copy would be counted as unsold and would not be taken into consideration while doing the final count of the newspaper circulation figures. To avoid this, newspapers take precautions, at least on paper, and try to maintain the commission ratio stipulated by the ABC. A recent strategy by newspapers to override the stringent guidelines of the ABC was to convince advertisers to take into account readership figures rather than circulation figures while releasing advertising. Since newspapers are ferociously competing with each other to increase their circulation and readership, they end up paying agents/hawkers more than the ABC-specified commission. This increases the circulation figure, but the sold copies are not counted by the ABC in its survey. Despite the strict regulation by the ABC, it hasn't been able to curb unfair practices by newspapers and it appears that the market has started to influence the function and operation of the news media.[43]

Gift schemes for readers were another strategy used by *Dainik Bhaskar* to increase its readership. These ranged from giving gifts to readers for a monthly subscription to lottery schemes where readers can win handsome prizes (Figure 5.4), similar to the lottery schemes found in Thai newspapers (McCargo, 2002). Under the scheme a monthly subscriber of the newspaper can collect a gift at the end of a month after submitting the coupon to a nearby agent of *Dainik Bhaskar*. The coupon was usually pasted at the top corner of the paper, which a reader needed to collect for the entire month.

---

42 The Audit Bureau of Circulations (ABC) is a voluntary organisation of publishers, advertisers and advertising agencies that operates in different parts of the world. Its main task is to verify the circulation data provided by newspapers and periodicals. The Bureau issues ABC certificates every six months to publishers whose circulation figures conform to the rules and regulations set out by the Bureau. This helps advertisers make their decision before investing money in advertising. According to the ABC's website, 'The ABC figures are not the outcome of opinions, claims or guesswork, but they are the result of rigid, in-depth and impartial audits of paid circulations of member publications by independent and leading firms of chartered accountants working in accordance with the rules/ procedures prescribed by the Bureau.' Available at: http://www.auditbureau.org/about.htm. However, in recent times, readership surveys have emerged as an important factor for advertisers in decision-making. N. K. Singh, the resident editor of the *Indian Express*, Ahmedabad, told us, 'No longer do the ABC figures command the same values because the readership survey has taken over the role of the ABC.' For a sound analysis of ABC, see Jeffrey (1994).

43 In the context of the US, Meyer (2004) remarks, 'the glory of the newspaper business in the United States used to be its ability to match its success as a business with self-conscious attention to its social service mission. Both functions are threatened today' (4).

Figure 5.4: Pamphlet for special promotion offered by *Dainik Bhaskar*

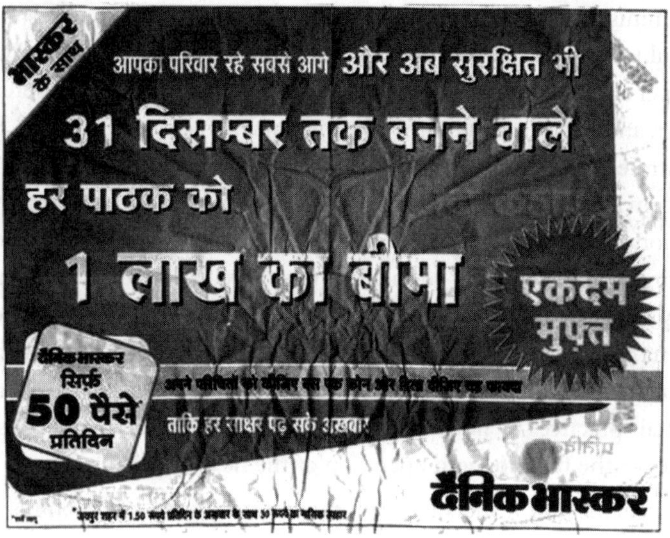

The reader might win a prize if he/she finds a lucky number after scratching the coupon, which was declared every day. Even if readers were unable to get the lucky prize, they were assured of a small gift at the end of a month that would be worth more than the monthly subscription.[44] The gifts included T-shirts, plastic jars, buckets, washing powder and other household items. Dinesh Maheshwari, Manager, SMD, told me, 'Usually gift items are selected to attract women, as our survey found that women are important in influencing newspaper subscription.[45]

Such schemes last for two to three months and help in developing a habit among readers for the newspaper. While explaining the significance of such schemes, Dinesh Maheshwari said,

> Through such schemes we are usually able to increase our circulation. Though it's difficult to retain all readers attracted to the newspaper because of the scheme, we are usually successful in retaining 70 to 80 per cent of readers after the completion of the scheme.[46]

---

44 Such a scheme is not unique to *Dainik Bhaskar* and is frequently adopted by several newspapers. For details, see Ninan (2007).

45 Interviewed on 6 November 2006, Bhopal.

46 Interviewed on 6 November 2006, Bhopal.

This strategy to increase circulation was first introduced by the English daily, the *Times of India*. Among Hindi newspapers, *Dainik Bhaskar* is believed to be the first to introduce this strategy, which was used during their launch of the Jaipur edition in 1996.

Another way to increase circulation is through hawkers who are provided with incentives, such as an increment of INR 30 per copy. To qualify for incentives, the increase in the number of newspaper copies must last for a period of three months. Dinesh Maheshwari explained:

> Because of the lure of money, some hawkers take extra copies with them, but are unable to continue beyond a month. Therefore, in order to ensure that the increase is real and it would continue, we have adopted the method of an observation period of three months.[47]

These precautions are taken to ensure that circulation does not fall back suddenly, which might affect advertising. As noted by S. K. Basu, in charge of training in *Dainik Bhaskar*, 'Printing more copies means making a loss because it increases the cost of production. Before increasing the circulation we ensure that there is a corresponding increase in advertising revenue.'[48]

Earlier, hawkers were provided small gifts, but now they ask for monetary incentives instead, explained Shoib Kareem, who was in charge of distribution at Lalghati, a suburb of Bhopal.[49] When asked whether agents or hawkers were more important for *Dainik Bhaskar*, Dinesh Maheshwari explained, 'We obviously give more importance to hawkers since they are the people who deal directly with readers. But at the same time we do not ignore agents.' Sometimes, agents did not inform hawkers about the incentives announced by the paper. To ensure that hawkers were informed about their incentives, *Dainik Bhaskar* appointed people who dealt directly with them as well as with agents. In Bhopal, it was difficult to hide information about the incentives from hawkers since they had a good network among themselves. But in small towns and rural areas, where there were few hawkers, such incentives were hidden by the agent. While talking to a hawker in Itarsi, who was a college student, I learnt that he had not received any extra incentive in the two years after he started working. His salary was fixed and did not depend on the number of copies he was able to sell in a day.

---

47 Interview with Dinesh Maheshwari, Manager, SMD, 6 November 2006, Bhopal.

48 Interviewed on 28 October 2006, Bhopal.

49 Interviewed on 26 November 2006, Bhopal.

This shows that in small towns agents usually take away a larger profit compared to cities where there is stiff competition and hawkers have strong networks. But one also has to take into account the number of copies that an agent is able to sell in small towns, which is far fewer in comparison with big cities.

Who decides the news? The editor vs. market

How far advertising has affected the content of a newspaper is an intriguing question that baffles many analysts. Several studies have highlighted the power of marketing in affecting media content (Bagdikian, 1983, 2004; Bennett, 2004; Gilens and Hertzman, 2000; Thussu, 2006b). Schudson (2011) argues that 'not just the state but the market, too, can threaten press freedom' (111). He though cautions from considering capitalism as 'the enemy of free expression'. Habermas (1989) in his analysis of the transformation of the bourgeois public sphere in Europe also lamented the commercialisation of the press, the 'preeminent institution' of the public sphere that precipitated its fragmentation. Habermas contends that with commercial interests becoming paramount for the press, issues related to 'public affairs, social problems, economic matters, education, and health, ... pushed into the background by "immediate reward news" (comics, corruption, accidents, disasters, sports, recreation, social events, and human interest)' (169–70). The supposed 'golden era' of rational-critical discourse before the commercialisation of mass media is a myth (see Schudson, 1998). Instead of viewing the relationship between the market and the press freedom as zero-sum game, I would argue that both could exist in a complementary and competitive way (see also Downey and Neyazi, 2014).

As noted, *Dainik Bhaskar* had a well-established marketing department to deal with advertising and circulation. During my fieldwork in Bhopal, reporters and sub-editors repeatedly told me that they were underpaid, whereas people in the marketing department were paid a decent salary right from the time when they joined. The preferential treatment given to marketing compared to the news/editorial department also reflects the deep structural bias and belief that marketing was superior to the production of the content for the paper. *Dainik Bhaskar* became the first Hindi newspaper that used marketing strategies and conducted a massive readership survey before making its foray into a new market. Marketing strategy to sell newspapers was adopted by *Dainik Bhaskar* in 1996 during the launch of the Jaipur edition, which has been continuing. Such techniques have brought commercial success for *Dainik Bhaskar*, but they also raise the question of autonomy for the institution of the editor. Has the editor lost his/her authority over the content of the newspaper, which has now been taken over by market forces? In other words, is the content of the newspaper driven by the market rather than by a concern for social and political happenings? Mahesh Shrivastav, editor of *Dainik Bhaskar* from 1990 to 2000, told me that when he was the editor, he used to go through all the content of the paper and provide informed comments on important local, regional or national issues. 'But today', he exclaimed, 'the editor does not even know what is inside the newspaper.'[50]

No doubt, he is raising the important problem of commercialisation that has afflicted Indian news media in the current context of globalisation. But such a view ignores the increase in varieties of news stories over the years that have to be provided space in the newspaper. Before 1991, Hindi newspapers largely focused on political news, with minor coverage of other issues. After 1991, a number of issues that were earlier given short shrift started getting more attention. Issues related to the market and the economy, careers, education, health and lifestyles received greater coverage and eventually squeezed the space provided to political news. Moreover, the number of pages in the newspaper has gone up in recent times. In 1980, *Dainik Bhaskar* was an eight-page newspaper that increased to 20 pages in 2006 and to 24 pages in 2011 including a four-page *City Bhaskar* supplement. Similarly, in the 1980s, newspapers hardly cared about readers preference and the editor would be asked to provide an opinion on any issue coming up. An editor was supposed to know something about everything. With increasing competition since the 1990s, professionalism started developing and the function of the editor became diversified. Instead of the editor giving comments on every issue, newspapers would now hire experts and columnists to write on issues deserving public attention.[51] The use of experts to write for the newspaper also helps in producing a simpler analysis of complex issues and reader-friendly material. According to Vipul Mudgal, Associate Editor of the *Hindustan Times*,

> The task of the editor has become more challenging in recent times than it used to be in earlier days. This has resulted in the devolution of the power of the editor and now we have more than one editor looking after different sections of the paper.[52]

---

50 Interviewed on 27 October 2006, Bhopal.

51 *Dainik Bhaskar* produces two leader page articles everyday. Each columnist is paid INR 2,500 for writing an article, explained Shiv Kumar Vivek, in charge of the editorial page. Interviewed on 1 November 2006, Bhopal.

52 Interviewed on 26 September 2006, Delhi.

Mudgal is making the point that functional specificity in the newspaper, which was absent earlier, has become important.

Moreover, with the amount of content growing in a newspaper, it is now impossible for an editor to go through all the content being produced in the newspaper. *Dainik Bhaskar* had an editor for each major section of the newspaper who was responsible for the content produced in that section. But it was still the chief editor who was legally responsible for all the content published in the newspaper. If any defamatory content appeared in the newspaper, a legal notice was served in the name of the chief editor. Nevertheless, one cannot ignore the market forces influencing the content of the newspaper. In order to increase its readership to attract more advertising, *Dainik Bhaskar* aggressively employed marketing strategies by conducting frequent surveys to understand the preferences of its readers. This meant that newspapers have to give greater weight to readers' expectations than to happenings in society. Similarly, monthly coupon schemes and prizes were introduced to increase readership, but such schemes are also used by several other newspapers. At the same time, hawkers have been rewarded to increase newspaper subscription.

Another important development that occurred in the 1980s is the liberation of newspapers from their dependence on government advertisements, which used to be an important source of revenue for newspapers until the 1970s (Jeffrey, 2000).[53] This also prevented small newspapers from criticising the government because it might affect the way government distributed advertising. The government briefly stopped advertisements to *Dainik Bhaskar* in the wake of the leak of toxic gas from a Union Carbide pesticide plant in Bhopal in 1984, that has been called the world's worst industrial disaster, when the newspaper vehemently criticised the government for negligence in preventing this tragedy. Instead of bowing down before the government, *Dainik Bhaskar* continued to support the cause of the people, which also established its credentials in Bhopal.[54] However, with growing advertising revenues from private sources in the late 1980s and 1990s, newspapers have become more confident about their independence. Mudid Gulati explained that one-third of advertisements comes from the government and two-thirds is generated through retail advertisements in Bhopal. The rate paid for government advertisements is much lower than the

---

53 The idea of government advertisement was created during the colonial period by the British, who used it as a way to control and provide patronage to newspapers. See Israel (1994).

54 The Bhopal gas tragedy is an important landmark in the history of the expansion of *Dainik Bhaskar*, as it provided them with an opportunity to establish their credentials in the homeland.

commercial rate, as it is the government that decides the advertising rate for the newspaper. The difference between government and commercial advertisement rates is almost 300 per cent, according to S. K. Jha. The lower rate of the government advertisement shows that retail or private advertisements are the most important source of revenue for a newspaper.

It would be gross generalisation, however, to assert that business pressures have taken over editorial decisions. During my fieldwork when I interviewed marketing professionals at *Dainik Bhaskar*, they complained to me that editorial department is often unwilling to adjust the last minute advertisement placement by removing a couple of news items. This shows the competitive nature of relationship between the market and editorial departments. There are cases where news media has been able to safeguard editorial independence from business pressures. It was also the stature of the resident editor that could have a determining influence; a strong editor is more likely to protect editorial independence as compared to a weak editor. Bowing down to the demands of the advertisers might drive away the audience and this fact influence the media owner to strike a balance between market pressures and editorial independence. Quality journalism does create wealth. There thus exists competitive and complementary relationship between the market and the press freedom. This intractable relationship between the market and the editorial independence is overlooked in the oversimplified narrative that views corporate ownership with suspicion and surrender to the whims of the market.

Conclusion

This chapter focussed on the political economy of the Hindi press and how it has transformed the larger perception of Hindi public. The growth trajectory of *Dainik Bhaskar* and *Dainik Jagran* shows the emergence of media conglomerates outside the English language media group. The changing ownership patterns of Indian media conglomerates with the significant presence of Hindi media conglomerates in India's top media groups is indicative of the rising power of the Hindi media. An interesting aspect of the rise of Hindi newspapers is the multi-faceted approach that takes advantage of both the rising market economy to cash in on local advertising as well as alignment with the issues of farmers and grassroots mobilisation in the wake of economic reforms. The success story of Hindi newspapers also throws light on the issue of journalism ethics as both *Dainik Bhaskar* and *Dainik Jagran* were involved in paid news controversies. The media that operates with the profit motive cannot be expected to grant equal access to subordinate or marginalised groups. The prevalence of multiple interests – economic, political and ideological – with each of them being emphasised according to exigencies, shows the polyvalent nature of the Hindi press.

Yet, it would be gross generalisation to disregard the rise of Hindi newspapers as purely driven by a profit motive that hasn't benefited small towns and rural areas where they expanded. The growth of Indian language newspapers since the 1980s contributed to a shift in the focus of Indian journalism from the English-speaking urban middle class to the majority of diverse people living in towns and rural areas speaking in vernacular languages. Looking at the past three decades, when newspapers were almost absent in rural areas, it would be incorrect to assume that there has been a fragmentation of the public sphere. Since the late 1980s, northern India has seen enormous growth in the readership of Hindi newspapers that has greatly enlarged the public sphere. One cannot ignore the growing awareness about various social and political issues in the countryside that came along with the increasing penetration of Hindi newspapers into the hinterlands driven by advertising revenues. Such a growing awareness among marginalised groups such as people in rural areas and small towns and farmers, which came about because of the consumption of news, also resulted in the growth of subaltern politics that widened the participation of people who had remained largely indifferent to politics. It was definitely Hindi newspapers that were facilitating the growth of grassroots mobilisation and the rise of a non-party political process, as English newspapers do not have any base in the countryside and small towns of north India. It is the increasing awareness among the rural masses that has further consolidated Indian democracy and triggered the rise of the subaltern sections of society. The duality embedded in the expansion of Hindi newspapers is quite evident; on the one hand, it has brought in the dominance of market and advertising, and on the other hand, it has further democratised the public sphere by including people who were earlier excluded from participation.

6

The Hybrid Media System, Anti-corruption Movement and Political Mobilisation

Thus far in this book, I have focused on traditional media and the ways in which they have affected political and social mobilisation in contemporary India. This and the following chapter move on to analyse the transformation in the process of political communication and mobilisation after the emergence of new media. In these chapters, I show how new information networks have transformed the dynamics of citizens' participation and supplemented the role of traditional media and face-to-face interaction, leading to the emergence of what Andrew Chadwick (2011, 2013) called a 'hybrid' media system. Political communication now takes place in a more complex hybrid space in which both traditional and newer media are utilised by a diverse array of actors such as political parties, protest movements, and professional news organisations to engage citizens and to influence public opinion and the political agenda.

Several studies have shown the ways in which the internet has transformed democratic politics (Chadwick, 2006; Hindman, 2008; Howard, 2005, 2010; Loader and Mercea, 2012; Mossberger, Tolbert and McNeal, 2007). The WikiLeaks online disclosure of US foreign policy demonstrated the disruption caused by social media, which is now forcing the mainstream news media to turn to political blogs and citizen users for material. Such disruption, according to Loader and Mercea (2012), has enabled citizens to discuss and share political information and 'critically monitor the actions of governments and corporate interests' (5) with friends and networked citizens. The rise of the internet also resulted in further fragmentation of media channels and led Bennett and Iyengar (2008) to pronounce the beginning of a new era of 'minimal media effects'. At the same time, the uneven level of access by different social groups to new media, a phenomenon known as the digital divide, has raised concerns regarding the limitations of its democratic potential. I propose that instead of focusing exclusively on either online media or traditional media, scholars should see the complexity as a result of a hybrid media environment, an environment in which traditional media continue to occupy an important place along with new media and face-to-face interactions. However, the hybrid media environment of India differs from the media environments in advanced economies in which most citizens access the internet.

This chapter, by focusing on the case of the anti-corruption movement, popularly known as Jan Lokpal Andolan, the first known movement in contemporary India to utilise the internet to mobilise support, argues that new media, combined with traditional media, have the potential to mobilise the public and influence policy-making.[1] The campaign was launched in 2011 by 74- year-old Indian social activist and self-styled Gandhian, Anna Hazare, to support the passage of legislation called Jan Lokpal Bill to combat the menace of corruption.[2] The campaign for the Jan Lokpal Bill received global attention because of the extensive media coverage of the protests. The interface between print, television, and the internet, as well as grassroots mobilisation, created a new space for political mobilisation, or a 'hybrid media system', which was witnessed during Anna Hazare's campaign against corruption. The mobile phone and short messaging service [SMS] were used effectively to coordinate the public protests and mobilise supporters. The emergence of a hybrid media system offers opportunities for social movements to mobilise public opinion rapidly ('virality') but also includes the danger of disappearing equally rapidly ('ephemerality'). This virality and ephemerality may, in the process, help the movements or vested interests achieve their goals.

The effective use of new media not only brought the anti-corruption campaign into cyberspace and rendered it more global, but also garnered huge support for anti-corruption protests, which *Time* magazine listed among the top 10 news stories of 2011. Simultaneously, media coverage of the event triggered actual political participation; people from different parts of India visited Jantar Mantar in New Delhi, where Anna Hazare commenced a fast-until-death protest to press for his demands. The site was reported to be India's Tahrir Square. In addition to Mr Hazare's personal undertaking, major protests were organised in several cities across India. In the initial phase, the protests were primarily confined to the urban middle-class and did not penetrate the hinterlands, which created doubts regarding the democratic credentials of the campaign. Contrary to the popular perception that the campaign was limited to the urban middle-class, I demonstrate that there was significant participation by a diverse public comprising people from the rural areas, towns and cities in addition to the middle classes.

---

1   Although I have used movement and campaign interchangebly in this research, I am mindful of the differences between these two concepts.

2   Although Anna Hazare became the face of the anti-corruption campaign, all organisational aspects of the campaigns were looked after by India Against Corruption (IAC), which essentially consisted of middle class with significant support from Non-resident Indian (NRIs).

What are the implications of mediated mobilisation for democratic politics and civil society? Can new media create new forms of political engagement by attracting the support of disengaged citizens? Are new forms of conducting politics emerging with the rise of new and traditional media? To address these and other questions, the chapter analyses the anti-corruption movement in two phases: the first phase began on 5 April 2011 when Anna Hazare began his fast-until-death protest and lasted until the end of April 2011; while the second phase began on 16 August 2011 with the arrest of Anna Hazare in New Delhi. Whereas the first phase of the movement was primarily confined to metropolitan cities and the urban middle class, with people offering their support without much critical debate, the second phase witnessed the emergence of a critical mass as well as more diversified support for the anti-corruption movement that reached beyond the urban middle class.[3]

Political participation in a hybrid media system

Mobilised citizens are more likely to participate in political activities; hence, mobilisation is an important precondition for political participation (Hooghe, Vissers, Stolle and Mahéo, 2010). Traditionally, political participation is confined to institutionalised activities such as voting, forming political groups, party membership, joining a protest or rally and contacting a politician (Verba and Nie, 1972). Huntington and Nelson (1976) defined political participation as 'activity by private citizens designed to influence government decision-making' (3). This definition of political participation, which is associated only with influencing government action, has been criticised as narrow and limited (Barnes and Kaase, 1979; Conge, 1988). The definition of political participation has since broadened to incorporate non-institutionalised activities and actions directed not only at influencing government decision-making but also at all political, societal, media and economic actors or elite.

Individual's political participation is often driven by the desire and expectation that their actions will have some influence on political outcomes.

---

3   Ironically, populist movements carry within themselves both progressive and reactionary forces in their hegemonic articulation of popular sentiments and hence, reflect the danger of disintegration in the long run by trying to hold diverse elements together. The disintegration also provides opportunities for the emergence of multiple coherent forces and thus shows the potential for the rise of a long-lasting alternative to the existing social order. The diverse and contradictory forces that came together to represent the anti-corruption movement and its gradual disintegration, and the emergence of the AAP from the movement reflect the trajectory that is often taken by a populist movement.

Yet, it would be incorrect to link the effects of political participation exclusively to political or legislative outcomes because altruistic values that increase individual life satisfaction and happiness for oneself and for others can also drive individual political participation. Political participation invariably has indirect effects. An important indirect effect of the mobilisation for the anti-corruption movement was the emergence of a new political party, the Aam Aadmi Party (AAP), in Delhi in 2012, whose leaders emerged from the movement. The new political party then surprised all by winning a high number of seats in the Delhi assembly election in 2013, and then went on to win the Delhi assembly election in 2015 with a landslide. Since the 2011 anti-corruption movement targeted the political class, particularly the Congress party, which was ruling at the centre, the movement further discredited and tarnished the image of the Congress party and may have influenced the outcome of the 2014 Lok Sabha election. Therefore, when analysing the process of political communication, we cannot ignore the role of exogenous factors in influencing political outcomes.

A lack of political participation results from various factors. Citizens may feel that their participation will not make any difference in the existing political system. According to Schlozman, Verba and Brady (2010), 'political participation is inhibited when individuals face deficits in time, money, or skills, thus making it difficult for them to take part' (488). On occasion, lack of access to means of political participation, discourages even politically interested citizens from participating in political activities. The arrival of digital media has helped overcome these hurdles of political participation for citizens.

With the escalation of digital media, the mobilisation processes have been considerably transformed, and new forms of political participation emerged that were not possible within the traditional media environment, such as supporting a movement online by signing a petition, joining social networks, or cyber attacks for a 'good' cause or to achieve a political goal, which is termed 'hacktivism'.[4] A person with a high level of political interest will participate in political activities regardless of exposure to the political issues and events. Similarly, post-materialist values, such as concerns for the environment, values of equality and personal integrity, inclusion of minorities and subaltern classes, human rights and sustainable development, encourage citizens to discover new avenues, greatly helped by the digital media, to express their private and public interests and identities. Some people regularly follow political events, whereas

---

4   For a very good study on anonymous hacktivist groups, see Beyer (2014).

others become interested only during a crisis or an important political event, such as an election. Among the internet users, substantial numbers may not be interested in the politics of the country or eager to participate in politics on the internet, but they are drawn into politics because a major personality is involved or there is a major crisis.

Studies have shown that politically interested citizens use the internet more frequently for political and civic engagement (Bimber, 1999; Norris, 2001; Polat, 2005). Here, new media does not directly affect the behaviour of the individual; instead, individual interests determine the use of new media for political communication. These complexities warrant the need to explore whether new media are able to entice disengaged citizens into civic and political participation, a point that is addressed later in the chapter.

There is an apparent paradox in the evolving media ecology and protest movements; although protest and activist groups have tried to use new media and bypass traditional media, which for them is pro-establishment and favours the established political groups, those groups depend on traditional media for the legitimacy of their actions (DeLuca, Lawson and Sun, 2012). It is, therefore, important to understand the hybrid media system that informs the majority of contemporary social and political mobilisation.

Chadwick's (2013) conceptualisation of the hybrid media system extended beyond the binary of traditional and new media and attempted to understand the media system in a more holistic manner that captures the interactions between political actors, journalists, broadcasters, bloggers and the public. Chadwick questioned the traditional understanding of the media logic that revolved around fixed norms, boundaries and hierarchies. Media logic, or the format and techniques used by the media to capture people's attention, have come to dominate media institutions. The media tends to reduce important messages into bylines by polarising, sensationalising and personalising the issues or taking advantage of their medium to survive in the existing hyper-competitive media market. Realising the importance of media logic, political parties, leaders and protest groups attempt to adapt to obtain maximum coverage. However, the concept of media logic that developed in the mass communication era, in which there was a single media cycle (Altheide and Snow, 1979), may not be helpful in understanding the complexity and fluidity of interactions among media and political actors in an emerging hybrid media system. For example, the majority of journalists today write on blogs or share their stories on social media. A live debate on television attracts reactions on Twitter. It is, therefore, important to use the plural, media logics, rather than of 'an all encompassing, hegemonic media logic' (Chadwick, 2013, 21).

In a hybrid media system, according to Chadwick (2013), political life is mediated by the web of networked actions involving offline and online communication as well as grassroots activism. Far from displacing the older media, the arrival of newer media facilitates the emergence of a hybrid media system in which interactions between older and newer media occur across various platforms. The new public created by the rise of newer media is often a hybrid, because that new public is also the consumer of older media, 'partly amalgamated combinations of groups, organisations, and social norms and practices that were previously associated with older media' (Chadwick, 2013, 24). In the new hybrid media environment, in which traditional journalistic processes compete with new citizen-driven digital media, it is difficult to identify the creators and sponsors of events because the majority of events today are co-created with different actors being involved simultaneously – political actors, media actors and the public – because communication now takes place in multiple places simultaneously.

Chadwick developed the framework to specifically understand the rapid transformation in political communication in the developed nations of Britain and the United States. However, this framework can be extended to developing countries such as India, where there is simultaneous growth of print, broadcast and social media. In today's globalised world, technological innovation migrates from one place to another in a short period of time that leads the elite of the country to adapt to a global lifestyles, rendering the earlier binaries of global north and underdeveloped south increasingly blurred. Take, for example, the rapid diffusion of mobile phones and the internet, which now has more users in developing countries than in developed countries.[5] The newer and older media not only compete but also complement and are interdependent of one another. The Anna Hazare campaign against corruption was the first known movement in India utilising the internet to mobilise support along with offline activism and must therefore be understood within the framework of a hybrid media system.

A report by the Internet and Mobile Association of India (IAMAI) indicates that as of October 2015, there were 375 million claimed internet users: 246 million in urban cities and 129 million in rural villages. In 2011, the number of internet users in India was just over 100 million. Despite the low penetration

---

5   There were 3.2 billion people using the internet globally at the end of 2015, 2 billion of whom were from developing countries (International Telecommunication Union [ITU], 2015).

of the internet in India, Team Anna decided to use new media. This decision was partially influenced by the fact that mobilising the internet public and the middle-class would certainly draw the attention of traditional media such as news channels and newspapers.[6]

The discourse on corruption

Anna Hazare-led movement fought against corruption, and it is pertinent here to understand the discourse on the prevalence of corruption in India. Corruption in India is prevalent at several levels, and ordinary citizens experience corruption on an everyday basis (Gupta, 1995; Jeffrey, 2002). Common forms of corruption in India include but is not limited to, bribing bureaucrats and government officials to obtain services, such as electricity supply, water supply, a ration card, or even a driver's licence or passport.[7] In addition, there has been a significant increase in political corruption among the elected representatives of the people, which has become the subject of much discussion because of the increase in both its magnitude and its frequency. For example, in referring to the magnitude of corruption, the Supreme Court of India in May 2011 in its remarks on the 2G Spectrum Scam said that the figures involved were 'mind boggling' and 'we haven't seen so many zeroes in our life.'[8] Until fairly recently, Transparency International, a corruption watchdog, has continuously ranked India in the more corrupt half of the countries in the Corruption Perception Index (CPI), which ranks countries annually since 1996 by their perceived levels of corruption by expert assessments and public opinion surveys (See Quah, 2008). Because it is difficult to measure actual levels of corruption, the CPI measures perceived corruption. Quah (2008) attributed the widespread prevalence of corruption in public offices in India to its

---

6   Several studies have indicated that the internet has mobilised disinterested citizens into civic and political participation (Barber, 2001; Delli Carpini, 2000; Krueger, 2002; Schlozman, Verba and Brady, 2010).

7   The literature on corruption has identified three primary types of definitions of corruption: public office-centred, market-centred and public interest-centred definitions (See Heidenheimer, 1989; also Clarke, 1983).

8   The 2G scam, in which the Congress party and its coalition government was embroiled, has been termed the biggest scam in the history of independent India, which *Time* magazine named among the world's top 10 abuses of power in 2011, is said to have caused the Indian government a loss of INR 1.76 lakh crore (roughly equivalent to US$39 billion). The Telecom Minister at that time, A. Raja, was accused of selling spectrum licences in 2009 to different companies at a price that was fixed in 2001. For his involvement in the scam Raja was arrested in February 2011, but was subsequently granted bail by Supreme Court in May 2012 with certain conditions. As of May 2017, the matter is still under consideration in a special court set up to investigate the 2G scam.

ineffective anti-corruption strategies, accentuated by a lack of political will and unfavourable policy context. By 2016, India was ranked 79 out of 176 countries on the CPI, which reflects the perception of India's movement from the more corrupt to the less corrupt half of the countries on the list.

Unlike other developing democracies, corruption in India is not generally considered to be a threat to its democratic regime (Jenkins, 2007). However, the process of democratic consolidation has certainly been affected because of the prevalence of corruption that has eroded the accountability of public institutions and hampered anti-poverty programmes (Jenkins, 2007). The Right to Information (RTI) Act, 2005, which empowered citizens to seek government information from a public authority, was an important landmark in the fight against public corruption. The Indian media effectively used the RTI to seek relevant government information. There was a significant increase in the magnitude of corruption scandals in the latter half of the 2000s. Pratap Bhanu Mehta (2003) argued that corruption is an important channel for social mobility in India and hence has a certain popular legitimacy. During my fieldwork in 2006, I asked the resident editor of a leading Hindi daily, *Dainik Bhaskar* Bhopal, how he selected the morning lead stories and whether a story on corruption could find its way to the front page. He told me, 'People are so fed up with the frequent occurrence of corruption that they have lost interest in it. So corruption is no longer a serious news story and it cannot make front-page news unless there is a mega scam.'[9]

India's news audiences were perceived as having corruption-fatigue, based on this editor's comments, unless the latest corruption story is bigger than the last mega corruption story. Although leading Hindi language newspapers are not included in a Factiva database search on the word 'scam' from 2006 to 2011, results from my search of the *Times of India* (TOI) over this period are suggestive of the *Dainik Bhaskar* editor's view that only mega-scams would generate headlines, and from 2009 to 2011 there was a deluge of stories on scams, including several mega-scams, their political and industrial origins, ongoing investigations and the judicial process. Over 6,000 stories mentioned the word 'scam' over the six-year period from 2006 to 2011. The annual distribution changed significantly over time from 430 in 2006, 277 stories in 2007 and 447 in 2008, to a number that more than tripled to 1,567 in 2009 with a not insubstantial amount of news given to the legal action on Satyam

---

9   Interviewed on 17 October 2006, Bhopal.

Computer Services and its auditors at PWC, which has been described as the biggest corporate scam in India's history, as well as the progress on investigation into the 2G spectrum scandal along with the Commonwealth Games (CGW) scam that hit Congress party in New Delhi. Scam stories declined by about one-third to 1,075 in 2010, and then more than doubled to 2,253 in 2011 when these three mega-scams and a host of other scams that impacted the reputations of established sources of power, including the military and political elite were reported. Why did Anna Hazare-led campaign against corruption attract such enourmous support? In Parliamentary debates, on 24 August 2011, M. B. Rajesh of the Communist Party of India (Marxist) said:

> Corruption is the most hotly debated topic in the country today. Whether it is in the media, social networking sites or in the streets, people are discussing this issue with deep concern. Actually, people have come out in tens of thousands against corruption. The recent corruption exposures have created a great deal of public anger and resentment. This public outrage is being reflected in the ongoing fast of Shri Anna Hazare.

There is certainly underlying angst regarding corruption because it affects both the middle class and the poor. Therefore, when Anna Hazare launched the campaign against corruption, it gathered huge public support. The campaign gave people the confidence that corruption could be eradicated and that people's representatives could be held accountable.

Media and the anti-corruption movement

Anna Hazare demanded that the government enact a law to create an effective anti-corruption institution called the Jan Lokpal that would have wide-ranging powers to investigate and prosecute powerful individuals without fear of political interference. The anti-corruption Lokpal (Ombudsman) Bill was introduced eight times in Parliament, beginning in 1968. Anna Hazare perceived the existing anti-corruption laws to be inadequate because they failed to curb the mega-corruption that the country had witnessed in recent times. In the first half of 2011, Hazare began calling for a strong Jan Lokpal Bill to be passed to fight corruption; his campaign gained momentum in the second half of 2011. The Bill was finally passed by the Lok Sabha in December 2011 and by the Rajya Sabha in December 2013.

The media played an important role in the anti-corruption movement led by

Anna Hazare and several analysts argued that it was a 'media-fuelled movement'. Rajagopal (2011a) asked, 'Am I still Anna when nobody is watching?' suggesting that people would not have come out in such large numbers had there been no 24X7 media coverage of the event. The social movement's heavy dependence on the media worked by both the rapid amplification (virality) and the rapid disappearance (ephemerality) of the movement. In this age of digital communication technologies, social movements, which often encounter difficulties obtaining space in traditional media, begin by using the new media in order to mobilise support for their cause. The internet and SMS technology help the movements instantly communicate with and mobilise potential supporters worldwide. Once the movement begins gaining visibility, it may get picked up by the traditional media, which has an amplification effect and mobilises a wider audience, thus leading to virality. This dependence on the media to mobilise public opinion instead of mobilising support at the grassroots level first also challenges the movement's sustainability. The long-term articulation of demands requires building grassroots support rather than beginning the movement with the media without having first established a solid support base. I later demonstrate how the anti-corruption movement obtained high visibility, but failed to steer the increasing support coming from disparate groups into a coherent articulation of demands because the channels for grassroots co-ordination were absent, leading to the disappearance of the movement in quite a short time.

There is little doubt about the role of the media during the campaign. A simple search on Factiva for newspapers globally with the keyword 'Anna Hazare' from January 2011 to February 2012 shows how stories about Anna Hazare came to dominate newspapers globally from April 2011 onwards. There were fewer than 200 stories about Anna Hazare from January 2011 to March 2011; however, during April, when Anna Hazare began his fast, newspaper coverage soared to 5,157 for the month of April (Figure 6.1). The most massive jump was in the month of August, and the total number of stories addressing Anna Hazare climbed to over 14,000. Even Anna Hazare's team acknowledged the role of the media after the government agreed to their demands. Thus, on 9 April, Kiran Bedi, core member of Team Anna who subsequently joined BJP in 2015, tweeted, 'Media is the fourth pillar and it's very powerful to spread the word to the entire nation.' She also wrote, 'I want to thank the media for spreading the word to the world about #corruption.'

Figure 6.1: Newspaper coverage of 'Anna Hazare' from January 2011 to February 2012

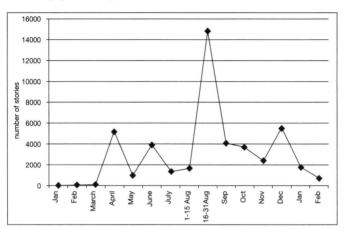

Source: Factiva global newspaper database.

Similarly, Ambika Soni, the-then Information and Broadcasting Minister, in a reference to the role of the media during Anna Hazare's campaign, said, 'It was generally perceived that reporters became participants' and:

> I don't know if it was excitement of the atmosphere or something new which was seen by many people. But the way commentaries were made, the way the broadcasts were made, you all generated a hype which was larger than what I feel was there (TNN, 5 November 2011a).

This perception of the role of media in the movement is reflected in the following analysis.

The first phase of fast-until-death began on 5 April 2011. Anna Hazare ended his fast four days later on 9 April after the government capitulated to Team Anna's demands, assuring Hazare that they would establish a 10-member joint committee comprising of ministers and civil society members to draft an effective Lokpal Bill. In the wake of the protests, Esha News Agency published a study reflecting how news channels supported the movement without critiquing the process. The study reported that between 3 April and 11 April there were a total of 5,657 clips with a total duration of 655 hours.[10] The tone of the coverage was overwhelmingly supportive of the Anna Hazare protest with 5,592 positive clips and only 65 negative clips.

---

10   The report, which is available for public access, does not provide details regarding the news channels covered in the survey.

When the government's draft of the Jan Lokpal Bill disappointed Team Anna, the second phase of the fast began. Anna Hazare started his second fast on 16 August but decided to break his fast on 28 August after the government accepted all demands and assured him that it would enact a strong Lokpal Bill. However, on 16 August, Anna Hazare was arrested and sent to Delhi's Tihar Jail. Anna Hazare decided to continue his fast from jail and appealed to his supporters to continue their protests. His arrest by the Congress-led government not only angered the citizens, but also helped reinvent the news and produce high drama by turning the arrest into a media event (Kumar, 2014). People began thronging outside Tihar Jail, and the live broadcasts of the event helped mobilise people throughout the country. By the time the government realised its mistake in arresting Anna Hazare and decided to release him a day later on 17 August, Hazare had been turned into a national icon, riding high on the legitimacy the government accorded him by considering him a serious threat. Several politicians and public figures also began visiting Hazare in jail, requesting that he break his fast during the 24X7 glare of the media spectacle, which created the illusion of unprecedented power commanded by the 74-year-old, self-proclaimed Gandhian. A study by the Centre for Media Studies (CMS), New Delhi indicated that between 16 and 28 August, two leading Hindi news channels, *Aaj Tak* and *Star News*, devoted 97 per cent of their total news time during primetime (7.00 pm to 11.00 pm) to Anna Hazare's anti-corruption movement; the corresponding figure for two English news channels, CNN-IBN and NDTV 24X7, was 87 per cent (Bhaskar, 2011; Muralidharan, 2011). This CMS study did not provide details regarding the tone of the coverage, but the sheer amount of visibility the movement received on news channels makes one wonder whether any other news was covered during primetime during those 13 days (CMS, 2011).

The newspapers played an equally important role in creating awareness of the anti-corruption campaign. Most newspapers provided extensive coverage and launched a campaign in support of Anna Hazare. *Times of India*, a leading English daily, played an important role and christened Anna Hazare as a man of the people. Even more important was the role of the Hindi and regional language newspapers in creating awareness among diverse people and taking the movement to small towns and rural areas in which news channels and English newspapers have limited penetration. The role of Hindi newspapers in grassroots mobilisation has been documented in previous studies (Kumar, 2011; Neyazi,

2010, 2011).[11] The CMS (2011) study of Hazare's 13-day fast from 17 to 29 August indicates that two leading Hindi dailies – *Dainik Bhaskar* and *Dainik Jagran* – devoted 64 per cent and 53 per cent of their front pages, respectively, to covering the movement compared to 45 per cent of stories on the movement on the front page of the *Times of India* in the same period. There are several instances of people organising protest marches in support of Anna Hazare's anti-corruption movement in small towns, which were covered in Hindi and regional language newspapers.[12]

Mobile phones proved to be even more instrumental in the anti-corruption movement. Team Anna developed the innovative idea of asking people to make a missed call (a missed call involves calling a number and cutting the call after a couple of rings, thus avoiding any charges) to a designated number to show their support for the movement.[13] The idea of a missed call was promoted as a strategy aimed at those who were unable to come to Delhi's Jantar Mantar to participate in the protest. The greater goal was to mobilise larger masses for the movement. During the campaigns, the team leaders received 6.6 million missed calls in three months, and nearly 25 million missed calls were received in six months from different parts of the country (Gowda and Prakash, 2014; Sharma, 2014). These calls helped the team build the database of numbers that were used to send bulk SMS to promote the cause and announce events. The threat emerging from mobilisation using mobile phones messages also resulted in the government creating a regulation banning the sending of bulk SMS.[14] The strategy of mobilisation by missed calls was subsequently used by Narendra Modi during his campaign in September 2011 when he was the Chief Minister of the state of Gujarat.[15] It was also alleged that Arvind Kejriwal of AAP, who

---

11 Kumar has shown how the Hindi newspapers played a significant role in mobilising the masses to support the demand for creating the independent state of Uttarakhand in 2000 (Kumar, 2011).

12 During my fieldwork in September 2011, I came across several news stories in the local edition of *Dainik Bhaskar* in Itarsi and Sohagpur, small towns in the state of Madhya Pradesh, which reported local protests organised against corruption in support of Anna Hazare's campaign.

13 This practice of missed call is also known as beeping, flashing, pranking, fishing or boom call, deliberate missed call, and has been used for instrumental and expressive purposes in various parts of the world (Donner, 2008; Fernández-Ardèvol, 2013; Geirbo and Helmersen, 2008).

14 In September 2011, Telecom Regulatory Authority of India (TRAI) published regulations directing all service providers to not send more than 100 SMS per SIM per day and more than 2,000 per SIM in a month. However, the limit of 100 SMS did not apply to messages transmitted by the government (for details see TRAI, 2011).

15 Narendra Modi during his Sadbhavana Mission in September 2011 used similar mobilisation tactics and asked his supporters to make missed calls to a designated number to show their support. The

was a core member of the anti-corruption movement, used the mobile numbers collected during the anti-corruption movement during his 2014 Lok Sabha election campaign (Sharma, 2014).

Social media, particularly social networking sites, are believed to have played an important role in the anti-corruption movement led by Anna Hazare. In a statement, Law Minister Salman Khurshid said, 'We were caught unawares because Anna's movement was a remarkable combination of traditional politics and unconventional modern practices. We were at a disadvantage because we did not use the social media as effectively as Anna's movement did' (Express New Service, 2011). Such a perception is not without reason; a report released by Facebook revealed that Anna Hazare and the Jan Lokpal Bill were the most mentioned in status updates in 2011 in India. In 2011 there were over 38 million Facebook users in India.[16] The general perception that people use social media largely for entertainment is not true in this case. Politics has certainly entered social networking sites, which have opened up new avenues for conducting politics.

Many pages sprang up on Facebook showing support for Anna Hazare. At the end of August 2011, when the movement was at its peak, it is estimated that there were more than 200 pages on Facebook dedicated to Anna Hazare, with over one million supporters and approximately 37,500 followers on Twitter; the Jan Lokpal Bill itself had approximately 2,11,000 followers.[17] 'India Against Corruption' had approximately 6,03,000 supporters on Facebook at the end of 2011.[18] There were more than 100 pages on Facebook on 'India Against Corruption' in addition to the official pages that had been created by supporters outside the official team. 'India Against Corruption' also had dedicated pages for different cities across India that each averaged 1,000 supporters. For example, a small city such as Ujjain had over 1,000 supporters, and the Hyderabad and

---

mission sought to promote social harmony by visiting all districts in Gujarat and fasting one day in each district.

16 I have used figures until November 2011 since the chapter talks about the anti-corruption movement between April 2011 and November 2011. As of March 2017, India has over 213 million Facebook users just behind the US, which had 219 million users.

17 Analysis of social media in this section is based on my personal observations of Twitter and Facebook done in August through December, 2011.

18 The decisive and all-out shift in the stance of 'India Against Corruption', the group that spearheaded the anti-corruption movement in favour of the BJP, shows that the movement was supported by Hindutva groups that wanted to discredit the legitimacy of the state and the ruling party to govern and to create a fertile ground for the rise of alternative parties, including the BJP. The selection of symbols on display also demostrated a strong version of Hindutva nationalism. However, the movement subsequently began using more inclusive symbols.

Pune pages had approximately 4,000 supporters. At the same time, 'India Against Corruption' pages existed outside India – in the US, Singapore, Malaysia, London, Dubai, Japan, Switzerland and Australia.

The official account of Jan Lokpal was one of the most influential brands on Twitter in India, with an aggregate score of 71.29 according to the Klout score of December 2011.[19] In terms of rank, it placed second after NDTV, which had an aggregate score of 80.08. The Twitter account of Jan Lokpal has continuously maintained the highest aggregate score since August 2011. The aggregate score was 68 on 15 August and increased to 74 on 17 August. After that, it ranged between 70 and 74 until the end of December 2011.

The more interesting aspect of the anti-corruption movement is the way in which social media were used in conjunction with mobile phones to continue informing the public about everyday activities, including details of the places in which protests were to be organised, support from different celebrities, the condition of Anna Hazare's fasting health, and documents comparing Jan Lokpal and the government's version of Lokpal. Similarly, within minutes of the arrest of Anna Hazare as he was preparing to fast on 16 August, a video was posted on YouTube with the message from Anna Hazare in which he appealed to the people to support the movement by non-violent means and spoke of the second line of leadership. This not only indicates that the video was pre-recorded in anticipation of his arrest but also the media-savvy nature of the movement. Similarly, within hours of the arrest of Anna Hazare, the #supportannahazare became the top-trending topic on Twitter in India for two days (TNN, 27 August 2011b).

Team Anna also used reality shows to create awareness of the anti-corruption movement and to draw the support of wider segments of society. On 18 June, Anna Hazare and Arvind Kejriwal appeared in *Aap ki Adalat* (Your Court) on India TV with Rajat Sharma, a political journalist, and Om Thanvi, editor of *Jansatta*, an important Hindi newspaper, as the judge. This hour-long programme invites politicians and important personalities for a mock trial in a mock courtroom and became an instant hit when it premiered in 1992. Anna Hazare and Arvind Kejriwal also appeared on *Sa Re Ga Ma Pa Little Champs*, a popular reality show on Zee TV on 12 August 2011.

However, the leading role of the media in the movement was criticised

---

19   Klout.com determines the social influence of people/brands on Twitter. The score for Indian people/ brands is published by pinstorm.com. I accessed the database on 12 December 2011.

during Parliamentary debates. In an obvious reference to the role of the media, Gurudas Dasgupta from the Communist Party of India said, 'I am saying with humility that the role that the electronic media is playing about the developments in the *Ramlila* ground is not conducive to the responsibility that the media owes to the nation' (17 August 2011). Similarly, T. K. S. Elangovan from the Dravida Munnetra Kazhagam party expressed his unhappiness with the media and stated:

> Earlier this issue was shown as a fight against corruption. Then, the media turned it into a fight against the Ruling Party. Third, the media converted it as a fight against Parliament. Now, it has become a fight against the Constitution of India. It is the work of the media. ... In a democracy, the people are the judges and not the media (27 August 2011).

In yet another reference to the role of the media, populist leader Lalu Prasad Yadav said, 'We are creator of news and you (media) are getting us down in front of the public' (27 August 2011). The widely shared anger of political class against the media indicates the perceived role of the media in the anti-corruption movement.

The middle class and political participation

Schlozman, Verba and Brady (2010) in their study of political participation in the US, demonstrated that the propensity for political participation is higher among economically and educationally upward groups, consistent with the findings from Verba and Nie's (1972) earlier study. This contrasts with India, in which economically and educationally backward groups are politically more active, particularly in electoral politics, than groups with higher socio-economic status (Hasan, 2000; Yadav, 2000). However, Anna Hazare-led anti-corruption movement witnessed greater participation by the middle class, whose participation in electoral politics has remained lower than the participation of marginalised groups.

When Anna Hazare launched the campaign against corruption, the middle class was the backbone of the movement. The enthusiasm of the middle class is not surprising when we analyse the characteristics of this class. The middle class in post-liberalisation India must be distinguished from the Nehruvian middle class. In post-independence India from 1950 to 1980, the middle class, which comprised the bureaucracy, civil servants, technocrats and other higher government employees, consolidated their position in the process of state building. During this period, this middle class directly benefitted from the policies of the government.

However, from the 1980s and more specifically after 1991, with the liberalisation of the Indian economy, there emerged a powerful middle class that grew despite the government. This middle class was primarily employed in the private sector, viewed the government with suspicion and considered the bureaucracy and civil servants to be inimical to their goal of achieving efficiency. The members of this middle class, who were the primary beneficiaries of economic reforms after 1991, are now more affluent, have transnational networks and desire more accountable governance (Fernandes, 2006; Sridharan, 2004). This role of the middle class has been emphasised in theories of democracy (Moore, 1966). It was this middle class that became the engine of the anti-corruption movement.

Rob Jenkins (2007) argued that the second wave of the anti-corruption movement in India from 2001 to 2006 helped bridge the gaps between the poor and the middle class, the NGOs and people's movements. Initially, the support base for Anna Hazare's-led anti-corruption movement was primarily composed of the metropolitan and urban middle class. This support base subsequently spread, and more poor people joined the fight. The interests of the poor in India are different from those of the middle class. The poor want the government to look after their welfare and provide all basic amenities, such as education, health and daily necessities. By contrast, the middle class wants all these basic amenities from the market; however, they expect the government to be efficient and help the market to function efficiently. The poor have been experiencing corruption in the very programmes that were meant to support them, such as the schemes under the Mahatma Gandhi National Rural Employment Guarantee Act (MGNREGA),[20] the Public Distribution System (PDS) and obtaining ration cards. The anti-corruption movement led by Anna Hazare, which promised to remove corruption from the government, began drawing support from these diverse constituencies composing a different mass of the poor – people from rural areas, towns and cities, and the middle class.

---

20 The MGNREGA seeks to enhance the livelihood security of people in rural areas by guaranteeing 100 days of wage-employment in a financial year to a rural household whose adult members volunteer to do unskilled manual work.

However, the people's movements did not fully support the anti-corruption movement, partially because of the nature and composition of Anna's team. Manoranjan Mohanty (2011), a leftist intellectual, lamented that the Anna Hazare's anti-corruption movement did not try to widen its base by including the people's movements. He blamed the people's movements as well for 'not recognising a clearly democratic element in the Anna upsurge, ... and thus missing an opportunity at this historical moment' (17). Critics argued that the corporate class supported the anti-corruption campaign (Nayak, 2011; Roy, 2011); consequently, the Jan Lokpal Bill drafted by Team Anna has kept the corporate houses, NGOs and media groups beyond the purview of the Bill. Anna supporters dismissed these criticisms because they believed that removing corruption in the government would go a long way towards establishing the accountability of non-government bodies.

In the second phase, people's movements did support Anna Hazare's anti-corruption movement. Medha Patkar, a noted social activist, lent her support to the movement with certain qualifications. Similarly, Aruna Roy, another noted social activist who was responsible for the passing of the RTI Act in 2005, supported the anti-corruption movement. Although neither Medha Patkar nor Aruna Roy fully agreed with the Jan Lokpal Bill drafted by Team Anna, they recognised a strong need for such an institution to curb corruption.

Support for Anna Hazare's anti-corruption movement also came from unexpected constituencies such as the *dabbawallas* (lunch-box carriers) of Mumbai and the auto-rickshaw drivers in Delhi. Ironically, although the *dabbawallas* of Mumbai are known for not halting their work even during a crisis such as the bomb blasts in Mumbai, they went on a one-day strike, the first in their 120-year history, to show their solidarity with the anti-corruption movement.[21] Similarly, the auto-rickshaw drivers in Delhi went on a one-day strike on 25 August; they also participated in a protest march in support of Anna Hazare's anti-corruption movement.

There was support for the anti-corruption movement even outside the metropolitan cities. For example, Sunil Mishra, popularly known as Dr Sunilam, who led *kisan* (farmer) politics in Madhya Pradesh, was active in the movement. He was a former MLA in Madhya Pradesh and founded the Kisan Sangharsh

---

21 The *dabbawalas* are a community of approximately 5,000 semi-literate people who efficiently deliver lunches daily from homes to offices and schools in Mumbai. For a detailed account, see Pathak (2010).

Samiti (Farmers' Struggle Committee). He won the election from Multai as the people's candidate from the farmers' community in 1998, but subsequently joined the Samajwadi Party of Mulayam Singh Yadav. He was included in the core committee of Team Anna as a special invitee. Dr Sunilam regularly organised *dharnas* (sit-ins) and protests in Madhya Pradesh in support of Anna Hazare's campaign against corruption. One such *dharna* was organised on 23 November in Bhopal to apply pressure to the state government to bring a Lok Ayukta[22] to the state; the *dharna* was attended by people from different parts of Madhya Pradesh.[23] There was a noticeable presence of farmers and the lower middle class in the *dharna*, although the majority of the participants were from the middle class. All participants used mobile phones as a principal channel of communication and had made a missed call to the designated number to register their support for the anti-corruption movement.

The majority of participants in the *dharna* did not regularly follow politics and had never participated in any political activities. These participants were attracted to the anti-corruption movement by the media because they regularly watched the coverage of the movement on television and read about it in the newspapers. In addition, the majority of the respondents did not participate in the first phase of the movement in April 2011; in the second phase of the movement in August 2011, however, they regularly organised meetings and protest marches in their towns and cities. Some of them also went to Delhi to participate in the actual protest with Anna Hazare.

This support indicates that Anna Hazare-led anti-corruption movement was able to draw disengaged citizens into civic activities. Visibility in the media was crucial in drawing a large amount of support for the movement, which Rajagopal (2011b) termed as an 'orchestrated spectacle'. One wonders whether the people would have given the same level of support to the anti-corruption movement had it not been regularly covered in the media. Social movements and other protest movements require coverage in the news media to attract wider mobilisation, publicity and validation (Gamson and Wolfsfeld, 1993). The first attempt of any protest movement today is to draw the attention of the media so that they can be heard in the corridors of power. Team Anna did use the avenues opened up by new media to give their voice wider publicity. The success of the movement in mobilising the people and capturing the attention of the political class was also a triumph for the media.

---

22   Lok Ayukta is the anti-corruption ombudsman at the state level.

23   All observations in this section are based on my personal interviews with the participants in the *dharna* (sit-in).

The overwhelming response to the anti-corruption movement took the political class by surprise and resulted in the passing of an unprecedented resolution in Parliament on 27 August 2011 urging Anna Hazare to break his fast and end the protest. Despite the support of the diverse public for the movement in the second phase, Team Anna failed to make the movement more inclusive by including other pressing issues that directly affected the poor, such as land acquisition for Special Economic Zones (SEZs) and unregulated mining by private companies, both of which affected poor rural farmers, the fishing community and tribal groups. However, the most important achievement of the anti-corruption movement was the creation of wider debates across the country regarding corruption by mobilising various sections of society, which has resulted in the emergence of a critical mass that was willing to confront their elected representatives if those representatives failed to deliver. The movement also created tension between the state and civil society and spurred debates about the legitimacy of the latter to confront the elected representatives which undermined the grammar of electoral politics and created anarchy (Mehta, 2011; Vajpeyi, 2011).

The rise of a hybrid media system and the implications for Indian protest politics

Anna Hazare-led anti-corruption movement not only drew the interest of people in India, but also attracted worldwide attention primarily because of the media coverage. The methods used – Twitter, Facebook, YouTube and media management – reflected the middle-class character of the anti-corruption movement. The first phase of the movement was criticised for being confined to the urban areas and the middle class. However, the movement in its second phase, which began in August 2011, saw the participation of diverse constituencies from small towns. The overwhelming support for the movement was hardly expected by Team Anna when they launched the movement. This is also evident by their strategies. In its first phase, Team Anna largely relied on social media, which helped them garner the support of the middle class and attract worldwide attention, as we noted from the support on Facebook. After the movement began being covered on television and in the newspapers, the support base of the movement swelled. By the time the movement entered the second phase, it had been converted into a mass movement with substantial support among people other than the middle class.

The inclusion in the core committee of persons from people's movements, such as Dr Sunilam and Medha Patkar, helped the movement widen its base.

One important fact emerging from the success of the Anna Hazare-led anti-corruption movement in attracting wider public attention is the effective use of new media in drawing the online public into political participation. The online public, who used social networking sites for entertainment and to stay in touch with friends, learned to use these sites to engage in politics. Such a development is new in India, but has been ongoing in developed countries. New media played an important role in the Arab Spring (Tufekci and Wilson, 2012). However, what is needed here is to locate and study the influence of new media in connection with traditional media such as newspapers and TV. In the case of Anna Hazare-led anti-corruption movement, it would not have been possible for new media alone to take the movement to the diverse public. It was the entry of newspapers and TV, which began providing extensive coverage, that helped to increase and broaden the base of public support.

Analysing this connectivity and convergence between traditional and new media and the emerging hybrid media system is imperative in developing countries where the reach of new media remains limited. New media can be more democratic than traditional media because anyone with access to the internet can raise an issue in the public arena. However, it would not be possible for new media alone to influence wider sections of society unless they are able to influence traditional media. Similarly, for traditional media to reach out to a transnational audience, it must accept the help of new media. Such connectivity and convergence between traditional and new media were quite evident in the Anna Hazare campaign against corruption.

The development of new media has certainly had a democratising effect on the functioning of newspapers and news channels. The earlier monopoly of newspapers and news channels on providing news and breaking stories was dismantled with the development and spread of new media. Newspapers and news channels now fear losing their credibility to the new media. It is now difficult for traditional news media to hide a story from the public because such stories may be published in a blog or be circulated on social networks. This pressure of the new media may help in addressing the issue of self-censorship, where the media black out certain stories or events for political or economic interests. The new media may also have democratised the existing public sphere and enhanced the accountability of public officials. In this context, Dahlgren (2005) argued that it is true that 'the internet extends and pluralises the public sphere' (148). The recent exposure in India of numerous scandals was greatly facilitated by the new media. Once an issue is exposed on the social networking sites and blogs, public pressure begins building for traditional media to address the issue. The exposure of the 2G Scam was one such case in which the new media played a leading role (Chadha, 2012).

New media also changed the manner in which the business of politics is conducted in India. Political parties acknowledged that they could learn from Team Anna how to use the new media effectively.[24] Congress, the then ruling party, leading the United Progressive Alliance (UPA), could not handle the challenge that began to emerge from the internet within the democratic framework and argued that the internet should be censored. The move was so severely criticised that the UPA government had to backtrack.[25] This response is typical when the state is confronted with new technology that challenges the existing authority.[26] The arrival of new media has certainly empowered protest groups globally to mobilise public opinion and raise support for their cause, which was difficult during the broadcast era. In the anti-corruption movement, it was the alignment of issue, personality and means that determined the success of the movement. In today's India, the poor, middle class and elite, have been equally besieged by corruption. All were looking for someone who could fight the menace of corruption and Anna Hazare's clean image rendered him acceptable to the majority of the people.

The movement took off as an organised middle-class campaign, but subsequently propelled the involvement of many related but autonomous movements initiated and participated in by the poor and lower middle classes without any central co-ordination. At one point, the anti-corruption movement appeared to be facile populism combined with a touch of totalitarianism represented by the slogan 'Anna is India, India is Anna'. However, this populism gradually led to public discussions on anti-corruption measures from diverse viewpoints in the media and received responses from government and the Parliament (Neyazi and Tanabe, 2014). The movement disintegrated in quite a short time because of internal dissension and disagreements among the core

---

24   The statement of Salman Khurshid, the Law Minister in the UPA II government.

25   Kapil Sibal, Minister of Communication and Information Technology in the UPA II government, proposed this idea.

26   This occured during the colonial period in India when the press came under censorship after it was used by political leaders to mobilise public opinion against colonial rule.

members, we cannot ignore the movement's long-term effects. The rise of the AAP from the movement challenged the established political parties (Congress and BJP) at the centre and formed the state-level government in Delhi in 2015. The BJP's electoral success in the 2014 Lok Sabha election may also be perceived as having been helped by Anna Hazare's anti-corruption movement because it primarily targeted the ruling Congress-led UPA government. The anti-corruption movement further eroded the legitimacy of the Congress party, which was already besieged with various corruption charges.

Conclusion

In this chapter, I have shown how digital and communication technologies opened up new avenues to mobilise public opinion and facilitated political participation. The success of Anna Hazare-led anti-corruption movement in obtaining wider visibility can be partially attributed to its successful campaign on the internet, particularly on social networking sites, which also prompted traditional media to take up the issue. The internet did play a strategic role in the mobilisation for the anti-corruption campaign by channelling messages to traditional media and to offline communities by interpersonal interactions. The transformation of the support base of the anti-corruption movement from a metropolitan and urban middle class to more diversified public can be attributed to the prevalence of a hybrid media system or the way in which both new and traditional media in combination with grassroots mobilisation have helped highlight the issue in the public arena. The expanding and complex media landscape provided fertile ground for Team Anna to use the media to mobilise the masses and encourage the political class to seriously consider enacting an effective Lokpal. The rise of the 24X7 media cycle has certainly exposed the government to unprecedented scrutiny.

The highly competitive, diversified and overlapping media avenues also reflect the unprecedented opportunities available to various groups, protest movements and political constituencies in today's political communication networks. Not only the news media but even reality TV shows are willing to accommodate politics in their programmes if doing so helps to attract a larger audience. The participation of the multitude of public in the market-driven media networks led to a change in the nature and function of the media, which must not only ensure their survival in a capitalist marketplace but also cater to the requirement to serve wider audiences rather than merely serving the interests of the elite. This led to a simultaneous presence in the public arena of viewpoints and interests of the urban middle classes, the poor and the marginalised. This hybrid character of the public arena is often overlooked in discussions of the democratic transformation in India.

The desire to influence the media or to adapt to be noticed by the media is one of the important strategies of recent protest movements and distinguishes them from earlier movements that believed in grassroots mobilisation as their primary weapon. The heavy dependence on the media by recent contemporary movements has been criticised, which also renders it difficult to sustain the movement for long once the movement loses the attention of the media. Media-dependent movements therefore are often marked by virality and ephemerality – rapid diffusion but difficulty in sustaining the movement.

The chapter also demonstrates that there was significant participation in the anti-corruption movement by disengaged citizens who were mobilised by the media. The findings not only corroborate earlier studies that the internet mobilised disengaged citizens but raises new research questions to study the effect of new media in connection with traditional media or the hybrid media system, particularly in developing countries where the penetration of the internet remains limited. A hybrid media system helps diverse public with different interests and values use various media according to their convenience to come together in a network and to press their demands more effectively than has previously been possible. Media, both new and traditional, have certainly emerged as an important institution of mediation in contemporary India as well as in other developing countries and have transformed the business of politics. Making one's presence felt in the media has become important for political parties as well as for oppositional politics such as protest movements to ensure wider validation for their cause.

7

Agenda-setting and Mobilisation in a Hybrid Media Environment

The 2014 Indian national election is considered unprecedented not least because of the extraordinary performance of the Narendra Modi-led Bharatiya Janata Party (BJP) and the formation of the first single-party majority government at the centre after 25 years. There was also an unprecedented use of new media and social networks, especially to mobilise support particularly by Narendra Modi and the digital unit in the BJP, compared to the Congress party which, unlike the BJP, did not boast about having a digital strategy in 2014. This has led scholars and commentators to regard the 2014 election as the first social media election.[1] Narendra Modi's extensive use of both online and traditional media for campaigning has been dubbed '*maidan* to media' ('from field to media'), referring to the greater emphasis on media than on traditional ways of campaigning in India, such as rallies and meetings (Sardesai, 2014). Narendra Modi used social media as an important feature in his campaign strategy, but it was only one part of his overall campaign strategy. This chapter unravels the hybrid logic involved in Mr Modi's election campaign that creatively combined the logic of older and newer media and integrated it with traditional campaigns that use grassroots mobilisation, rallies and volunteer activism, both within and outside India. The 2014 election campaign was not just about Mr Modi, but about a new era in political communication practices in India where professional campaign managers, journalists, volunteer activists, entertainment media and ordinary citizens together played an important role. The Congress party and its campaign leader Rahul Gandhi had a professional firm advising on campaign strategy. The extraordinary performance of the Narendra Modi-led BJP in the Hindi heartland, where the party won 183 of the 218 seats in the region, gave the BJP an absolute majority in Parliament with a total of 282 seats. The Hindi heartland assumed significance during the campaign not only because of its electoral significance, but because most of the controversies in the run-up to the national election – including communal riots – that took place in the region.[2]

---

1   A few commentaries and articles that magnify the role of social media in the victory of Narendra Modi in the 2014 Lok Sabha election are Kaul, 2014; Pandey, 2014; Thakurta, 2014b; and Willis, 2014.

2   According to the Ministry of Home Affairs (MHA) data, communal riots increased by 25 per cent

Did the political parties succeed in getting their issues across in the media? In this chapter, I assess the battle for the news agenda and the agenda-setting power of the political parties to shape the news agenda drawing on content analysis of primetime television news on the most popular Hindi channel, *Aaj Tak*. I use post-election survey data from Delhi and a content analysis of media data along with a critical analysis of Twitter use to discuss the processes of influence and political communication in the 2014 national election.[3]

Since the early work of Katz and Lazarsfeld (1955), whose seminal 'two-step flow' model of personal influence set the agenda for researchers for decades, there have been several empirical studies in the context of the US and Europe that have shown limited effects of the media on voting behaviour (Finkel, 1993; Hillygus and Jackman, 2003; McGuire, 1986). Media, at best, could have an indirect effect on a voter's choice; most of the trusted information citizens received about politics was through friends, relatives and community members who were considered to have some authority on the topic (Katz and Lazarsfeld, 1955). The mid-twentieth century was a time of strong party identification in the US. It was believed that political campaigns could at best reinforce existing party predispositions and perhaps mobilise voters (Valentino, 2013).

As party identification in the US declined over the next decades, political campaigns advanced to become more professional and targeted. Today, the advances in campaigning can be found largely in digital communication technologies. Political campaigns in most of the advanced democracies have been extensively using the internet to reach their voters and mobilise support (Stromer-Galley, 2014). In a hybrid media environment, we are also witnessing the return of 'two-step flow' model where personal influence is getting

---

in 2013. The worst affected state was Uttar Pradesh with 247 cases as compared to 118 in 2012. Out of six worst affected states four were in northern India; Uttar Pradesh, Madhya Pradesh, Rajasthan and Bihar. The other two states included Karnataka in the south and Gujarat in the west. One of the major riots took place in Muzaffarnagar that drew national attention and led to complete polarisation in Uttar Pradesh. (For details see Tripathi, 2014). Nellis, Weaver and Rosenzweig (2016) in a recent study shows the BJP's vote share saw 0.8 per cent average increase following a communal riot in the year prior to an election.

3   The campaign could really only influence the choice of undecided voters. Our survey data shows that over 26 per cent of Delhi voters were undecided at the end of the campaign – that is 48 hours before election day. The percentage of undecided voters who made up their mind in the last 48 hours in our survey is close to the percentage of undecided voters reported by the National Election Studies (NES) 2014 survey, which is 24.5 per cent. See http://www.lokniti.org/pdf/All-India-Postpoll-2014-Survey-Findings.pdf. The Delhi 2014 survey data used in this chapter was funded by a grant from the Emory University Research Committee.

channelled through online communities to traditional media and face-to-face interactions. Personal influence via social media was exploited by Obama in the 2008 and 2012 US presidential election campaigns but this did not reduce the importance of grassroots campaigns involving doorstep canvassing (Chadwick, 2013; Nielsen, 2012; Stromer-Galley, 2014).

In India, a country in which different media – print, television and the internet – all continue to grow, can we expect to find a similar emphasis on grassroots face-to-face campaigning? We have seen the emergence of a hybrid media system where political actors try to reach potential supporters through various media depending on exigencies.[4] The hybrid articulation of political campaigns was also witnessed in India's 2014 national election. It was not just traditional platforms such as rallies, door-to-door canvassing, neighbourhood meetings, newspaper, radio and television reporting and advertising, but newer channels such as Twitter, Facebook and other social media, as well as WhatsApp, that were used by political parties to reach out to voters. The mobile phone and short messaging service (SMS) were used to transmit recorded messages from party leaders, while 'missed call' advertising was an integral part of the campaign strategies used by all three of the main parties. However, it was the Narendra Modi-led BJP that exploited the hybrid media ecology better than other political parties (Neyazi, Kumar and Semetko, 2016).

In this chapter, I also focus on the emergence of the hybrid media environment in India – an environment in which traditional media continues to occupy an important place along with new media and face-to-face interactions, and how it was exploited by the three main parties to reach out to voters and how voters engaged with the hybrid campaigns. I first focus on the ways the Hindi news media provided coverage to the political contest among the three main parties in Delhi – the BJP, the Indian National Congress (INC) and the Aam Aadmi Party (AAP). By drawing on a content analysis of two hours of primetime evening news from 8.00 pm to 10.00 pm daily on *Aaj Tak*, a popular Hindi news channel, the chapter examines how the leaders, parties and issues were reported in the news.[5] Eight weeks of news items on the campaign from 13 March to 12 May 2014 were analysed.[6]

---

4   For a detailed discussion of a hybrid media system, see Chapter 6.

5   The content analysis of *Aaj Tak* was done by two trained coders and Cohen's Kappa was used to test intercoder reliability. After intensive coder training with the author, intercoder reliability on the substantive variables used here ranged from .81 to .92, based on 48 randomly selected news items from the sample.

6   We analysed headlines of news stories as in many cases in *Aaj Tak* the lengthy and numerous

Aaj Tak ranks among the top two news channels in the Hindi heartland (BARC, 2015). Our Delhi survey showed that 42.3 per cent of respondents watched *Aaj Tak* as their first preferred news channel and for another 19.7 per cent it was their second or third preferred news channel. I also discuss how social media, particularly Twitter, was exploited by the BJP more than by other parties; this influenced traditional media and helped reach out to those who were not using the internet. Newspapers carried a separate column to report the happenings on social media and to provide sentiment analysis of Twitter every day throughout the election campaign. The election campaign was held in nine phases across the country. This meant that for weeks after Delhi residents had voted in Phase 2 on 10 April, they experienced the campaign as spectators given that it continued for seven more phases of voting in other parts of the country.

In the following pages, I first discuss the party strategies and agenda-setting in the emerging hybrid media environment. This is followed by a discussion on the ways voters engaged with the campaigns in order to understand the nature of hybrid interactions between the campaigns and voters. The discussion of the content analysis of *Aaj Tak* news stories helps in understanding the agenda-setting power of the parties, and whether the issues raised by each of the three parties – BJP, INC, and AAP – found resonance in the news media. Finally, I provide a critical analysis of the strategies used and the influence of hybrid media campaigns in mobilising voters.

Party strategies, agenda-setting and hybrid campaigns

The daily battle over who controls the campaign agenda in the news media among political parties is mediated through multiple channels. The agenda-setting power of the mass media has been the subject of decades of research in the field of political communication. Cohen (1963) described this power as telling the public not what to think but rather what to think about, especially in the context of issues that are far removed from their personal experience such as foreign affairs. A few years later in a 1968 election study in Chapel Hill, North

---

headlines that open the show do not lead to detailed coverage in the main stories. For example, only 24.5 per cent of the opening headlines became longer detailed stories in the primetime bulletin. So most of the many headlines opening the show can be understood as short stories themselves, some items lasting nearly a minute. There were total of 1,617 news items during the primetime in our sample period of eight weeks, out of which 1,329 or 82.2 per cent of stories were about the 2014 political campaign. Remaining news items were non-political or not related to the campaign.

Carolina, McCombs and Shaw (1972) named the concept of agenda-setting, and established a correlation between media issue agendas during the campaign and public issue agendas based on citizens' responses to the 'most important problem' questions in a post-election cross-sectional survey. Agenda-setting research advanced methodologically to move beyond a correlation between issues on media and public agendas, to provide evidence of causality, that the media agenda leads the public agenda, first by utilising panel survey data (Weaver, Graber, McCombs and Eyal, 1981) and later with experiments (Iyengar and Kinder, 1987). I have cited only some of the hundreds of studies that have shown support for the agenda-setting hypothesis (for reviews see Dearing and Rogers, 1996; McCombs 2014).

A related line of research concerns how the media agenda is formed and ultimately asks: Does the news media set the public agenda, or is the media simply passing on the priorities of news sources? Many studies of election campaigning in different national political contexts in Europe and North America demonstrate that political parties do indeed influence media agenda (for example, Brandenburg, 2002; Semetko, Blumler, Gurevitch and Weaver, 1991; Semetko and Schoenbach, 1994; Soroka, 2002; Walgrave and van Aelst, 2006). Taking into account the methodological advances and approaches taken by political scientists and communication scientists on agenda-setting, Green-Pedersen and Walgrave (2014) bring together experts and evidence from various national contexts to focus on the links between party politics, the media, and policy or issue agendas. They also conclude with a discussion of agenda-setting as a concept or an approach.

Research comparing the agenda-setting power of the media versus political parties in UK and US election campaigns in the 1980s attributed the differences found between the two countries to the strong public service broadcasting ethos of reporting in Britain and the strong news values-driven culture backed by the strong commercial media system in the US. These system-level differences, along with a host of traditions and campaign reporting practices, contributed to more openness to party agendas in the news in the UK than the US (Semetko, Blumler, Gurevitch and Weaver, 1991). India moved decades ago from a monopoly public service media system with the arrival of cable and satellite in the early 1990s, and India's public service channel Doordarshan lost audiences early on to those new commercial or private channels. As India's media system continues to grow, there are few studies on the culture of news production in the context of the country's election campaigns (Thorsen and Sreedharan, 2015) and liberalisation and globalisation (Batabyal, 2014; Mehta, 2008; Neyazi, 2010; Rao, 2008, 2009; Roy, 2011; Thussu, 2006a; Udupa, 2015).

I contribute to the dearth of literature on agenda-setting in India with a focus on party, media and public issue agendas in the 2014 national election campaign. Political parties attempt to set the agenda in the daily news by highlighting certain issues, or statements by their leaders and top candidates, and by framing certain issues in particular ways to suit their interests. But the news agendas may not often correspond with party agendas. There is continuous contestation between political and media actors during the daily campaign to ensure both are able to get the maximum benefit from each other; political parties want to obtain voter attention and support, while media wants to increase ratings and audiences. Along with the rapid rise of new technologies and the internet, the 'single daily news cycles' (Chadwick, 2013, 62) have become a thing of the past. The involvement of mass participation in the creation of online content demonstrates that political elites alone no longer control the messaging that emerges from political events. Instead, engaged and opinionated non-elites – including supporters and those against the party – are contributing equally in shaping political events, which have transformed power relationships in the news production process. The internalisation of the norms, behaviour and expectations as warranted by the media leads to a change in the behaviour of political actors. What might work for television might not be conducive for going viral on the internet, because television demands short sound bites. What is considered good for English news channel audiences is not necessarily good for Hindi news channels.

The 2014 Lok Sabha election was a contest among political parties and candidates for visibility, space and time, in the media by making controversial statements. Even if a candidate was addressing a rally in the most remote location, the aim usually was to attract the attention of TV studios in Delhi. Narendra Modi was more successful in placing himself in the agenda because his campaign made better use of hybrid media ecology and more effectively used Twitter in addition to the strategic placement of advertisements on different platforms.

The three main parties aggressively tried to place their agenda in the news in order to remain visible. The Narendra Modi-led BJP pushed the themes of 'development' and 'good governance' framed within the larger context of the ostensibly successful 'Gujarat model'. The Rahul Gandhi-led INC attempted to dispute Mr Modi's claim with a hard-hitting negative campaign that emphasised 'communalism' by reminding voters of the Gujarat riots in 2002 when Mr Modi was the Chief Minister of Gujarat. The INC's decision to opt for a negative campaign was also the result of confusion about whether to focus on achievements under the Congress-led United Progressive Alliance II (UPA II), or to attack Mr Modi for his communal and sectarian agenda and his 'Gujarat model' of development. The Arvind Kejriwal-led AAP pushed the agenda of corruption by dubbing both the BJP and the INC as corrupt parties that were implicated in various corruption scandals and had links with corrupt corporates. Kejriwal repeatedly talked about 'crony capitalism', insinuating that the link between the politicians and the corporate class undermines the interests of the common people who constitute the vast majority of the Indian population.

The BJP's innovative Mission 272+ strategy signaled the party's goal of achieving an absolute majority in the Lower House of Parliament. Mission 272+ was largely driven by a national programme of volunteers who were connected with the mission headquarters in Bengaluru. They obtained cell phone numbers of potential voters who wanted to hear from Narendra Modi, and ensured they were sent a continuous stream of SMS messages from the party leader and his live speeches from across the country via cellphone. At the start of 2016 in January, the BJP's Mission 272+ was not taken seriously since published polls suggested that there was confusion in the public mind – more voters preferred Narendra Modi as Prime Minister than either Arvind Kejriwal or Rahul Gandhi – but support for the BJP and AAP was closer.[7] These polls left the impression that the election could have an uncertain outcome and even potential for a hung parliament.

---

7   The confusion was the result of two polls published a week apart. The 9 January 2014 publication of a *Times of India-IPSOS* poll of the country's eight most populous cities found that 44 per cent claimed they would vote for AAP in the 2014 national election, but 58 per cent believed that the BJP's Narendra Modi would be the best Prime Minister compared to only 25 per cent who named AAP's Arvind Kejriwal and 14 per cent who named the Congress' Rahul Gandhi (TNN, 2014a). A week later the same newspaper published an AC Nielsen poll conducted in the national capital region and in the Mumbai-Greater Mumbai areas for Ananda Bazaar Patrika (ABP) News, which showed the public preference for Modi as the best Prime Minister varied greatly between Delhi and Mumbai (TNN, 2014b). Mr Modi was only slightly ahead of Mr Kejriwal with 45 per cent and 42 per cent, respectively, among residents of the capital city, whereas in the Mumbai-Thane area the comparable figures were 58 per cent and 18 per cent, respectively (TNN, 2014b). Mr Gandhi came a distant third in both locations, with 22 per cent in Mumbai-Thane and 16 per cent in Delhi picking him as the best candidate for Prime Minister.

AAP's campaign appeared to lack any well-thought-out strategies based on ground realities; this is evident from their decision to contest 432 seats, which only established political parties could afford. It was easy for Mr Kejriwal to attack the ruling Congress party, which was besieged by corruption charges that were a prime reason for the rise of AAP. The Congress party mainly relied on grassroots campaigns and had a low presence on social media. The party Vice-President and campaign leader, Rahul Gandhi, did not even have a Twitter account during the run-up to the election.

The BJP had a far more advanced campaign strategy compared to the INC and AAP and was able to get more space in the media (Centre for Media Studies, 2014). Since there was hardly any credible alternative to Mr Modi for the position of Prime Minister according to published opinion polls and because Mr Modi was the most active campaigner of the three candidates, most of the coverage in the media revolved around Mr Modi. According to the magazine *India Today*, an estimated 234 million people had direct interactions with Narendra Modi compared to 13.3 million with Rahul Gandhi (Pradhan and Mahurkar, 2014). The perceived weaknesses of Mr Gandhi, his reluctance to take leadership of the INC and his few campaign appearances and public contacts diminished the visibility of the party in the news.

After being declared the BJP's prime ministerial candidate, Mr Modi ran the campaign in a presidential way, making the campaign individual-centric. Most of the BJP's advertising emphasised the leader instead of the party.[8] This was a departure from the BJP's previous campaigns in which the party was equally in focus along with the leader. For example, in the 2009 election the BJP slogan was *'Abki baar vajpa sarkar'* (This time, BJP government), but this was changed in 2014 to *'Abki baar, Modi sarkar'* (This time, Modi government). Mr Modi's campaign strategies were dynamic; there was constant reflection and reassessment based on feedback and responses from volunteers and the public leading to immediate corrections or changes to the plan which was evident from Mr Modi's sudden adoption of television and newspaper interviews in the middle of the campaign.

The first television interview that Mr Modi gave was to *News X* on 29

---

8   In the 2014 campaign, the media paid constant attention to party leaders, whose perspectives on issues and potential to persuade were arguably important. Mughan (2001) has described the outcome of this media attention to party leaders in the UK context as a more presidential parliamentary election, and British campaigns have been found to be more presidential than those in other European parliamentary contexts (Boumans, Boomgaarden and Vliegenhart, 2013).

March 2014. The interview was highly publicised but it turned out to be a monologue. The interview did not go down well with the audience since it lacked interactivity, which is an important feature of interviews. Instead of adapting to media logic, Mr Modi had tried to tweak the rules of an interview.

Mr Modi corrected his mistake in his second television interview that he gave to Rajat Sharma of India TV on their flagship programme, *Aap ki Adalat* (People's Court) on 12 April. This is a popular weekly programme that attracts a substantial number of viewers.[9] The interview became very popular and was widely shared across social media; it became as one of the top-10 most watched political videos from India at the end of April (Express News Service, 2014).[10] This apparently made Mr Modi realise the importance of television interviews and he gave more interviews to television news channels after this, with preference given to the more widely watched regional networks instead of English news channels, which have smaller audiences than vernacular news shows. Mr Modi gave nearly 50 interviews to both print media and television after his second interview on India TV (Sardesai, 2014, 230). What is important to note is the strategic placement of interviews during the campaign. Mr Modi would give an interview just before voting day in each of the nine phases of the election, and especially to the regional networks where voting was to take place in order to reach the largest number of relevant voters.

The INC started its campaign with a focus on its past economic performance but had to change strategy midway when they realised that (a) public opinion was becoming more negative towards them and (b) the party was getting less space in the news media. The Congress switched to an offensive campaign and started negative campaigning by personally attacking Mr Modi for his 'sectarian politics'. To counter the attack, the BJP emphasised Mr Modi's strong leadership and his ability to deliver governance and inclusive development. And on the campaign trail, Mr Modi chose to personally attack INC's Rahul Gandhi and his mother Sonia Gandhi for 'dynasty politics'.

Did the party campaigns influence media agendas and mobilise voters?

---

9   According to viewership rating, at one point this interview with Narendra Modi was watched by nearly 74 per cent of Hindi news television viewers (Afaqs, 2014). Rajat Sharma's fame is in fact due to *Aap ki Adalat* (see Mehta, 2008). The programme is designed in a court format and became an instant hit when it first aired on television in 1992. Many famous personalities were grilled through uncomfortable questions and the judgement was given towards the end.

10 The video had more than four million viewers on YouTube at the end of April 2014, which is quite remarkable even by Indian viewing standards.

Measuring the impact of campaigns in the media agenda has become more complicated with the emergence of a hybrid media environment in which political actors not only try to influence the media directly, but also through other channels such as Twitter and mobile SMS.

As shown in the previous chapter, internet penetration still remains low in India, though it is considered huge in terms of the absolute number – 462 at the end of 2016 (Internet Live Stats, 2017).[11] Most of these new internet users are located in urban India where they have been drawing the attention of political parties and traditional news organisations. In India's hybrid media system, mobile phones are perhaps the most crucial for our understanding of information flows and symbiotic relationships among all actors in an electoral campaign. This seems to be the case especially when we look at the share of mobile internet access, which is about 239 million or 71 per cent of all internet users in India (IAMAI, 2015; quoted in Neeraj, 2016).

The significance of mobile phones and access to social media applications on such devices was not lost on the political parties during the campaign. The use of Twitter and texting via SMS in the campaign to influence and shape information flows was widely witnessed and reported, especially in urban constituencies (Goyal, 2014; Pal, 2015). Social media was extensively used by the BJP as compared to other political parties. Table 7.1 shows that the BJP was much more active on Twitter, followed by AAP and INC during the campaign period (Semetko, Kumar, Neyazi, Mellon, Shah and Sangar, 2016a).[12] For example, based on a 10 per cent sample of random tweets in the wake of the 2014 national election, it was found that 70.5 per cent of the total tweets were about the BJP, while 21 per cent tweets were about AAP. The Congress party stood at distance third with only about 9.5 per cent tweets.

---

11   There were 243 million internet users at the beginning of 2014 (Internet Live Stats, 2017).

12   I am grateful to Professor Dhavan Shah and his team at the University of Wisconsin-Madison for collecting this Twitter data, based on a random sample of 10 per cent of tweets from each party.

Table 7.1: Party tweets based on a random sample of 10 per cent of tweets from each party in the 2014 Lok Sabha campaign

AAP (21%):		
Total number of Tweets sent	=	1,906
Re-tweeted by AAP or leaders of AAP	=	551 (29%)
Re-tweeted by others	=	652 (34.2%)
Not re-tweeted	=	703 (36.8%)
BJP (70.5%):		
Total number of Tweets sent	=	6,422
Re-tweeted by BJP or leaders of BJP	=	1,774 (27.5%)
Re-tweeted by others this includes a large number of celebrities	=	2,432 (37.5%)
Not re-tweeted	=	2,246 (35%)
INC (9.5%):		
Total number of Tweets sent	=	770
Re-tweeted by INC or leaders of INC	=	225 (28%)
Re-tweeted by others	=	194 (25%)
Not re-tweeted	=	283 (37%)

Source: Semetko, Kumar, Neyazi, Mellon, Shah and Sangar (2016a).

The emergence of the hybrid media ecology did result in the flow of information from new media to traditional media and vice versa. Most of the happenings on social media were subsequently rechanneled in the traditional media and offline, a process known as remediation. The *Times of India* regularly carried a Tweet box on its Election page, and sometimes on the front page, that extracted tweets from citizens, famous personalities and politicians on the election scenario. Several of the personal attacks and controversies were started online and then picked up by traditional media such as television. Although Hindi newspapers did not carry special sections on social media, they picked up stories and controversies from social media. This suggests that users of traditional media were aware of activities in the online world. For example, Narendra Modi on 16 April tweeted in English, 'Shahzada [referring to Rahul Gandhi as the prince] has not got over his childhood days, which is why he can't see beyond balloons and toffees. Development is a non-issue for him.' Another tweet by Mr Modi says, 'Coming from a poor family, I never had luxury of having toffees but in the last decade Gujarat has won several trophies for good governance.' These tweets from Mr Modi were widely covered in newspapers as well as television and reflect how he tried to utilise the agenda of development and good governance by repeatedly highlighting the 'Gujarat model'.

Mr Modi's marketing strategy was praised by all political parties, including Mr Gandhi in an interview with *Aaj Tak* on 6 April. According to *India Today*, Narendra Modi, through his multi-faceted campaigns that included rallies, road shows, 3D hologram appearances at simultaneous rallies in 53 cities on 10 April and direct phone calls to citizens on their mobiles, contacted about 18 times more voters than Mr Gandhi (nearly 234 million voters compared with the 13.3 million) (Pradhan and Mahurkar, 2014). Constant coverage in the newspapers and channels allowed Mr Modi's visibility to grow. Such an all-encompassing campaign strategy to influence public perceptions of the direction of the election was an important focus in the election campaign coverage of 2014.

Voters' engagement with campaigns

The engagement by Delhi voters with the campaign provides insights on the evolving hybrid media system. Campaigns in India, even in Delhi, remain for the most part on the streets, with the most important aspect being face-to-face contact with multiple political parties. We asked a series of questions about party contact and media use (Table 7.2). Traditional media sources (newspapers, TV and radio) still remain the most common sources of information, but the reliance on social media and SMS accessed via mobile phones was an important part of the mix in 2014.

Table 7.2: Delhi voters' sources of campaign information

	Delhi (n=1,557)			
	Daily+	**One to five days**	**Less often**	**Never**
Television	75.3	15.9	4.3	4.4
Newspapers	49.7	16.5	8.9	24.9
Posters	34.2	21.8	17.0	27.0
Pamphlets	20.0	28.9	20.1	31.0
Radio	9.1	18.4	22.3	50.2
SMS	7.7	14.5	20.7	57.1
Social media	6.9	7.6	15.7	69.7
WhatsApp	3.1	2.4	13.8	80.7
Email	2.2	4.0	16.0	77.8

Note: Actual wording of the question: Thinking about news and information about the Lok Sabha election, how often would you say you get your information from (a) television, (b) newspapers, (c) posters, (d) pamphlets, (e) radio, (f) SMS, (g) social media, (h) WhatsApp, (i) email? Multiple times a day, once a day, three to five days a week, one to two days a week, once in two weeks, less often, or never.

First, the rate of regular use of social media to obtain campaign information was low in Delhi since only 14.5 per cent of respondents used social media either daily or one to five days a week. More people obtained information through pamphlets and posters on the streets than social media. Second, traditional media remained the most frequently used channel for obtaining campaign information. The majority of respondents used television regularly for information about the campaign (75.3 per cent and 15.9 per cent) and newspapers were the second important source of campaign information used regularly (49.7 per cent and 16.5 per cent). Third, the frequency of SMS use, either daily or one to five days a week, is low among Delhi voters (7.5 per cent and 14.5 per cent); there may have been more active on-the-ground campaigning in the city involving printed materials since Delhi also had the highest rate for obtaining campaign information regularly from pamphlets (48.9 per cent daily or one to five days a week) and posters (56 per cent daily or one to five days a week). The campaign was probably more visible in traditional national news media (newspapers, TV and radio) in Delhi than elsewhere, because most of the national news organisations are headquartered in the city. The more intense coverage of the local electoral contests in Delhi may also be explained in part by the perceived national significance of the rise of the AAP over the previous year.

The reliance by voters on digital sources of information also depends on the volume and quality of the coverage of campaigns by the traditional media. This may be evident to news organisations that recognise and respond on a daily basis to the shifts in their audiences.

Table 7.3: Frequency of sharing campaign information with family and friends among Delhi voters

	Delhi (n= 1,556)			
	Daily+	One to five days	Less often	Never
Face-to-face	23.4	20.3	14.5	41.8
SMS	3.5	6.7	13.2	76.6
Social media	3.0	4.8	10.2	82.0
WhatsApp	1.1	2.2	9.8	86.8
Email	0.6	2.5	9.5	87.3

Note: Actual wording of the question: How often did you share news and information with your family and friends about the national elections via (a) face-to-face conversations, (b) SMS, (c) social media, (d) WhatsApp, (e) Email?

Whereas party campaigning and media use reflect a somewhat reactive role by voters, Table 7.3 refers to the frequency with which voters share information through various means of communication: social media, SMS, WhatsApp, email and face-to-face discussion. We find that face-to-face interaction remains most important, while digital media is less important for sharing information about election campaigns: 43.7 per cent of respondents in Delhi shared campaign information either daily or one to five days a week through face-to-face interactions, but only 10.2 per cent did so through SMS and 76.6 per cent never shared campaign information through SMS.

Table 7.4: Party campaigning activities in Delhi Lok Sabha 2014:
Mean number of times and forms of voter reported contact (n=1,557)

	AAP	BJP	INC
Face-to-face (street)	1.17	1.21	1.18
SMS	.53	.57	.51
Face-to-face (home)	.47	.53	.55
Telephone/mobile	.44	.47	.41
Social media	.12	.15	.13
Emails	.08	.08	.06
WhatsApp	.02	.02	.02

Note: Cells contain the mean score for each form of contact by each party, based on the following question: 'Parties and candidates reach out to voters in election campaigns. In this Lok Sabha election campaign, how often were you contacted through the following methods, and by which parties or candidates? 0=never contacted, 1=contacted at least once, 2=twice, 3=more often.'

Respondents were asked how often they were contacted through different modes and by which parties or candidates. A mean score for each medium and party was computed from 0=never contacted, 1=contacted at least once, 2=twice and 3=more often. The findings presented in Table 7.4. show a clear sign of hybrid campaigns with one party standing out as the most active in terms of frequency of contacting voters electronically or face-to-face. The BJP was ahead of other parties in terms of reportedly using digital media, both mobile phones and the internet, to reach out to voters. However, all three parties emphasised grassroots campaigns. They preferred to contact voters on the street compared to visiting their homes. The mean score of BJP for face-to-face contact at home was (M=0.53), AAP (M=0.47) and INC (M=0.55). However, the mean score for face-to-face contact on the street for BJP was

(M=1.21), AAP (M= 1.17) and INC (M=1.18). Similarly, the mean for BJP contacts through mobile (M=0.47) and SMS (M=0.57) was higher compared to AAP (M=0.44) and (M=0.53) and INC (M=0.41) and (M=0.51). This shows that grassroots campaigns in terms of face-to-face contacts were the most important for all political parties even in a predominantly urban setting, and hence 'ground wars' or grassroots campaigns still remain important alongside mediated campaigns to mobilise voters.[13] Below I present the analysis from the content of *Aaj Tak* to understand how each of the three parties was covered in the most watched news channel.

Parties, leaders and campaigns in the news

Aaj Tak nightly news has three components. The first component is the headlines. These are long, opening headlines that run from 15 seconds to 1 minute each and include story visuals and anchor voiceover. So in many cases these headlines are longer than TV news stories in many US and European news bulletins. The headlines are followed by the 'Top 25' stories of the day with visuals, delivered in a rapid bullet style that are usually shorter than the headlines and the entire segment runs for nearly 25 minutes. The third component contains lengthy news analysis stories by leading political reporters and anchors. Usually, three or four stories are shown and sometimes include interviews and in-studio discussions before the end of the programme. This format is not found in North America or Europe and may be unique to *Aaj Tak*.

We chose to analyse the headline items at the start of the programme as these provide film and commentary from the anchor to explain the issue and also evaluate the main actors in the story. From these lengthy headline items, we coded each as favourable or unfavourable towards the party or candidate. The content analysis shows that the BJP was more often the focus of headline items than the INC or AAP. When we examine the main actor in these news items, we find that nearly 50.6 per cent of stories included the BJP, compared with 40.8 per cent on the INC and only 8.6 per cent on AAP (Table 7.5). However, as Table 7.5 shows, this visibility bonus was not matched by a bonus in terms of a positive tone towards the BJP. Only 12.8 per cent of stories had positive tone towards BJP, while the same was 15.5 per cent for AAP; INC

---

13 Writing in the context of the US, Nielsen (2012) has shown that door-to-door canvassing and mobile phone banking were the most important methods used by candidates to reach out to voters.

received least positive coverage with 7 per cent. There was not much difference when it came to negative coverage of the BJP and INC; it was 46.2 per cent for the former and 48.4 per cent for the latter, but AAP received more negative coverage with 51.5 per cent. Interestingly, AAP received maximum positive and negative coverage since the neutral coverage was least among all with 33.3 per cent. While the neutral stories for the INC was 44.6 per cent and the BJP was 41 per cent. The balance ratios, the balance of positive to negative news for each party, reveal a clear emphasis on negative news on *Aaj Tak*. The ratio was -36 for AAP, -33.4 for BJP, and -41.4 for INC.

Table 7.5: Tone of news items towards the party, Lok Sabha 2014 election campaign, *Aaj Tak* primetime news (8.00 to 10.00 pm) 13 March to 12 May 2014

	Positive	Negative	Neutral	n
AAP	15.5	51.5	33.3	33
BJP	12.8	46.2	41	195
INC	7	48.4	44.6	157

Note: Stories in which the party was a main actor, defined as the first, second or third actor in the story, are included here. n=number of actors. Cells contain the percentages.

Looking at the coverage of leaders in *Aaj Tak*, Narendra Modi received disproportionately more coverage than Rahul Gandhi or Arvind Kejriwal, both as first, second and third most important actors in overall coverage. Narendra Modi accounted for 67.7 per cent of leader coverage, while Rahul Gandhi and Arvind Kejriwal received 17.6 and 14.7 per cent coverage, respectively (Table 7.6). However, there was not much difference between Mr Modi and Mr Kejriwal in terms of the positive tone of reporting: Mr Modi received 27.1 and Mr Kejriwal 27.7 per cent, while Mr Gandhi received 30.3 per cent. Negative stories about Mr Kejriwal amounted to 41.1 per cent, compared with 40.2 per cent for Mr Modi. Mr Gandhi received least negative coverage with 30.4 per cent. There was more neutral coverage of Mr Gandhi (39.9 per cent) than of Mr Modi (31 per cent) and Mr Kejriwal (31.3 per cent). Overall, Mr Modi was more prominent in these extended news headlines at the top of the programme at a time that garnered the largest audiences. In some cases, even if the headline was about Mr Gandhi attacking Mr Modi, the visuals would carry only Mr Modi. Similarly, Table 7.5 shows that BJP received more coverage than INC; AAP received disproportionately less coverage than the BJP and the

INC. Interestingly, the tone of the coverage towards AAP was more positive as compared to BJP and INC.

Table 7.6: Tone of news items towards the party leader, Lok Sabha 2014 election campaign, *Aaj Tak* primetime news (8.00 to 10.00 pm), 13 March to 12 May 2014

	Positive	Negative	Both positive and negative	Neutral	n
Arvind Kejriwal	27.7	41.1	0	31.3	141
Narendra Modi	27.1	40.2	1.7	31	649
Rahul Gandhi	30.3	30.4	0	39.9	168

Note: Stories in which a leader was the main actor, defined as the first, second or third actor in the story, are included here. n=number of actors. Cells contain the percentages.

The content analysis of the most watched Hindi TV news programme shows that the BJP and Narendra Modi received more coverage than other parties and leaders, but the balance ratios (positive – negative news) show that the news was generally more negative. For example, the balance ratio for each leader was: -13.4 for Mr Kejriwal, -13.1 for Mr Modi, and -0.1 for Mr Gandhi. Compared to balance ratio for each of the three parties – AAP, BJP and INC, news was less negative for their leaders.

In the next section I discuss whether the parties were successful in influencing the issue agenda of the media, with a focus on the *Aaj-Tak* agenda.

Party strategies and media agenda

The coverage on *Aaj Tak* during the two hour prime time daily news programme suggest that at least this very popular news channel, and probably many of its competitors in the news media, are inclined to report on issues and leaders in ways that do not necessarily correspond with the agendas of the parties. Television news media in India arguably play an important part in shaping public perceptions on the importance of issues and the images of the party leaders. As the most watched Hindi news channel, *Aaj Tak* is seen by the parties as an important source of influence on party support in the nation's large Hindi-belt which was the kingmaker in 2014.

Political parties use different stories and rhetoric to appeal to different sections of society. Some politicians in the BJP used communal rhetoric to appeal to its core supporters, but used the slogan of development and governance to appeal to youth and the aspiring middle classes. Narendra Modi was careful to keep the BJP campaign on-message and to rebut controversial statements when needed. On 22 April he tweeted, 'Petty statements by those claiming to be BJP's well-wishers are deviating the campaign from the issues of development and good governance.' This tweet came in the context of reported hate speeches from BJP leaders. Griraj Singh, a BJP candidate in the Lok Sabha election from Nawada in the state of Bihar, said in rally, 'Modi critics belong in Pakistan' (Yadav, 2014). Similarly, Praveeen Togadia, leader of the Vishwa Hindu Parishad (VHP), made a controversial statement targeting the Muslim community (Gaikwad, 2014). In a strong rebuttal, Mr Modi tweeted, 'I disapprove [of] any such irresponsible statements and appeal to those making them to kindly refrain from doing so.' This instant reaction from Mr Modi was not an isolated event; he was proactive throughout the campaign either in relation to his own party or in attacking rival parties and candidates.

The contest between the two main political parties was exemplified in the war of words between Narendra Modi and Rahul Gandhi, where Mr Modi repeatedly called Mr Gandhi *shehzada* (prince of a political dynasty). With this term, Mr Modi not only pointed to the undemocratic nature of the Congress party, but also tried to remind voters of Muslim rule in India.[14] In response, the Congress party described Mr Modi as *sahebzada* (lord or master) for his alleged role in the 'Snoopgate' affair, in which Mr Modi was accused of illegal surveillance of a young woman in Gujarat.

There were personal attacks on individual politicians throughout the campaign. Both the Hindi and English media presented the news stories by attaching personal attributes instead of reporting them objectively. All political parties and leaders tried to influence the media agenda to attract voters' attention. One example is the exchange of arguments between Narendra Modi and Priyanka Gandhi, daughter of the Congress party leader Sonia Gandhi and assassinated Prime Minister Rajiv Gandhi and, perhaps more importantly in the public mind, the granddaughter of Indira Gandhi. During her campaign in the city of Amethi, Priyanka Gandhi remarked, 'Each polling booth in Amethi will take revenge for this *neech rajniti* (low-level politics), the people of Amethi will not forgive him [Modi] for insulting my martyred father in Amethi.' In response, Mr Modi said, 'Yes, I was born into a *neechi jaati* [backward class] but is it a crime?' Through his use of rhetoric, Modi demonstrated his ability

---

14 In an earlier remark, Mr Modi compared Congress Party-led UPA government at the centre with 'Delhi Sultanate' – a reminder of Muslim past and undemocratic nature of the Gandhi dynasty.

to transform attacks into benefits. Although Priyanka Gandhi intended to show up the 'dirty politics' of the BJP and Mr Modi by framing him negatively, Mr Modi turned her remarks to his advantage by highlighting his lower caste background.[15]

Mobilisation through negativity

Not only was news content negative throughout the campaign, but party strategies also hinged on negativity. Attacking the rival party and candidates and issuing controversial statements were the most important subjects to emerge from the content analysis. In relation to news content, there is a plethora of studies in the context of advanced democracies that show a tendency towards negative stories in the news media (Diamond, 1978; Fallows, 1997; Lichter and Noyes, 1995; Robinson and Levy, 1985; Soroka, 2014). Similarly, negative campaigns are believed to be more influential in a competitive race (Able, Herrnson, Magleby and Patterson, 2001; Goldstein, Krasno, Bradford and Seltz, 2001; Saroka and McAdams, 2015). These studies suggest that negativity both in news content and campaign messages are commonly used to mobilise support.

Communalism is one of the central issues around which negative campaigns are framed during elections. Studies on communal riots have shown a spike in communal riots before an election, at least prior to 2004 (Brass, 2005). This time a communal riot took place in Muzaffarnagar in Uttar Pradesh in August-September 2013. There were several heated exchanges between political leaders on the issue of communalism. For example, Amit Shah, Narendra Modi's campaign manager, was banned by the Election Commission of India (ECI) from electoral rallies and meetings on 5 April for 'hate speech' when he said: 'If you want to take revenge, you should vote for the BJP.' Such comments from Mr Modi's close aide stirred tensions in areas affected by communal riots, drew national attention and provided opportunities to secular parties such as the INC, the Bahujan Samaj Party (BSP) and the Samajwadi Party (SP) to sharpen their attack against the BJP. On 5 April, *Aaj Tak* covered this story in its primetime slot for an entire half-hour at the beginning of the programme. It broadcast the controversial statement, while observing that despite his

---

15 On 12 May, the *Times of India* editorial criticised Mr Modi for this twist of rhetoric to gain votes, pointing out that Mr Modi was trying to polarise the election campaign and in effect dismissing his own theme of 'India is one'. Some of these incidents have also been discussed in Neyazi, Chakraborty and Chandra, 2015.

contentious remark no action had yet been taken against Amit Shah and the news anchor questioned the effectiveness of the ECI in deterring candidates from making controversial statements.[16]

Similarly, fake encounters remained an important issue throughout the campaigns.[17] The Congress party's P. Chidambaram created a furore when he dubbed Mr Modi an 'encounter minister' in reference to an alleged encounter that took place in Gujarat when Mr Modi was Chief Minister. At the same time, the attack was a response to Mr Modi's jibe at P. Chidambaram as the 'recounting minister', which was a reference to the 2009 Lok Sabha election where Chidambaram won the election only after a recount of the vote in his constituency.

Yet another example of negativity was evident when the Shahi Imam of Delhi's largest mosque, the Jama Masjid, came out in support of the Congress party after meeting with Sonia Gandhi, president of the Congress party. Soon after the meeting, the Shahi Imam accused the BJP of being a 'communal force' and criticised other secular parties, particularly the SP and the BSP, for not doing enough to check the rising communal tensions in Uttar Pradesh. Interestingly, Shahi Imam also labelled the AAP as 'communal' and claimed that it was supported by a right-wing Hindu nationalist organisation, the Rashtriya Swayamsevak Sangh (RSS). However, the BJP counter-attacked by criticising the Congress party for the meeting between the party president Sonia Gandhi and Shahi Imam and accused the party of 'spreading the poison of communalism.'

The issues of illegal Bangladeshi Muslim migrants in Assam and the exchange between different parties over the issue also reflect the prevalence of negativity. This issue received extensive coverage in the news media during the campaign. On one hand, the INC and a regional party, the Trinamool Congress (TMC), which has been ruling in the state of West Bengal, accused the BJP of 'communalising' the issue. On the other hand, the BJP accused the Congress and the TMC of protecting the interests of illegal immigrants for their 'vote bank politics'.

---

16 The ban on Amit Shah from campaigning was lifted after he requested the ECI to reconsider the decision as his remarks were 'misrepresented' and he did not violate the model code of conduct. A charge sheet was filed against Shah at the behest of the ECI in September 2014 (Ghosal, 2014). On 20 January 2016, the Uttar Pradesh police gave a clean chit to Shah because they did not find any evidence against him in the case (Press Trust of India, 2016a).

17 The term 'fake encounter' is used in India to describe the police killing of suspects or criminals while in custody or when suspects are unarmed. Such killings are considered to be 'extra-judicial' and have been strongly criticised by human rights activists.

The use of rhetoric allowed the Hindi media to increase its effectiveness and outreach, because it allowed them to appeal to the inner code of the Hindi-speaking masses. Such rhetoric does get translated in other languages, but it loses its appeal when it is printed or broadcast in the English media. It is not surprising that most of the English media preferred to use the original rhetoric along with a translation.

To what extent each of the three parties was able to influence the agenda of *Aaj Tak*? The content analysis of *Aaj Tak* offers some interesting facts about the coverage of the campaign. Of the three main subjects that we coded in our content analysis of *Aaj Tak*, nearly 17.1 per cent of stories were related to attacking the rival candidate or the party while another 4.6 per cent of stories were about hate speech and controversial statements as the first main subject in the news headlines. Similarly, the figure for the same was 10.9 and 2.3, respectively, as the second main subject.

There was hardly any mention of policy in the news headlines of *Aaj Tak*, with nearly 94 per cent of the headlines containing no reference to policy. Similarly, news headlines during primetime hardly covered any issues and instead focused on the spectacle of the rallies, road shows and campaign rhetoric. We, therefore, cannot say that the party policy agenda was actually able to influence the media agenda with respect to the most watched and important items that were in the headlines. The majority of the coverage in *Aaj Tak* was negative and tended to emphasise negativity. *Aaj Tak* offered nothing to parties in terms of reporting on party positions on key issues. A focus on leadership helped in getting a good platform and coverage in the media. The content analysis findings seem to confirm the importance of leadership in 2014, noted in the study by Semetko, Kumar, Neyazi and Mellon (2016). The *Aaj Tak* content emphasised leadership, leader characteristics and leader activities above all other issues, and if that was the norm for most TV news, then TV helped to presidentialise the election.

Table 7.7: Most Important Problem (MIP) reported by Delhi voters, 2014 Lok Sabha election

Most Important Problem (MIP)	MIP1	Rank	MIP2	Rank	MIP3	Rank	MIP123	Rank
Inflation/price rises	36.9	1	22.2	2	15.7	4	24.9	2
Corruption	30.0	2	27.6	1	20.6	2	26.1	1

Most Important Problem (MIP)	MIP1	Rank	MIP2	Rank	MIP3	Rank	MIP123	Rank
Jobs	10.0	3	13.2	4	18.6	3	16.7	3
Women's Safety	8.9	4	21.3	3	23.6	1	15.2	4
Economy	2.8	5	2.2	6	2.6	6	2.5	6
Law and Order	2.0	6	4.6	5	8.3	5	5.0	5
Total per cent	**90.6**		**91.1**		**89.4**		**90.4**	
n	1557		1557		1557		4671	

Note: Actual words of the question: As you know, we face many serious problems in this country and in other parts of the world. What do you think is the most important issue facing India today? (PROBE: Can you think of any other important issues facing the country? REPEAT UNTIL RESPONDENT SAYS 'NO' OR 3 ISSUES HAVE BEEN MENTIONED)

When it comes to media shaping the perceptions of voters on the salience of an issue, our survey shows mixed results.[18] Table 7.7 indicates that the concerns of people in Delhi revolved primarily around four issues – inflation, corruption, jobs, women's safety, – which together account for about 90 per cent of responses for the three most important problems both individually and collectively. These refer to the spontaneous answers provided by respondents to the first three questions on the survey, see the note to Table 7.7. From the first most important problem question (MIP1) alone, we can see that inflation (named by 36.9 per cent) and corruption (named by 30.0 per cent) are the primary concerns of more than two-thirds of respondents. These two issues alone remain the top two responses to MIP2, and when we take all three of the MIP questions together. However, these four issues were hardly discussed in the prime-time news bulletins of *Aaj Tak*. Instead *Aaj Tak* was focusing more on daily campaigning by the parties, that included many negative comments from one party about another, and there was only the occasional reporting on the issue of corruption and even less on the issue of inflation. There is, thus, a discernible gap between what potential voters see as the most important problems facing the country at the outset of the campaign and what the

---

18   The results reported here are from a post-poll survey data in Delhi during the 2014 national election. The sample was based on probability proportional to size (PPS) sampling and is demographically representative of the residents of the city. We did not weight the data. The survey was administered with structured questionnaires in Hindi by a Delhi-based market research firm, with trained interviewers working with our research team on all aspects of the sample and implementation of the survey.

popular Hindi news programme delivers in campaign reporting based on what party leaders were saying daily in rallies. If the party leaders were talking about these issues, then *Aaj Tak* rarely featured those soundbites and opted for attacks instead. The reason the issue of communalism is missing from Table 7.7, an issue the Congress party used to attack the BJP and Narendra Modi, is because it was hardly ever mentioned by Delhi voters in our sample. This is also an indicator of the gap between the Congress party's campaign strategy and the reality on the ground. It also may have been an important factor in the party's decimation in the 2014 Lok Sabha election.

The findings serve as a caution about making generalisations about the power of the media in influencing the perceptions of voters on issues and call for exploring other sources of influence. The agenda-setting research might have to look beyond media to find out other sources of influence to provide a more compelling analysis of media effects on audience.[19] This is where the hybrid media ecology becomes important, because each of the actors – political actors, the media and individual citizens – is entangled in a web of networks and trying to influence the others. Moreover, in a hybrid media environment, the process of agenda-setting is becoming more complex since voters are exposed to multiple sources of information. People not only analyse messages based on their own predispositions, but they also analyse media messages based on their own real life personal experiences. While predispositions create more polarised public, analysing media messages in light of personal experiences may moderate the agenda-setting power of the media. This is not to imply that media effects do not exist; rather we need to study multiple sites of interactions among media actors, political actors and diverse public that are influencing the process of political communication in a hybrid media environment.

Conclusion: The future of hybrid campaigns

The simultaneous integration and fragmentation of spaces in the emerging hybrid media system has opened up new opportunities for political actors to utilise different media based on exigencies to influence voters. Despite the fact that only a very small fraction of Indians were online, who were an even smaller number of the population in 2014, Twitter and Facebook derived public sentiment scores were published on the front pages of many newspapers and websites of TV news channels, suggesting that these are representative

---

19   For a critical analysis of agenda setting research, see Walgrave, Aelst and Bennett, 2010.

of the public as a whole. Traditional media coverage lent credibility to social media as a reliable source of pubic sentiment. People who are not using the internet are getting information about the activities on social media through traditional media. What is remarkable in the BJP's campaign strategy is that the contents were tailored to suit the requirements of a particular medium and communication was relayed simultaneously across a wide range of outlets. This helped in reaching not only journalists, but also their supporters and web surfers. The BJP not only aggressively used traditional techniques of campaigns such as face-to-face contacts with voters, but also new media such as mobile phones and the internet to reach out to voters. Most voters were more comfortable with the grassroots campaigns and used traditional media as their primary means of getting campaign information. While *Aaj Tak* provided more space to the BJP and Narendra Modi, the party's issue agenda was unable to influence the media agenda. Most of the coverage in *Aaj Tak* revolved around campaign activities with more emphasis on negative stories instead of talking about issues.

The battles over the news agenda among different parties and leaders in an effort to influence Delhi voters showed that more than the BJP, it was Narendra Modi who was successful in getting disproportionate coverage in the Hindi news channel compared to other leaders. Despite the media having their own agenda, having a strong leader helped the BJP influence coverage in the news media. The Narendra Modi-led BJP pushed the agenda of 'development' and 'good governance' with a positive view of economic growth in the future, while the INC pushed the negative agenda of 'communalism' suggesting that the violence in Gujarat in 2002 could return if the BJP came to power. AAP pushed the agenda of corruption to counter both the INC and the BJP. All political parties tried to contest the projection of Mr Modi as the man who could take India forward by invoking the right-wing political ideology of the BJP and Mr Modi's involvement in the 2002 Gujarat riots. The so-called secular parties questioned the safety of the Muslim minority under the BJP government, their social exclusion, higher rates of poverty and illiteracy. In the campaign, the battle to characterise Mr Modi's record as Chief Minister was the key weapon used by anti-BJP parties to frame the party and its leader as communal and irresponsible, while the BJP and its allies framed his record in office as one of strong leadership resulting in successful economic growth.

Yet, it would be incorrect to believe that it was only the BJP's past that allowed the rival parties to push the agenda of communalism to attack the BJP. Rather, BJP party leaders such as Amit Shah often brought up the issue of communalism. One might question whether there was a deliberate strategy to have Narendra Modi focused on development and good governance to attract the rising middle class and the youth, while other high-profile politicians such as Amit Shah used a communal agenda to appeal to BJP core voters.

The calibrated party strategies along with hybrid media campaigns did pay a dividend for the BJP. Historically, some political parties have always been quicker to adopt new technologies in their campaign strategies and tactics to compete with their opponents and influence the voters. The early adopter, in this case the BJP, might have an advantage in one electoral cycle, but would be difficult to continue their comparative advantage over the longer term and in subsequent electoral cycles. We expect to see more political parties adopting digital media in their hybrid campaign strategies, which would level the comparative advantage enjoyed by one party in one electoral cycle.

8

Conclusion
Politics, Power and Mobilisation in Digital India

The diversity and complexity of the Indian media is clearly reflected in the ways in which Hindi media operated and continue to operate in this comparatively young democracy by treading a complex space and influencing social and political mobilisation. By aligning themselves with the freedom struggle against the British, Hindi newspapers were able to establish themselves as a significant vehicle for political communication during the colonial period. The battle for public opinion took new turns after independence because the power equations between the vernacular press and the English press had altered. The findings in this book suggest that Hindi media is not a homogenous entity – neither in the past nor in contemporary contexts – in terms of its internal politics, ideological perspective and market influence. The Hindi media played an important role in the political and social mobilisation beginning in the 1980s in addition to exploding caste, regional and religious identities. The shifting focus of politics from the centre to the regional levels since the 1980s would not have been possible without the rise of the regional public sphere mediated in the vernacular languages, including Hindi. The Hindi media consolidated its position within Indian politics and society by acting as an agent of mobilisation and helped mediate local voices within the larger macro-institutions, which aided in the development of more productive interactions between the elite and the mass public. Political mobilisation mediated by the Hindi news media reflects the ongoing conflicts among various actors who want to wield power and influence public policies.

The binary between the Hindi and English media, if not completely disappearing, is becoming increasingly blurred. The political significance of the Hindi media was previously established, with political leaders not shying away from giving exclusive interviews to Hindi press and news channels. Certain journalistic practices that are embedded within the transorganisational field of journalism practices such as the objectivity and professionalism often associated with English media are now observed in Hindi media organisations.

The changes occurring in the media environment with the arrival of the internet have created a new era in the ways content flows have been taking place across different platforms, affecting both Hindi and elite English media.[1] This trend resulted in the emergence of a hybrid media system and has made it difficult to understand the functioning of a particular medium in isolation. For example, the headlines in the newspapers may have been influenced by what was discussed during the evening primetime news on television, whereas the morning news bulletin on television may discuss headlines from important newspapers. Similarly, a number of stories shared on the internet are sourced through traditional news media, as traditional news media regularly carry important tweets from politicians and celebrities and develop their stories further after initial feedback from Twitter. Traditional media regularly carry sentiments and stories on important political issues from Twitter and Facebook. The increasingly messy and overlapping sources of information mediated within the hybrid media system are not only affecting journalism practices; the process of political communication is becoming more complex. In this book, I have integrated the process model of political communication adapted from Pippa Norris (2002) with Andrew Chadwick's (2011, 2013) concept of a hybrid media system to study Hindi media-mediated mobilisation in a rapidly transforming media environment. I have argued that we must understand mobilisation in the context of this new hybrid and complex media environment and unravel the process of political communication by critically analysing the sources of messages, channels of communication and their effects on political mobilisation. I have shown how in a hybrid media environment, there is growing convergence between sources of messages and sites of conversations, not only creating a more interactive communicative process, but also making it difficult to disentangle the processes of political communication. As such, the process of agenda-setting has become more convoluted.

Despite the limited number of India's rural population with internet access, digital strategies have wider influence because of the contextual hybridity in information flows, with the daily press and broadcast media often trumpeting what may appear to be a robust online campaign. The use of digital strategies is becoming more widespread in urban India's robust and rapidly expanding media environment and has been used by marginalised groups, social movements, election campaigns and individual citizens. A hybrid media system helps a

---

1   Rapid growth in internet penetration in India to 462 million in 2016 did not solve the urban/rural divide with nearly 75 per cent of the internet users still concentrated in urban India (Internet Live Stats).

diverse public with different interests and values to use different media according to the level of convenience, to come together in a network and to press its demands more effectively than has previously been possible. In a hybrid media environment, politics is mediated by multiple elite and non-elite actors and enthrones the media as the central agent of mobilisation.

The success of the anti-corruption movement led by Anna Hazare in garnering attention can be partially attributed to the movement's successful campaign on the internet, particularly on social networking sites, which also prompted traditional media to take up the issue. As noted in Chapter 6, the changing support base of the anti-corruption movement from a metropolitan and urban middle class to a more economically and geographically diversified public was primarily the result of the prevalence of a hybrid media system or the way in which both new and traditional media, along with grassroots mobilisation, have helped highlight the issue in the public arena. The hybrid media environment provided fertile ground for Team Anna to use the media to more quickly attract attention and mobilise the masses so that the political class would seriously consider enacting an effective Lokpal or ombudsman to curb corruption in public life. The increasing use of the internet and social media in the context of India's 24X7 media cycle, which emerged in India during the First Gulf War in 1991 when cable and satellite television, and CNN, were introduced in businesses and five-star hotels, has certainly placed the government under unprecedented scrutiny.

The propensity among the recent social movements such as Anna Hazare-led anti-corruption movement to influence media or to adapt to be noticed by the media also distinguishes such movements from earlier movements that believed in grassroots mobilisation as their primary weapon. The heavy dependence on the media by recent contemporary movements has been criticised, which also renders it difficult to sustain the movement for long once the movement loses the attention of the media. The Right to Information (RTI) movement, which was equally uncomfortable for the government, adopted multi-pronged strategies, including grassroots mobilisation, rather than simply attempting to influence the media, which made it successful. Media-dependent movements such as the anti-corruption movement, therefore, are often marked by virality and ephemerality – rapid diffusion but difficulty in sustaining the movement.

Political actors have long been using the media extensively and hiring public relations firms to design their campaigns to win elections, but this is taken to a new level in a hybrid media environment. The 2014 Lok Sabha election witnessed the unprecedented use by political parties and individual politicians of different media to influence voters. Certainly, BJP's campaign strategies were quite sophisticated and content was tailored to suit the requirements of a particular medium yet sufficiently versatile to be easily adaptable across a wide range of outlets. This helped the party reach not only journalists, but also their supporters and web surfers. The BJP not only aggressively used traditional techniques such as face-to-face contact with voters, but also used new media such as mobile phones and the internet to reach out to voters. Most voters were more comfortable with the grassroots campaigns and used traditional media as their primary means of obtaining campaign information in the 2014 Lok Sabha election, as shown in Chapter 7. Although there is no evidence of the direct effect of social media on voting behaviour, research on the 2014 election determined that sharing information – both face-to-face and digitally – was an important predictor for engagement in the political parties' campaigns (Neyazi, Kumar and Semetko, 2016).

It would be inappropriate to conclude that the rise of the internet has empowered the non-elite actors to exercise power and articulate their demands in the public sphere. Studies in other national contexts have shown that actors who were empowered in the mass-media era are the actors becoming vocal in the digital media era; hence, the same advantages and disadvantages that exist politically offline are becoming reproduced online (Margolis and Resnick, 2000; Stromer-Galley, 2014). The case of India is more complex and nuanced than the development that has occurred with the rise of digital media in the developed world. Dalits, the lowest caste, who were forced to look beyond the traditional media at alternative strategies for mobilisation, are now increasingly using digital media to voice their demands in the public sphere. The nearly three decades of the story of the growth of private television have not been able to produce a single nationally recognised Dalit journalist. This is not to argue that the Dalit issues have been completely erased from the mainstream media. Rather, Indian media do cover Dalit issues within two dominant frames – victimhood or privileged – as we have seen in Chapter 4.

Unlike traditional media in which communication is filtered through various organisational channels, digital media allows a flow of communication with no intermediaries and hence offer opportunities for previously marginalised groups such as Dalits to intervene in the public debates. Digital media has enabled

Dalits to tell their own stories in their own language, ensuring that their stories will not be erased from the memory. In the mass-media era, it was possible for the elite actors to control the flow of information in their favour. In the current post-broadcast era, non-elite actors such as Dalits in India have been effectively using the internet to voice their grievances and bypass mainstream media.

In the past when there was no internet, Dalits developed their own alternative media in the form of magazines and small booklets and pamphlets to mobilise support. In the emerging hybrid media space, the internet has emerged as a significant platform of alternative media and voices. The potential of the internet to influence traditional media is much greater because of the increase in the algorithmic culture in which keywords are fed into the system to monitor events in the online world. In the past, magazine and booklets were confined to a limited audience; the online platform, however, is not bounded by space and operates as a deterritorialised medium, reaching a diverse audience. The emergence of a small group of digital Dalits among the Dalit middle class, which has been vigorously involved in highlighting atrocities committed against Dalits, is also questioning the silence of mainstream media on Dalit issues.[2] Thirumal and Tartakov (2010) argued that with the emergence of digital technologies, Dalits have developed a 'means of communicating with each other beyond the control of others' (22). The web presence of organised Dalits has increased recently.[3] The Rohith Vemula suicide case, which became a national issue, was first discussed and debated on online platforms, and subsequently taken up by the traditional media. Rohith Vemula was a Dalit student pursuing his PhD at Hyderabad Central University. He allegedly committed suicide on 17 January 2016. In his suicide note, he blamed the university administration for harassing him because of his caste (Dipti, 2016; Kaushik, 2016). Protest marches in support of Rohith Vemula were organised in several parts of the country. Caste discrimination as the reason behind the

---

2   The atrocities against Dalits includes public flogging of Dalits, raping Dalit women, parading Dalits naked and killing of Dalits for raising their voices. There is an act called the SCs and STs Atrocities Prevention Act enacted in 1989 to safeguard Dalits from atrocities; however, the law has not proved to be sufficient to prevent atrocities against Dalits.

3   Some of the important Dalit online platforms are Dalit Camera (www.dalitcamera.com); Round Table India (www.roundtableindia.co.in); National campaign for Dalit Human Rights (www. ncdhr.org.in); Dalit Freedom Network (www.dalitnetwork.org); Ambedkar and His People (www. ambedkar.org); Dalit Nation (www.dalitnation.com); Ambedkar Caravan (www.ambedkarcaravan. com). The existence of these online platforms indicate that educated Dalits are taking advantage of the new opportunity to share their experiences, plights and issues in the public sphere.

suicide of Rohith Vemula came to dominate national mainstream media and was debated in the Parliament and this process reflected the prevalence of a hybrid media system. The issue was brought to the public sphere by the internet and influenced the debates in the mainstream media, which were subsequently adopted by political parties and civil society actors, leading to major protests in different areas of the country.

In addition to the increase in digital media outlets, the sphere of democratic interactions has not only deepened into regional and local levels, but also expanded to the global level. There are now multiple issues of common interest discussed in the ever-expanding interactions among multiple viewpoints enabled by a hybrid media system. What we see here is the mediation among the discourse, concerns and activities of various sections of societies and those of the public and political institutions, enabled by various political and civil organisations, public institutions and traditional and new media.

The highly competitive, diversified and overlapping media avenues also reflect the unprecedented opportunities available to various groups, protest movements and political classes in today's political communication networks. The participation of a multitude of citizens in the market-driven media networks led to a change in the nature and function of the media, which not only must ensure their own survival in a capitalist marketplace, but also cater to the requirement to serve wider audiences instead of serving only the interests of the elite. The need to cater to both elite and non-elite actors led to a simultaneous presence in the public arena of the viewpoints and interests of the urban middle classes, the poor and the marginalised. News across media platforms may be similar during a crisis; however, on routine days, there are differences in news stories and various agendas. The rise of large commercial media conglomerates with implicit political interests over the years has cast doubt on whether these media houses would espouse the interests of the poor, which has been a criticism often made by scholars of the media in India (Thakurta, 2014a). There are also cases in which news media have been able to safeguard editorial independence from business pressures, as noted in Chapter 5. The process of news production is more complex than simply being driven by self-interests or profit. The relationship between commercialisation of the media and the editorial independence is therefore not a zero-sum game, in which more of one necessarily requires less of the other; both can coexist in a complementary and competitive manner.

Internet vernacularisation and the future of mobilisation

Internet content that initially was largely only in English has grown dramatically with contributions in vernacular languages attracting new internet users from smaller cities and towns. According to the latest available data on internet users' geographical locations, rural India accounted for 87 million internet users, and the urban India had 219 million internet users by the end of December 2015 (Press Trust of India, 2016b). The year-on-year growth rate of internet users in rural India was 93 per cent, and 71 per cent for urban India. This trend will continue in the coming years, and rural India is likely to experience an exponential growth in users with an estimated 315 million internet users predicted by 2020, accounting for 48 per cent of total connected Indians (Jain and Sanghi, 2016). Internet growth in India will be facilitated by the growth of the internet content in regional languages, not English: Google launched the ILIA in 2014, which promotes Indian languages on the web. The initial partners in this Google initiative included leading Indian media companies such as ABP News, Network 18 and Jagran Prakashan Ltd., all of which have a strong presence in the Indian language media market, including Hindi (Sriram, 2015).

With an estimated 127 million, the growth of Indian language internet users has been greater than English language internet users (BS Reporter, 2016). Of these 127 million Indian language internet users, nearly half, or more than 60 million, were using the internet in the Hindi language (BS Reporter, 2016). In the year 2014–15, the year-on-year growth rate of Hindi language content on the web was 97 per cent compared with 19 per cent for English language content. Although the number of internet users in all Indian languages is growing rapidly, the transformation is more pronounced among Hindi language internet users. This trend of internet vernacularisation in India is consistent with the global trend of the decentralisation and de-Americanisation of the worldwide web and the rise of the global south in terms of the number of web users, as noted in the study by Wu and Taneja (2016). Two important social networking sites now have a significant presence in Indian languages, Facebook is available in 11 Indian languages, and Twitter allows tweets in 6 Indian languages.

The profile of the first 100 million internet users was predominantly urban English-speaking middle class. However, the profile of the most recent 100 million internet users is quite diverse, with a majority coming from small towns and rural areas and accessing the internet in their local vernacular languages (Shah, Nimisha and Bajpai, 2015). Looking back at the growth trajectory of newspapers and television in India, we observed a similar trend of diversification of the audience base after the initial concentration. It took nearly three decades after independence for the Indian language newspapers to surpass the English language newspapers in terms of circulation, which occurred in 1979. The massive increase in Indian language newspaper circulation in the 1980s was accompanied by a parallel trend of increasing mobilisation of the masses in India. Similarly, when private television broadcasters entered India in 1990, the majority of their programming in the first decade was in English, catering to the urban middle class. It was the late 1990s and early 2000s that witnessed the growth of Indian language programming on private television. The increase in Indian language news channels and newspapers since the early 2000s also resulted in the mediatisation of politics, a phenomenon that encourages sensationalism, simplification and personalisation. I have previously demonstrated how this massive transformation in the press and broadcast media affected the process of political communication.

For example, the vernacularisation of the internet is leading to a transformation at India's rural areas where close to 70 per cent of the population currently reside. Rural access to the internet will have a massive effect on mobilisation with contextual hybridity in information flow, in which a number of messages first emerging in a particular medium become translated and remediated by other media reaching beyond their primary audience. Internet vernacularisation may lead to even greater mobilisation when compared with the mobilisation witnessed after the rise of the Indian language newspapers and news channels; the use of digital technologies through the internet has become more diffused and personalised, having the potential to influence non-internet users. Internet users reading and processing content in their own languages without any intermediary also create space for greater participation because individual citizens are able to monitor and evaluate government policies and programmes. This process would allow citizens to experience a more fertile ground in which to engage in the political process and governance and share their daily experiences with both one another and the outside world. In terms of creating a more informed and engaged citizenry, the success of Digital India initiative, which seeks to connect all the villages by an internet network, would mostly be determined by how well the government is able to deliver more personalised content in local languages. In the ever-changing media environment, personal and social networks, in addition to the proliferation of vernacular internet content, will affect the competing ideas of articulating one's demands in the public arena and allowing a disparate public to unite in a web of networks and intervene in the ongoing debates.

Communicating power in digital India

India has entered a post-broadcast era in which various actors have been using the media to influence public opinion, a process that has been described as the mediatisation of politics (Downey and Neyazi, 2014; Esser, 2013; Strömbäck, 2008). As with other institutions, there are political, professional and economic interests within the media institutions. The existence of professional interests has certainly allowed the Indian media to highlight injustices time and again, whether it is the case of paid news, Radia-gate, coal and other mega scams or farmer suicide. If journalists always reported the news according to the desires of the powerful and as dictated by the market, Indian journalism would have lost its vibrancy and legitimacy. However, the political interests in which media groups strive to seek political favour and the economic interests of profit maximisation are adversely affecting the functioning of the media as the fourth estate.

The instrumentalisation of media in which outside groups such as political parties, politicians and corporate groups attempt to use media to intervene in the decision-making process, as reflected in paid-news scandals, is another concern for the functioning of the Indian media.[4] The use of media by political actors to further their political and policy goals has increased recently, facilitated by the rise of modern communication technologies and more professionalised political public relations. The earlier personalised relations between journalists and political actors are increasingly being replaced by strategic planning in which political actors are using experts to design political strategies, frame issues and establish the media agenda.[5] One of the first changes introduced after the advent of the BJP-led government at the centre was the discontinuing the earlier practice of taking journalists along on their diplomatic tours. Only the public service broadcaster, Doordarshan, has been allowed to accompany government officials on diplomatic tours. Similarly, Prime Minister Narendra Modi has been using social media, particularly Twitter, to communicate the

---

4   For a theoretical discussion of media instrumentalisation, see Mancini (2012).

5   This development may appear new in the context of India, but has been occurring in developed countries. For a study of European government strategies for news management, see Pfetsch (2007).

government's stance on various issues directly to the public. Narendra Modi launched the programme called '*Mann Ki Baat*' in October 2014 in which he addresses the people of the nation every month by radio and Doordarshan. The programme is now broadcast in 19 Indian languages. All ministers in the current government have been instructed to communicate their achievements to the people by social media.

India has entered an era of 'permanent campaign', in which political actors forget the distinction between governance and campaign. Governance with publicity has been used as a strategy to compensate for declining public trust in the government as in many other Western and Asian nations (Pfetsch, 2007; Sanders and Canel, 2013). Such a development is not good for a democracy because evaluations of issues, policies and programmes should primarily be judged by their implementation and performance rather than their newsworthiness.

The shift in the Indian government's communication policy was to ensure strategic communication planning to influence public opinion by controlling the flow of information. This top-down approach to influencing public opinion by the media may not be successful in the long run because it is difficult to control the flow of information because of the emergence of hybrid media systems, which have experienced mass participation in the creation of online content and demonstrated that the political elite alone no longer control political events. Rather, non-political elite have been able to significantly contribute to shaping political events, which has transformed power relationships in news production. The case of WikiLeaks is a clear rupture in the evolution of news making and political mobilisation and shows how digital technologies can enable even a small group of semi-elite individuals with access to information to wield substantial organisational power. According to Thorson and Wells (2016), the rise of digital technologies has placed individuals at the centre of 'personal information networks embedded in multiple, intersecting content flows curated by various actors in varying proportions' (310). Digital media has enabled citizens to act as news producers and provide interpretations of politics, challenging the top-down process of communication.

The simultaneous growth of print, television and the internet in India has not only mediatised politics, but has enabled a diverse citizenry to participate more actively in this process of mediatisation. This participation, in turn, is challenging both media actors and political actors, who must to be careful of the unpredictable nature of the Indian public, which is evident from not only the results of the 2015 assembly elections in Delhi and Bihar, where the BJP remained out of power in both state assemblies after doing well in these states in the 2014 national election, but also the 2017 state assembly election in Uttar Pradesh where the BJP won by a large margin.[6] As political polarisation has increased in many democracies, including India, what was once described as an incumbency advantage can no longer be assumed. Citizens are becoming more engaged through alternative channels of political expression and are not limiting their participation to electoral politics, using both traditional and digital media. With the launch of low-cost smartphones in 2015, the prospects continue to grow for marginalised and low-income citizens to express themselves through online platforms. Internet vernacularisation has further democratised the communication process, attracting new internet users from rural areas, small towns and cities beyond the urban middle class. The conflict among political actors regarding the yielding of political power will become more pronounced as the dynamics of political communication continue to remain fluid in the profoundly complex hybrid media environment.

---

6   The BJP lost election in both these states after winning all seven seats in Delhi and 31 out of 40 seats in Bihar in the 2014 Lok Sabha election.

Bibliography

Aalberg, Toril and James Curran. eds. 2012. *How Media Inform Democracy: A Comparative Approach.* London: Routledge.

Aarts, Kees and Holli A. Semetko. 2003. 'The Divided Electorate: Media Use and Political Involvement.' *The Journal of Politics* 65(3): 759–84.

Able, Owen. G., Paul S. Herrnson, David B. Magleby and Kelly Patterson. 2001. 'Are Professional Campaigns More Negative?' In *Playing Hardball: Campaigning for the U.S. Congress,* edited by Paul S. Herrnson, 70–91. Saddle River, NJ: Prentice Hall.

Afaqs. 2014. 'Modi's "Aap Ki Adaalat" Fetches High Viewership for India TV.' *Afaqs,* 24 April. Accessed 26 August 2016. Available at http://www.afaqs.com/news/story/40660_Modis-Aap-Ki-Adaalat-fetches-high-viewership-for-India-TV.

Ahmed, Waquar, Amitabh Kundu and Richard Peet. eds. 2011. *India's New Economic Policy: A Critical Analysis.* London: Routledge.

Almond, Gabriel and Sydney Verba. 1963. *The Civic Culture: Political Attitudes and Democracy in Five Nations.* Princeton, NJ: Princeton University Press.

Altheide, David L. and Robert P. Snow. 1979. *Media Logic.* Beverly Hills, CA: Sage Publications.

Anderson, Benedict. 1991. *Imagined Community: Reflections on the Origin and Spread of Nationalism,* revised edition. London: Verso.

Athique, Adrian. 2012. *Indian Media.* Cambridge: Polity Press.

Bagdikian, Ben H. 1983. *The Media Monopoly.* Boston: Beacon Press.

_____. 2004. *The New Media Monopoly.* Boston: Beacon Press.

Baishya, Anirban K. 2015. '#NaMo: The Political Work of the Selfie in the 2014 Indian General Election.' *International Journal of Communication* 28(9): 1686–1700.

Bajpai, Shailaja. 2016. 'The World Came Home: The History of Television in India.' *The Indian Express,* 24 July. Accessed 14 August 2016. Available at http://indianexpress.com/article/entertainment/television/the-world-came-home-2932048/.

Balakrishna, P. and B. Sidharth. 2004. 'Selling in Rural India.' *Business Line,* 16 February.

Barber, Benjamin. 2001. 'The Uncertainty of Digital Politics: Democracy's Uneasy Relationship with Information Technology.' *Harvard International Review* 23(1): 42–48.

Barnes, Samuel H. and Max Kaase. 1979. *Political Action: Mass Participation in Five Western Democracies*. London: Sage Publications.

Barns, Margarita. 1940. *The Indian Press: A History of the Growth of Public Opinion in India*. Liverpool: George Allen and Unwin Limited.

Barrier, Gerald N. 1974. *Banned: Controversial Literature and Political Control in British India, 1907–1947*. Missouri: University of Missouri Press.

Barro, Robert J. 1996. 'Democracy and Growth.' *Journal of Economic Growth* 1(1): 1–27.

Baruah, Sanjiv. 1999. *India against Itself Assam and the Politics of Nationality*. Philadelphia: University of Pennsylvania Press.

Basu, Amrita. 1997. 'When Local Riots are Not Merely Local: Bringing the State Back in, Bijnor 1988–1992.' In *State and Politics in India*, edited by Partha Chatterjee, 390–435. Delhi: Oxford University Press.

Batabyal, Somnath. 2014. *Making News in India: Star News and Star Ananda*. New Delhi: Routledge.

Bayly, Chris. A. 1975. *The Local Roots of Indian Politics: Allahabad 1880–1920*. Oxford: Clarendon Press.

———. 1988. *Rulers, Townsmen and Bazaars: North Indian Society in the Age of British Expansion, 1770–1870*. Cambridge: Cambridge University Press.

———. 1996. *Empire and Information: Intelligence Gathering and Social Communication in India*. New York: Cambridge University Press.

Bennett, Lance W. and Shanto Iyengar. 2008. 'A New Era of Minimal Effects? The Changing Foundations of Political Communication.' *Journal of Communication* 58(3): 707–31.

Bennett, Lance W. 1998. 'The Uncivic Culture: Communication, Identity, and the Rise of Lifestyle Politics, P.S.' *Political Science and Politics* 31(04): 41–61.

———. 2004. 'Global Media and Politics: Transnational Communication Regimes and Civic Cultures.' *Annual Review of Political Science* 7(1): 125–48.

———. 2007. *News: The Politics of Illusion*. New York: Longman.

Besley, Timothy and Andrea Prat. 2006. 'Handcuffs for the Grabbing Hand? The Role of the Media in Political Accountability.' *American Economic Review* 96(3): 720–36.

Beteillé, André. 1965. *Caste, Class, and Power: Changing Patterns of Stratification in a Tanjore Village*. Berkeley: University of California Press.

———. 1969. *Castes: Old and New: Essays in Social Structure and Social Stratification*. Mumbai, New York: Asia Publishing House.

Beyer, Jessica. 2014. *Expect Us: Online Communities and Political Mobilization*. Oxford: Oxford University Press.

Bhaskar. 2011. 'News Channels' Prime Time Coverage of Anna Hazare's Fast: Study

Report.' *Bhaskar*, 30 August. Accessed 28 August 2016. Available at http://brpbhaskar.blogspot.in/2011/08/news-channels-prime-time-coverage-of.html.

Bhatnagar, Ramratan. 2003 (1947). *The Rise and Growth of Hindi Journalism (1826–1945)*. Varanasi: Vishwavidyalaya Praakashan.

Bhushan, Sandeep. 2013. 'Manufacturing News.' *Economic and Political Weekly* 48(23): 12–15.

_____. 2014. 'How the Television News Industry Scripted the Indian Elections.' *The Caravan*, 15 May. Accessed 6 May 2015. Available at http://www.caravanmagazine.in/vantage/television-scripted#sthash.PXmKtgim.dpuf.

_____. 2015. '"Regulation" and "Non-Media" Money in Media.' *Economic and Political Weekly* 50(7): 19–22.

Bijapurkar, Rama. 2007. *We are Like that Only: Understanding the Logic of Consumer India*. New Delhi: Penguin.

Bimber, Bruce. 1999. 'The Internet and Citizen Communication with Government: Does the Medium Matter?' *Political Communication* 16(4): 409–29.

Bose, Ajoy. 2008. *Behenji: A Political Biography of Mayawati*. New Delhi: Penguin.

Boumans, Jelle W., Hajo G. Boomgaarden and Rens Vliegenthart. 2013. 'Media Personalisation in Context: A Cross-national Comparison between the UK and the Netherlands, 1992–2007.' *Political Studies* 61(1): 198–216.

Boyce, Merill, T. 1988. *British Policy and the Evalution of the Vernacular Press in India, 1835–1878*. Delhi: Chanakya.

Brandenburg, Heinz. 2002. 'Who Follows Whom? The Impact of Parties on Media Agenda Formation in the 1997 British General Election Campaign.' *Harvard International Journal of Press/Politics* 7(3): 34–54.

Brass, Paul. 2005. *The Production of Hindu-Muslim Violence in Contemporary India*. Seattle: University of Washington Press.

Broadcast Audience Research Council (BARC). 2015. 'TV Weekly Viewership.' Accessed 14 May 2015. Available at http://www.barcindia.co.in/statistic.aspx.

Bromley, Michael and Angela Romano. 2005. *Journalism and Democracy in Asia*. London: Routledge.

BS Reporter. 2016. 'Hindi Internet Users Estimated at 60 Million in India: Survey.' *Business Standard*, 4 February. Accessed 28 August 2016. Available at http://www.business-standard.com/article/current-affairs/hindi-internet-users-estimated-at-60-million-in-india-survey-116020400922_1.html.

Butcher, Melissa. 2003. *Transnational Television, Cultural Identity and Change: When STAR Came to India*. New Delhi, Thousand Oaks: Sage Publications.

Census of India. 2001a. *Distribution of 10,000 Persons by Language – India, States and Union Territories 2001*. New Delhi: Office of the Registrar General and Census Commissioner, Government of India.

_____. 2001b. *Distribution of Population by Scheduled and Other Languages-India, States and Union Territories-2001*. New Delhi: Office of the Registrar General and Census Commissioner, Government of India.

_____. 2011a. *Literacy in India, 2011*. New Delhi: Office of the Registrar General and Census Commissioner, Government of India.

_____. 2011b. *Houses, Household Amenities and Assests 2011*. New Delhi: Office of the Registrar General and Census Commissioner, Government of India.

_____. 2011c. *Primary Census Abstract: Scheduled Castes and Scheduled Tribes*. New Delhi: Office of the Registrar General and Census Commissioner, Government of India.

_____. 2011d. *Population Enumeration Data*. New Delhi: Office of the Registrar General and Census Commissioner, Government of India.

Centre for Media Studies (CMS). 2011. 'Face of Corruption in News Media: A Report on their Coverage.' Accessed 28 August 2016. Available at http://www.cmsindia.org/publications/face-of-corruption-in-news-media-2011.pdf.

_____. 2014. 'Coverage of 2014 Lok Sabha Polls By News Channels.' New Delhi. Accessed 14 December 2016. Available at http://www.cmsindia.org/publications/Monograph_Coverage_2014_LokSabha_Polls.pdf.

Chadha, Kalyani. 2012. 'Twitter as Media Watch-dog: Lessons from India's Radia Tapes Scandal.' *Global Media and Communication* 8(2): 171–76.

Chadwick, Andrew. 2006. *Internet Politics: States, Citizens, and New Communication Technologies*. New York: Oxford University Press.

_____. 2011. 'The Political Information Cycle in a Hybrid New System: The British Prime Minister and the "Bullygate" Affair.' *International Journal of Press/Politics* 16(1): 3–29.

_____. 2013. *The Hybrid Media System: Politics and Power*. Oxford: Oxford University Press.

Chakravartty, Paula and Srirupa Roy. 2013. 'Media Pluralism Redux: Towards New Frameworks of Comparative Media Studies "Beyond the West".' *Political Communication* 30(3): 349–70.

Chandra, Bipin, Mridula Mukherjee, Aditya Mukherjee, K. N. Panikkar and Sucheta Mahajan. 1988. *India's Struggle for Independence*. New Delhi: Penguin.

Chandra, Kanchan. 2004. *Why Ethnic Parties Succeed: Patronage and Ethnic Headcounts in India*. Cambridge: Cambridge University Press.

Chatterjee, Ramananda. 1929. 'Origin and Growth of Journalism among Indians.' *Annals of the American Academy of Political and Social Science* 145(2): 161–68.

Chaturvedi, J. P. 1970. 'Inherent Handicap.' In *What Ails the Indian Press: Diagnosis and Remedies*, edited by D. R. Mankekar, 65–74. New Delhi: Somaya Publications.

Chaturvedi, Jagdish Prasad. 2004. *Hindi Patrakarita ka Itihas*. Delhi: Prabhat Prakashan.

Chhibber, Pradeep, Francesca Jensensius and Pavithra Suryanarayan. 2014. 'Party Organisation and Party Proliferation in India.' *Party Politics* 20(4): 489–505.

Chong, Dennis and James N. Druckman. 2007. 'Framing Theory.' *Annual Review of Political Science* 10: 103–26.

Clarke, Michael. ed. 1983. *Corruption: Causes, Consequences and Control.* London: Burns & Oates.

Codell, Julie, F. 2004. 'Introduction: The Nineteenth-Century News from India.' *Victorian Periodicals Review* 37(2): 106–23.

Cohen, Bernard C. 1963. *The Press and Foreign Policy.* Princeton, NJ: Princeton University Press.

Conge, Patrick, J. 1988. 'The Concept of Political Participation: Toward a Definition.' *Comparative Politics* 20(2): 241–49.

Cook, Timothy. E. 1998. *Governing with the News.* Chicago: University of Chicago Press.

Dahl, Robert A. 1956. *Preface to Democratic Theory.* Chicago: University of Chicago Press.

_____. 1971. *Polyarchy: Participation and Opposition.* New Heaven, CT: Yale University Press.

_____. 1982. *Dilemmas of Pluralist Democracies: Autonomy vs. Control.* New Haven, CT: Yale University Press.

_____. 1989. *Democracy and Its Critics.* New Haven, CT: Yale University Press.

Dahlgren, Peter. 2005. 'The Internet, Public Spheres, and Political Communication: Dispersion and Deliberation.' *Political Communication* 22(2): 147–62.

Dalmia, Vasudha. 1997. *The Nationalisation of Hindu Traditions: Bharatendu Harischandra and Nineteenth-century Banaras.* New Delhi: Oxford University Press.

De Vreese, Claes H. 2004. 'The Effects of Strategic News on Political Cynicism, Issue Evaluations, and Policy Support: A Two-wave Experiment.' *Mass Communication and Society* 7(2): 191–214.

_____. 2005. 'News Framing: Theory and Typology.' *Information Design Journal + Document Design* 13(1): 51–62.

Dearing, James W. and Everett Rogers. 1996. *Agenda-setting.* Volume 6. Thousand Oaks: Sage Publications.

della Porta, Donatella. 2012. 'Communication in Movement: Social Movements as Agents of Participatory Democracy.' In *Digital Media and Political Engagement Worldwide: A Comparative Study,* edited by Eva Anduiza, Michael James Jensen and Laia Jorba, 39–53. Cambridge: Cambridge University Press.

Delli Carpini, M. X. 2000. 'Gen.com: Youth, Civic Engagement, and the New Information Environment.' *Political Communication* 17(4): 341–50.

DeLuca, Kevin M., Sean Lawson and Ye Sun. 2012. 'Occupy Wall Street on the Public Screens of Social Media: The Many Framings of the Birth of a Protest Movement.' *Communication, Culture and Critique* 5(4): 483–509.

DeSouza, Peter R. and E. Sridharan. eds. 2006. *India's Political Parties*. New Delhi: Sage Publications.

Di Tella, Rafael and Ignacio Franceschelli. 2011. 'Government Advertising and Media Coverage of Corruption Scandals.' *American Economic Journal: Applied Economics* 3(4): 119–51.

Diamond, Edwin. 1978. *Good News, Bad News*. Cambridge, MA: MIT Press.

Diamond, Larry. ed. 1993. *Political Culture and Democracy in Developing Countries*. Boulder, CO: Lynne Rienner.

Dimock, Michael and Samuel Popkin. 1997. 'Political Knowledge in a Comparative Perspective.' In *Do the Media Govern?*, edited by Shanto Iyengar and Richard Reeves, 217–24. Thousand Oaks, CA: Sage Publications.

Dipti, Nagpaul. 2016. 'Writing Back in Anger.' *The Indian Express*, 21 January. Accessed 14 August 2016. Available at http://indianexpress.com/article/india/india-news-india/write-back-in-anger/.

Donner, Jonathan. 2008. 'The Rules of Beeping: Exchanging Messages via Intentional "Missed Calls" on Mobile Phones.' *Journal of Computer Mediated Communication* 13(1): 1–22.

Donovan, Robert J. and Raymond L. Scherer. 1992. *Unsilent Revolution: Television News and American Public Life, 1948–1991*, new edition. Cambridge: Cambridge University Press.

Downey, John and Taberez A. Neyazi. 2014. 'Complementary and Competitive Logics of Mediatization: Political, Commercial and Professional Logics in Indian Media.' *International Journal of Press/Politics* 19(4): 476–95.

Doyle, Gillian. 2002. 'Media Ownership: The Economics and Politics of Convergence and Concentration in the UK and European Media.' *Journal of Cultural Economies* 27(3): 290–93.

Druckman, James N. 2001. 'The Implications of Framing Effects for Citizen Competence.' *Political Behaviour* 23(3): 225–56.

Dua, Hans R. 1993. 'The National Language and the Ex-colonial Language as Rivals: The Case of India.' *International Political Science Review/Revue Internationale de Science Politique* 14(3): 293–308.

Dumont, Louis. 1970. *Homo Hierarchicus: The Caste System and Its Implications*. Translated from the French by Mark Sainsbury. London: Weidenfeld & Nicolson.

Economic Times. 2011. 'India's Middle Class Population to Touch 267 Million in Five Years', 6 February. Accessed 6 September 2016. Available at http://articles.economictimes.indiatimes.com/2011-02-06/news/28424975_1_middle-class-households-applied-economic-research.

Elder, Joseph W. 1971. 'The Decolonization of Educational Culture: The Case of India.' *Comparative Education Review* 15(3): 288–95.

Engineer, Ashghar Ali. ed. 1990. *Babri-Masjid Ramjanabhoomi Controversy.* Delhi: Ajanta Publication.

_____. 1991. 'Press on Ayodhya "Kar seva".' *Economic and Political Weekly* 26(20): 1263–66.

Entman, Robert M. 1993. 'Framing: Toward Clarification of a Fractured Paradigm.' *Journal of Communication* 43(4): 51–58.

_____. 2010. 'Improving Newspaper's Economic Prospects by Augmenting their Contributions to Democracy.' *International Journal of Press/Politics* 15(1): 104–25.

Esha News Monitoring Services. 2011. *Television Monitoring Intelligence Report for 3rd to 11th April 2011.* Mumbai.

Esser, Frank. 2013. 'Mediatization as a Challenge: Media Logic versus Political Logic.' In *Democracy in the Age of Globalization and Mediatization*, edited by Hanspeter Kriesi, Daniel Bochsler, Jörg Matthes, Sandra Lavenex, Marc Bühlmann and Frank Esser, 155–76. Hampshire, UK: Palgrave Macmillan.

Eveland Jr, William P. and Dietram A. Scheufele. 2000. 'Connecting News Media Use with Gaps in Knowledge and Participation.' *Political Communication* 17(3): 215–37.

Express News Service. 2011. 'Team Anna's Use of Social Media Caught Us Unawares, Says Khurshid.' *The Indian Express*, 19 October. Accessed 14 December 2016. Available at http://archive.indianexpress.com/news/team-anna-s-use-of-social-media-caught-us-unawares-says-khurshid/861900.

_____. 2014. 'Top 10 Political Videos on YouTube.' *The Indian Express*, 8 May. Accessed 26 August 2016. Available at http://indianexpress.com/article/india/politics/top-10-political-videos-on-youtube/.

Fallows, James. 1997. *Breaking the News: How the Media Undermine American Democracy.* New York, NY: Vintage.

Fernandes, Leela. 2000. '"Nationalizing the Global": Media Images, Cultural Politics and the Middle Class in India.' *Media, Culture and Society* 22(5): 611–28.

_____. 2006. *India's New Middle Class: Democratic Politics in an Era of Economic Reform.* Minneapolis and London: University of Minnesota Press.

Fernández-Ardèvol, Mireia. 2013. 'Deliberate Missed Calls: A Meaningful Communication Practice for Seniors?' *Mobile Media and Communication* 1(3): 285–98.

FICCI-KPMG. 2016. *Indian Media and Entertainment Industry Report, 2016.*

Finkel, Steven E. 1993. 'Reexamining the Minimal Effects Model in Recent Presidential Campaigns.' *Journal of Politics* 55(1): 1–21.

Frankel, Francine. R. 2000. 'Introduction: Contextual Democracy: Intersections of

Society, Culture and Politics in India.' In *Transforming India: Social and Political Dynamics of Democracy*, edited by Francine R. Frankel, Zoya Hasan, Rajeev Bhargava and Balveer Arora, 1–25. New Delhi: Oxford University Press.

_____. 2005. *India's Political Economy, 1947–2004: The Gradual Revolution*. New Delhi: Oxford University Press.

Freitag, Sandria. B. 1989. *Collective Action and Community: Public Arenas and the Emergence of Communalism in North India*. Berkeley: University of California Press.

_____. 1996. 'Contesting in Public: Colonial Legacies and Contemporary Communalism.' In *Contesting the Nation: Religion, Community, and the Politics of Democracy in India*, edited by David Luden, 211–34. Philadelphia: University of Pennsylvania Press.

_____. 2007. 'More than Meets the (Hindu) Eye: The Public Arena as a Space for Alternative Visions.' In *Picturing the Nation: Iconographies of Modern India*, edited by Richard H. Davis, 92–116. Delhi: Orient Longman.

Gaikwad, Rahi. 2014. 'Togadia's "Hate Speech" Video under EC Scanner.' *The Hindu*, 21 April. Accessed 15 December 2016. Available at http://www.thehindu.com/news/national/togadias-hate-speech-video-under-ec-scanner/article5934581.ece?homepage=true&ref=relatedNews.

Gambaro, Marco and Riccardo Puglisi. 2009. 'What Do Ads Buy? Daily Coverage of Listed Companies on the Italian Press.' *Departmental Working Papers 2009–36*. Italy, Milan: Department of Economics, University of Milan.

Gamson, William A. and Andre Modigliani. 1987. 'The Changing Culture of Affirmative Action.' In *Research in Political Sociology*, Volume 3, edited by Richard D. Braungart, 137–77. Greenwich, CT: JAI.

Gamson, William and Gadi Wolfsfeld. 1993. 'Movement and Media as Interacting Systems.' *Annals of the American Academy of Political Science* 528: 114–25.

Gandhi, M. K. 1965. *Our Language Problem*. Edited and published by Anand T. Hingorani. Mumbai: Bhartiya Vidya Bhavan.

Gehlbach, Scott and Konstantin Sonin. 2008. 'Government Control of the Media.' New Economic School. Mimeo.

Geirbo, Hanne C. and Per Helmersen. 2008. 'Turning Threats into Oppotunities—The Social Dynamics of Missed Calls.' *Telektronikk* 2: 77–83.

Ghosal, Aniruddha. 2014. 'Amit Shah is Chargesheeted in Election "Hate Speech" Case.' *The Indian Express*, 11 September. Accessed 15 December 2016. Available at http://indianexpress.com/article/india/politics/amit-shah-chargesheetd-for-objectionable-speech-during-ls-polls/.

Giddens, Anthony. 1991. *Modernity and Self-Identity: Self and Society in the Late Modern Age*. Stanford: Stanford University Press.

Gilens, Martin and Craig Hertzman. 2000. 'Corporate Ownership and News Bias:

Newspaper Coverage of the 1996 Telecommunications Act.' *The Journal of Politics* 62(2): 369–86.

Gitlin, Todd. 1980. *The Whole World is Watching: Mass Media in the Making and Unmaking of the New Left.* Berkeley, CA: University of California Press.

Goffman, Erving. 1974. *Frame Analysis: An Essay in the Organization of Experience.* Cambridge, MA: Harvard University Press.

Goldstein, Ken. M., Jonathan S. Krasno, Lee Bradford and Daniel Seltz. 2001. 'Going Negative: Attack Advertising in the 1998 Elections.' In *Playing Hardball: Campaigning for the US Congress*, edited by Paul S. Herrnson, 92–107. Saddle River, NJ: Prentice Hall.

Gopal, Madan. 1990. *Freedom Movement and the Press: The Role of Hindi Newspapers.* New Delhi: Criterion Publications.

Gopal, Ram. 1966. *Linguistic Affairs of India.* Bombay: Asia Publishing House.

Gould, William. 2004. *Hindu Nationalism and the Language of Politics in Late Colonial India.* Cambridge: Cambridge University Press.

Government of India. 1954. *Report of the First Press Commission.* New Delhi: Ministry of Information and Broadcasting.

———. 1977. *White Paper on Misuse of Mass Media during the Internal Emergency.* New Delhi: Jain Book Agency.

———. 1982. *Report of the Second Press Commission.* New Delhi: Ministry of Information and Broadcasting.

———. 2011. *Basic Road Statistics of India, 2011.* New Delhi: Ministry of Road Transport and Highways.

Gowda, M. V. Rajeev and Purnima Prakash. 2014. 'The India against Corruption Movement.' In *Handbook of Research on Political Activism in the Information*, edited by Ashu M. G. Solo, 240–57. Hershey: IGI Global.

Goyal, Malini. 2014. 'How BJP, AAP, Congress and their Candidates are Using Social Media to Woo Voters.' *The Economic Times*, 6 April. Accessed 15 May 2015. Available at http://articles.economictimes.indiatimes.com/2014-04-06/news/48908610_1_social-media-it-cell-fekuexpress.

Green-Pedersen, Christoffer and Stefaan Walgrave. eds. 2014. *Agenda Setting, Policies, and Political Systems: A Comparative Approach.* Chicago: University of Chicago Press.

Guha, Ramachandra. 2008. *India after Gandhi: The History of the World's Largest Democracy.* New Delhi: Picador.

Gupta, Akhil. 1995. 'Blurred Boundaries: The Discourse of Corruption, the Culture of Politics and the Imagined State.' *American Ethnologist* 22(2): 375–402.

———. 1998. *Postcolonial Developments: Agriculture in the Making of Modern India.* Durham: Duke University Press.

Gupta, Dipankar. 2000. *Interrogating Caste: Understanding Hierarchy and Difference in Indian Society*. New Delhi, New York: Penguin Books.

Gupta, Jyotirindra Das. 1970. *Language Conflict and National Development*. Berkeley: University of California Press.

Gupta, Nilanjana. 1998. *Switching Channels: Ideologies of Television in India*. New Delhi: Oxford University Press.

Gupta, Renu. 2006. 'Technology for Indic Scripts: A User Perspective.' *Language in India* 6(7): 1–16.

Gupta, Renu and V. Sornlertlamvanich. 2007. 'Text Entry in South and Southeast Asian Scripts.' In *Text Entry Systems: Mobility, Accessibility, Universality*, edited by I. Scott MacKenzie and K. Tanaka-Ishii, 227–49. Amsterdam: Morgan Kaufmann.

Gupta, Uma Das. 1977. 'The Indian Press 1870–1880: A Small World of Journalism.' *Modern Asian Studies* 11(2): 213–35.

Habermas, Jurgen. 1989. *The Structural Transformation of the Public Sphere: An Inquiry into a Category of Bourgeois Society*. Translated by Thomas Burger with the assistance of Frederick Lawrence. Cambridge, MA: The MIT Press.

Haider-Markel, Donald P. and Mark R. Joslyn. 2001. 'Gun Policy, Opinion, Tragedy, and Blame Attribution: The Conditional Influence of Issue Frames.' *Journal of Politics* 63(2): 520–43.

Hallin, Daniel C. and Paolo Mancini. 2004. *Comparing Media Systems*. Cambridge: Cambridge University Press.

Hamilton, James. 2004. *All the News That's Fit to Sell: How the Market Transforms Information into News*. Princeton, NJ: Princeton University Press.

Hansen, Kasper M. and Rasmus Tue Pedersen. 2014. 'Campaigns Matter: How Voters become Knowledgeable and Efficacious during Election Campaigns.' *Political Communication* 31(2): 303–24.

Hansen, Thomas B. and Christophe Jaffrelot. eds. 1998. *The Compulsions of BJP Politics*. Delhi: Oxford University Press.

Hansen, Thomas, B. 1999. *The Saffron Wave: Democracy and Hindu Nationalism in Modern India*. Princeton: Princeton University Press.

Hasan, Zoya. 1998. *Quest for Power: Oppositional Movements and Post-Congress Politics in Uttar Pradesh*. Delhi: Oxford University Press.

_____. 1995. 'Shifting Ground: Hindutva Politics and the Farmers' Movements in Uttar Pradesh.' In *New Farmers Movements in India*, edited by Tom Brass, 165–94. Ilford, Essex, UK: Frank Cass.

_____. 2000. 'Representation and Redistribution: The New Lower Caste Politics of North India.' In *Transforming India: Social and Political Dynamics of Democracy*, edited by Francine R. Frankel, Zoya Hasan, Rajeev Bhargava and Balveer Arora, 146–75. New Delhi: Oxford University Press.

_____. ed. 2004. *Parties and Party Politics in India*. New Delhi: Oxford University Press.

Hay, Colin. 2007. *Why We Hate Politics*. Cambridge: Polity Press.

Hazarika, Sanjoy. 1988. 'The Media Business; India's Advertising Industry Surges.' *The New York Times*, 23 May.

Heidenheimer, Arnold. J. 1989. 'Terms, Concepts, and Definitions: An Introduction.' In *Political Corruption: A Handbook*, edited by Arnold J. Heidenheimer, Michael Johnston and Victor T. LeVine, 3–14. New Brunswick: Transaction Publishers.

Hewitt, Vernon. 2008. *Political Mobilisation and Democracy in India: States of Emergency*. London: Routledge.

Hillygus, D. Sunshine and Simon Jackman. 2003. 'Voter Decision-making in Election 2000: Campaign Effects, Partisan Activation and the Clinton Legacy.' *American Journal of Political Science* 47(4): 583–96.

Hindman, Mathew. 2008. *The Myth of Digital Democracy*. Princeton: Princeton University Press.

Hooghe, Marc, Sara Vissers, Dietlind Stolle and Valérie-Anne Mahéo. 2010. 'The Potential of Internet Mobilization: An Experimental Study on the Effect of Internet and Face-to-Face Mobilization Efforts.' *Political Communication* 27(4): 406–31.

Howard, Philip N. 2005. *New Media Campaigns and Managed Citizen*. Cambridge: Cambridge University Press.

_____. 2010. *The Digital Origins of Dictatorship and Democracy: Information Technology and Political Islam*. New York: Oxford University Press.

Huntington, Samuel P. 1991. *The Third Wave: Democratisation in the Late Twentieth Century*. Oklahoma: University of Oklahoma Press.

Huntington, Samuel, P and Joan M. Nelson. 1976. *No Easy Choice: Political Participation in Developing Countries*. Cambridge, MA: Harvard University Press.

Indian Readership Survey. 2014. *Media Consumption*. Mumbai. Media Research Users Council.

Inglehart, Ronald. 1997. *Modernisation and Postmodernisation: Cultural, Economic and Political Change in 43 Societies*. Princeton: Princeton University Press.

International Monetary Fund (IMF). 2015. *World Economic Outlook Database*. Last modified April 2015. Aaccessed 26 August 2016. Available at http://www.imf. org/external/pubs/ft/weo/2015/01/index.htm.

International Telecommunication Union (ITU). 2015. 'ICT Facts and Figures: The World in 2015.' Accessed 14 December 2016. Available at https://www.itu.int/ en/ITU-D/Statistics/Documents/facts/ICTFactsFigures2015.pdf.

Internet and Mobile Association of India (IAMAI). 2015. *Report on Internet in India*. New Delhi.

Internet Live Stats. 2016. Accessed 14 December 2016. Available at http://www. internetlivestats.com/.

Israel, Milton. 1994. *Communications and Power: Propaganda and the Press in the Indian Nationalist Struggle, 1920–1947*. Cambridge: Cambridge University Press.

Iyengar, Shanto. 1991. *Is Anyone Responsible? How Television Frames Political Issues*. Chicago: University of Chicago Press.

Iyengar, Shanto and Donald R. Kinder. 1987. *News that Matters: Television and American Opinion*. Chicago: University of Chicago Press.

Jaffrelot, Christophe and Sanjay Kumar. eds. 2009. *Rise of the Plebeians? The Changing Face of Indian Legislative Assemblies*. New Delhi: Routledge.

Jaffrelot, Christophe. 1993. *The Hindu Nationalist Movement in India*. New York: Columbia University Press.

_____. 2002. *India's Silent Revolution: The Rise of the Lower Castes in North India*. London: C. Hurst.

_____. 2009. 'The Uneven Rise of Lower Castes in the Politics of Madhya Pradesh.' In *Rise of the Plebeians? The Changing Face of Indian Legislative Assemblies*, edited by Christophe Jaffrelot and Sanjay Kumar, 103–48. New Delhi: Routledge.

_____. 2010. *Religion, Caste and Politics in India*. New Delhi: Primus Books.

Jagannathan, N. S. 1999. *Independence and the Indian Press: Heirs to a Great Tradition*. Delhi: Konark Publishers.

Jain, A. K. 1970. 'Credibility Gap.' In *What Ails the Indian Press: Diagnosis and Remedies*, edited by D. R. Mankekar, 59–64. New Delhi: Somaya Publications.

Jain, Nimisha and Kanika Sanghi. 2016. 'The Rising Connected Consumers in Rural India.' BGC Perspective. Accessed 15 December 2016. Available at https://www. bcgperspectives.com/content/articles/globalization-customer-insight-rising-connected-consumer-rural-india/#chapter1.

Jain, Ramesh. 2006. *Hindi Patrakarita: Itihas Aur Sanrachna*. Jaipur: Avilash Publishers.

Jakubowicz, Karol. 2007. 'Public Service Broadcasting in the 21st Century. What Chance for a New Beginning?' In *From Public Service Broadcasting to Public Service Media*, edited by Gregory Lowe and Joe Bardoel, 29–50. Goteborg: Nordicom.

Jeffrey, Craig. 2002. 'Caste, Class and Clientelism: A Political Economy of Everyday Corruption in Rural North India.' *Economic Geography* 78(1): 21–41.

Jeffrey, Robin. 1993. 'Indian-Language Newspapers and Why They Grow.' *Economic and Political Weekly* 28(38): 2004–11.

_____. 1994. 'Monitoring Newspapers and Understanding the Indian State.' *Asian Survey* 34(8): 748–63.

_____. 2000. *India's Newspaper Revolution: Capitalism, Politics and the Indian-Language Press 1977–99*. New Delhi: Oxford University Press.

_____. 2009. 'Testing Concepts about Print, Newspapers, and Politics: Kerala, India, 1800–2009.' *The Journal of Asian Studies* 68(2): 465–89.

Jenkins, Rob. 1999. *Democratic Politics and Economic Reform in India*. Cambridge: Cambridge University Press.

_____. 2007. 'India's Unlikely Democracy: Civil Society versus Corruption.' *Journal of Democracy* 18(2): 55–69.

Jha, Prem Shankar and Arvind N. Das. 2000. *History in the Making: 75 Years of The Hindustan Times*. New Delhi: Hindustan Times.

Johnson, Kirk. 2000. *Television and Social Change in Rural India*. New Delhi: Sage Publications.

Kagal, Ayesha. 2016. *More News is Good News: The Untold Stories from 25 Years of Television News*. New Delhi: HarperCollins.

Kalpagam, Uma. 2002. 'Colonial Governmentality and the Public Sphere in India.' *Journal of Historical Sociology* 15(1): 35–58.

Kamra, Sukeshi. 2002. *Bearing Witness: Partition, Independence, End of the Raj*. Calgary: University of Calgary Press.

_____. 2011. *The Indian Periodical Press and the Production of Nationalist Rhetoric*. New York: Palgrave Macmillan.

Karkhanis, Sharad. 1981. *Indian Politics and the Role of the Press*. New Delhi: Vikas Publishing.

Karlekar, Hiranmay. 1986. 'The Great Advertising Boom.' *The Indian Express*, 11 September.

Katz, Elihu and Paul F. Lazarsfeld. 1955. *Personal Influence: The Part Played by People in the Flow of Communication*. New York: Free Press.

Kaul, Chandrika. 2002. *Reporting the Raj: The British Press and India, c. 1880–1922*. Manchester: Manchester University Press.

Kaul, Mahima. 2014. 'India Obsessed with Social Media Role in Elections.' *Index on Censorship*, 21 May. Accessed 15 December 2016. Available at https://www.indexoncensorship.org/2014/05/india-obsessed-with-social-media-role-in-elections/.

Kaushik, Martand. 2016. 'Missing the Story: Lessons for Indian Journalism from Dalit Mobilisation Online.' *The Caravan*, 1 March. Accessed 15 December 2016. Available at http://www.caravanmagazine.in/perspectives/missing-the-story-lessons-indian-journalism-dalit-mobilisation-online.

Kiihberger, Anton. 1998. 'The Influence of Framing on Risky Decisions: A Meta-analysis.' *Organizational Behaviour and Human Decision Processes* 75(1): 23–55.

Kinder, Donald R. and Lynn M. Sanders. 1990. 'Mimicking Political Debate with Survey Questions: The Case of White Opinion on Affirmative Action for Blacks.' *Social Cognition* 8(1): 73–103.

King, Robert. D. 1997. *Nehru and the Language Politics of India.* New Delhi: Oxford University Press.

Kohli, Atul. 1990. *Democracy and Discontent.* Cambridge: Cambridge University Press.

———. 2006a. 'Politics of Economic Growth in India, 1980–2005, Part I: The 1980s.' *Economic and Political Weekly* 41(13): 1251–59.

———. 2006b. 'The 1990s and Beyond: Part II.' *Economic and Political Weekly* 41(14): 1361–70.

Kohli, Vanita. 2006. *The Indian Media Business,* second edition. New Delhi: Sage Publications.

Kothari, Rajni. 1964. 'The Congress "System" in India.' *Asian Survey* 4(12): 1161–73.

———. 1974. 'The Congress System Revisited: A Decennial Review.' *Asian Survey* 14(12): 1035–54.

Krueger, Brian. S. 2002. 'Assessing the Potential of Internet Political Participation in the United States: A Resource Approach.' *American Politics Research* 30(5): 476–98.

Kudaisya, Gyanesh. 2006. *Region, Nation, 'Heartland': Uttar Pradesh in India's Body Politic.* New Delhi: Sage Publications.

Kudaisya, Medha. 2006. *The Life and Times of G. D. Birla.* New Delhi: Oxford University Press.

Kumar, Anup. 2011. *The Making of a Small State. Populist Social Mobilisation and the Hindi Press in the Uttarakhand Movement.* New Delhi: Orient BlackSwan.

———. 2014. 'Jan Andolans and Alternate Politics in India: Symbiotic Interactions: Vernacular Publics and News Media in Jan Lokpal Andolan.' In *The Vernacular Public Arena and Democratic Transformation in India,* edited by Taberez A. Neyazi, Akio Tanabe and Shinya Ishizaka, 95–112. London: Routledge.

Kumar, Krishna. 1990. 'Quest for Self-Identity: Cultural Consciousness and Education in Hindi Region, 1880–1950.' *Economic and Political Weekly* 25(23): 1247–55.

———. 2005. *Political Agenda of Education: A Study of Colonialist and Nationalist Ideas,* revised edition. New Delhi: Sage Publications.

Kumar, Shanti. 2005. *Gandhi Meets Primetime: Globalisation and Nationalism in Indian Television.* Urbana-Champagne: University of Illinois Press.

Lasswell, Harold. 1948. 'The Structure and Function of Communication in Society.' In *The Communication of Ideas,* edited by Lyman Bryson, 215–28. New York: Institute for Religious and Social Studies.

Lazarsfeld, Paul Felix, Bernard Berelson and Hazel Gaudet. 1948. *The Peoples Choice: How the Voter Makes Up His Mind in a Presidential Campaign.* Cambridge: Cambridge University Press.

Lelyveld, David. 1993. 'The Fate of Hindustani: Colonial Knowledge and the Project of a National Language.' In *Orientalism and Postcolonial Predicament: Perspectives on South Asia*, edited by Carol A. Breckenridge and Peter van der Veer, 189–214. Philadelphia: University of Pennsylvania Press.

Lichter, S. Robert and Richard Noyes. 1995. *Good Intentions Make Bad News*. Lanham, MD: Rowman and Littlefield.

Lipset, Seymor Martin, Kyoung-Ryung Seong and John Charles Torres. 1993. 'A Comparative Analysis of the Social Requisites of Democracy.' *International Social Science Journal* 45(2): 154–75.

Lipset, Seymor Martin. 1960. *Political Man: The Social Bases of Politics*. Garden City, NY: Doubleday.

Liu, Yung-I., Fei Shen, William P. Eveland and Ivan Dylko. 2013. 'The Impact of News Use and News Content Characteristics on Political Knowledge and Participation.' *Mass Communication and Society* 16(5): 713–37.

Loader, Brian D. and Dan Mercea. eds. 2012. *Social Media and Democracy: Innovations in Participatory Politics*. London: Routledge.

Lohia, Ram Manohar. 1972 (1958). *Notes and Comments*, Volume I. Hyderabad: Rammanohar Lohia Samata Vidyalaya Nyas.

Londregan, John B. and Keith T. Poole. 1996. 'Does High Income Promote Democracy?' *World Politics* 49(1): 1–30.

Loynd, Maxine. 2008. 'Politics without Television: The Bahujan Samaj Party and the Dalit Counter-public Sphere.' In *Television in India: Satellites, Politics and Cultural Change*, edited by Nalin Mehta, 62–86. London: Routledge.

Maclean, Kama. 2011. 'The Portrait's Journey: The Image, Social Communication and Martyr-Making in Colonial India.' *The Journal of Asian Studies* 70(4): 1051–82.

Malhan, Sangita P. Menon. 2013. *The TOI Story: How a Newspaper Changed the Rules of the Game*. New Delhi: HarperCollins.

Malhotra, Inder. 2008. 'Changing Face of Indian Media.' *Media Mimansa* October–December: 67–72.

Malik, Yogendra K. 1977. 'North India Intellectuals' Perceptions of their Role and Status.' *Asian Survey* 17(6): 565–80.

Mancini, Paolo. 2012. 'Instrumentalization of the Media vs. Political Parallelism.' *Chinese Journal of Communication* 5(3): 262–80.

Mani, A. D. 1954. 'Introduction.' In *Journalism in Modern India*, edited by Roland E. Wolseley, xiv–xxiii. Mumbai: Asia Publishing House.

Mankekar, Purnima. 1999. *Screening Culture, Viewing Politics: Television, Womanhood and Nation in Modern India*. New Delhi: Oxford University Press.

Margolis, Michael and David Resnick. 2000. *Politics as Usual: The Cyberspace "Revolution"*. Thousand Oaks: Sage Publications.

Mazzarella, William. 2003a. *Shovelling Smoke: Advertising and Globalisation in Contemporary India*. Durham and London: Duke University Press.

_____. 2003b. 'Critical Publicity/Public Criticism: Reflections on Fieldwork in the Bombay Ad World.' In *Advertising Cultures*, edited by Timothy deWaal Malefyt and Brian Moeran, 55–74. New York: Oxford University Press.

McCargo, Duncan. 2002. *Media and Politics in Pacific Asia*. London: Routledge.

_____. 2011. 'Partisan Polyvalence: Characterising the Political Role of Asian Media.' In *Comparing Media Systems beyond the Western World*, edited by Daniel C. Hallin and Paolo Mancini, 201–23. Cambridge: Cambridge University Press.

McChesney, Robert W. 2007. *Communication Revolution: Critical Junctures and the Future of Media*. New York: New Press.

_____. 2008. *The Political Economy of Media: Enduring Issues, Emerging Dilemmas*. New York: Monthly Review Press.

McChesney, Robert W. and Dan Schiller. 2003. 'The Political Economy of International Communications: Foundation for the Emerging Global Debate about Media Ownership and Regulation.' *Technology, Business and Society Programme Paper No. 11*. Geneva: United Nations Research Institute for Social Development.

McCombs, Maxwell and Donald Shaw. 1972. 'The Agenda-setting Function of Mass Media.' *Public Opinion Quarterly* 36(2): 176–87.

McCombs, Maxwell. 2014. *Setting the Agenda: Mass Media and Public Opinion*. Cambridge: Polity Press.

McGuire, William. 1986. 'The Myth of Massive Media Impact: Savaging and Salvaging.' *Public Communication and Behaviour* 1: 173–225.

McMillan, John and Pablo Zoido. 2004. 'How to Subvert Democracy: Montesinos in Peru.' *Journal of Economic Perspectives* 18(4): 69–92.

Mehta, Alok. 2006. *Bharat Mein Patrekarita*. Delhi: National Book Trust.

Mehta, Nalin. 2008. *India on Television: How Satellite News Channels Have Changed the Way We Think and Act*. New Delhi: HarperCollins.

_____. 2015. *Behind a Billion Screens: What Television Tells Us about Modern India*. New Delhi: HarperCollins.

Mehta, Pratap. B. 2003. *The Burden of Democracy?* New Delhi: Penguin.

_____. 2011. 'Of the Few, by the Few'. *The Indian Express*, 7 April. Accessed 16 June 2014. Available at http://www.indianexpress.com/news/of-the-few-by-the-few/772773.

Meyer, Philip. 2004. *The Vanishing Newspaper: Saving Journalism in the Information Age*. Columbia and London: University of Missouri Press.

Micheletti, Michele. 2003. *Political Virtue and Shopping: Individuals, Consumerism, and Collective Action*. New York: Palgrave Macmillan.

Mill, John Stuart. 1861 (1958). *Considerations on Representative Government*. New York: Liberal Arts Press.

Mishra, Krishna Bihari. 2011. *Hindi Patrakarita: Jatiya Chetna Aur Khariboli Sahitya Ki Nirmanbhumi*. New Delhi: Bharatiya Jnanpith.

Mishra, V. M. 1971. 'The Hindi Press in India: an Interpretative History.' *International Communication Gazette* 17(4): 243–49.

Mohanty, Manoranjan. 2011. 'People's Movements and the Anna Upsurge.' *Economic and Political Weekly* 46(38): 16–19.

Moore, Barrington Jr. 1966. *Social Origins of Dictatorship and Democracy: Lord and Peasant in the Making of the Modern World*. Boston: Beacon.

Mossberger, Karen, Caroline J. Tolbert and Ramona S. McNeal. 2007. *Digital Citizenship: The Internet, Society and Participation*. Cambridge: MIT Press.

Mughan, Anthony. 2001. *Media and the Presidentialization of Parliamentary Elections*. London and New York: Palgrave Macmillan.

Mukherji, Rahul. 2007. 'Introduction: The State and Private Initiative in India.' In *India's Economic Transition*, edited by Rahul Mukherji, 1–24. New Delhi: Oxford University Press.

Muralidharan, Sukumar. 2011. 'Media as Echo Chamber: Cluttering the Public Discourse on Corruption.' *Economic and Political Weekly* 46(37): 19–22.

Nair, S. Tara. 2003. 'Growth and Structural Transformation of Newspaper Industry in India: An empirical Investigation.' *Economic and Political Weekly* 38(39): 4182–89.

Nandy, Asish, Shikha Trivedy, Shail Mayaram and A. Yagnik. eds. 1995. *Creating a Nationality: The Ramjanmabhumi Movement and Fear of the Self*. Delhi: Oxford University Press.

Narain, Prem. 1970. *Press and Politics in India 1885–1905*. Mumbai: Munshiram Manoharlal.

Narayan, Badri. 2011. *The Making of the Dalit Public Sphere in North India*. New Delhi: Oxford University Press.

Natarajan, S. 1962. *A History of the Press in India*. London: Asia Publishing House.

Nayak, Birendra. K. 2011. 'People's Movements and the Anna Upsurge: A Comment.' *Economic and Political Weekly* 46(38): 83–84.

Nayyar, Baldev Raj. 1969. *National Communication and Language Policy in India*. New York: Frederick A Praeger Publishers.

NCAER. 2002. *India Market Demographic Report*. New Delhi.

Neeraj, M. 2016. 'Mobile Internet Users In India 2016: 371 Mn by June, 76% Growth In 2015.' *DazeInfo*, 8 February. Accessed 14 December 2016. Available at https://dazeinfo.com/2016/02/08/mobile-internet-users-in-india-2016-smartphone-adoption-2015/.

Nellis, Gareth, Michael Weaver and Steven Rosenzweig. 2016. 'Do Parties Matter for Ethnic Violence: Evidence from India.' *Quarterly Journal of Political Science* 11(3): 249–77.

Newton, Kenneth. 1999. 'Mass Media Effects: Mobilisation or Media Malaise?' *British Journal of Political Science* 29(4): 577–99.

Neyazi, Taberez A. 2010. 'Cultural Imperialism or Vernacular Modernity? Hindi Newspapers in a Globalising India.' *Media, Culture and Society* 32(6): 907–24.

_____. 2011. 'Politics after Vernacularisation: Hindi Media and Indian Democracy.' *Economic and Political Weekly* 46(10): 75–82.

_____. 2014. 'News Media and Political Participation: Re-evaluating Democratic Deepening in India.' In *Democratic Transformation and the Vernacular Public Arena in India*, edited by Taberez A. Neyazi, Akio Tanabe and Shinya Ishizaka, 76–94. London: Routledge.

Neyazi, Taberez A. and Akio Tanabe. 2014. 'Introduction: Democratic Transformation and the Vernacular Public Arena in India.' In *Democratic Transformation and the Vernacular Public Arena in India*, edited by Taberez A. Neyazi, Akio Tanabe and Shinya Ishizaka, 1–25. London: Routledge.

Neyazi, Taberez A., Sanchita Chakraborty and Tripti Chandra. 2015. 'The Election Campaign in the Hindi News Media: Issues, Rhetoric and Leadership.' In *India Election 2014: First Reflections*, edited by Einar Thorsen and Chindu Sreedharan, 191–203. Bournemouth: the Centre for the Study of Journalism, Culture and Community, Bournemouth University.

Neyazi, Taberez Ahmed, Anup Kumar and Holli A. Semetko. 2016. 'Campaigns, Digital Media, and Mobilization in India.' *The International Journal of Press/ Politics* 21(3): 398–416.

Nielsen, Rasmus K. 2012. *Ground Wars: Personalized Communication in Political Campaigns*. Princeton: Princeton University Press.

Ninan, Sevanti. 1995. *Through the Magic Window*. New Delhi: Penguin.

_____. 2007. *Headlines from the Heartland: Reinventing the Hindi Public Sphere*. New Delhi: Thousand Oaks, CA: Sage Publications.

Norris, Pippa. 1996. 'Does Television Erode Social Capital? A Reply to Putnam.' *PS: Political Science and Politics* 29(3): 474–80.

_____. 2000. *A Virtuous Circle: Political Communications in Postindustrial Societies*. Cambridge: Cambridge University Press.

_____. 2001. *Digital Divide: Civic Engagement, Information Poverty, and the Internet World-wide*. New York: Cambridge University Press.

_____. 2006. 'Did the Media Matter? Agenda-setting, Persuasion and Mobilization Effects in the 2005 British General Election.' *British Politics* 1(2): 195–221.

Orsini, Francesca. 2002. *The Hindi Public Sphere 1920–1940: Language and Literature in the Age of Nationalism*. New Delhi: Oxford University Press.

Packard, Vance. 1957. *The Hidden Persuaders*. London: Longmans, Green.

Page, David and William Crawley. 2001. *Satellites over South Asia: Broadcasting, Culture and the Public Interest*. New Delhi: Sage Publications.

Pal, Joyojeet. 2015. 'Banalities Turned Viral: Narendra Modi and the Political Tweets.' *Television and New Media* 16(4): 378–87.

Pandey, Gyanendra. 1975. 'Mobilization in Mass Movement: Congress "Propaganda" in the United Provinces (India), 1930–34.' *Modern Asian Studies* 19(2): 205–26.

Pandey, Vikas. 2014. 'Narendra Modi: India's Social Media PM.' *BBC*, 26 May. Accessed 15 December 2016. Available at http://www.bbc.com/news/world-asia-india-32874568.

Pathak, Gauri. 2010. 'Delivering the Nation: The Dabbawalas of Mumbai.' *South Asia* 33(2): 235–57.

Paul, Subin. 2017. 'When India was Indira: Indian Express's Coverage of the Emergency (1975-77).' *Journalism History* 42(4): 201–11.

Peterson, Paul E. 1981. *City Limits*. Chicago: University of Chicago Press.

Petrova, Maria. 2009. 'Newspapers and Parties: How Advertising Revenues Created an Independent Press.' *The American Political Science* 105(4): 790–808.

Pfetsch, Barbara. 2007. 'Government News Management: Institutional Approaches and Strategies in Three Western Democracies.' In *The Politics of News: the News of Politics*, edited by Doris A. Graber and Denis McQuail, 71–97. Washington: Congressional Quarterly Press.

Pickard, Victor. 2014. *America's Battle for Media Democracy: The Triumph of Corporate Libertarianism and the Future of Media Reform*. Cambridge: Cambridge University Press.

Pinney, Christopher. 2004. '*Photos of the Gods': The Printed Image and Political Struggle in India*. London: Reaktion Books.

Polat, Rabia. K. 2005. 'The Internet and Political Participation: Exploring the Explanatory Links.' *European Journal of Communication* 20(4): 435–59.

Pradhan, Kunal and Uday Mahurkar. 2014. 'Maximum Campaign: Modi Unleashes a Blitzkrieg Never Seen before in Indian Electoral History.' *India Today*, 9 May. Accessed 15 December 2016. Available at http://indiatoday.intoday.in/story/narendra-modi-bjp-campaign-indian-electoral-history-lok-sabha-elections-2014/1/359920.html.

Prasad, Rajendra. 1958 (1956). *Speeches of President Rajendra Prasad, 1952–1956*. New Delhi: The Publications Division.

Press Council of India. 1991. *Annual Report*, 1 April 1990 – 31 March 1991. New Delhi.

_____. 2010. *'Paid News': How Corruption in the Indian Media Undermines Democracy*, 1 April. New Delhi.

Press in India. 1996. *40th Annual Report*. New Delhi: Registrar of Newspapers for India, Ministry of Information and Broadcasting, Government of India.

_____. 2015. *59th Annual Report*. New Delhi: Registrar of Newspapers for India, Ministry of Information and Broadcasting, Government of India.

Press Trust of India. 2016a. 'Clean Chit to Amit Shah in 2014 Hate Speech Case.' *The Hindu Businessline*, 20 September. Accessed 6 November 2016. Available at http://www.thehindubusinessline.com/news/clean-chit-to-amit-shah-in-2014-hate-speech-case/article8128378.ece.

_____. 2016b. 'Mobile Internet Users in India to Reach 371 Million by June 2016.' *The Indian Express*, 4 February. Accessed 15 December 2016. Available at http://indianexpress.com/article/technology/tech-news-technology/mobile-internet-users-in-india-to-reach-371-mn-by-june-2016/.

Przeworski, Adam, Michael Alverez, Jose. A Cheibub and Fernando Limongi. 1996. 'What Makes Democracies Endure?' *Journal of Democracy* 7(1): 39–55.

Putnam, Robert. 1995. 'Tuning in, Tuning out: The Strange Disappearance of Social Capital in America.' *PS: Political Science and Politics* 27(4): 664–83.

Quah, Jon S. T. 2008. 'Curbing Corruption in India: An Impossible Dream?' *Asian Journal of Political Science* 16(3): 240–59.

Rajagopal, Arvind. 2001. *Politics after Television: Hindu Nationalism and the Reshaping of the Public Sphere in India*. Cambridge: Cambridge University Press.

_____. 2011a. 'Am I Still Anna When Nobody is Watching?' *The Hindu*, 7 September.

_____. 2011b. 'Visibility as a Trap in Anna Hazare Campaign.' *Economic and Political Weekly* 46(47): 19–21.

Ranganathan, Maya and Usha M. Rodrigues. 2010. *Indian Media in a Globalised World*. New Delhi: Sage Publications.

Rao, Shakuntala. 2008. 'Accountability, Democracy, and Globalization: A Study of Broadcast Journalism in India.' *Asian Journal of Communication* 18(3): 193–206.

_____. 2009. 'Glocalization of Indian Journalism.' *Journalism Studies* 10(4): 474–88.

Rau, M. Chalapathi. 1974. *The Press*. New Delhi: National Book Trust.

Reed, Stanley. ed. 1914. *Indian Year Book 1914*. Kolkata: Bennett, Coleman & Co.

Robinson, Michael. J. and Margaret A. Sheehan. 1983. *Over the Wire and on TV: CBS and UPI in Campaign '80*. New York: Russell Sage Foundation.

Roy, Arundhati. 2011. 'I'd Rather Not Be Anna.' *The Hindu*, 21 August. Accessed 16 June 2015. Available at http://www.thehindu.com/opinion/lead/article2379704.ece.

Roy, Srirupa. 2011. 'Television News and Democratic Change in India.' *Media, Culture and Society* 33(5): 761–77.

Rudolph, Lloyd I. and Susanne Hoeber Rudolph. 1987. *In Pursuit of Lakshmi: The Political Economy of the Indian State*. Chicago: University of Chicago Press.

Ryan, Timothy. 1990. 'At the Barricades: Press-state Relations in Modern India.' *South Asia Bulletin* 10(1): 54–60.

Ryfe, David M. 2006. 'Guest Editor's Introduction: New Institutionalism and the News.' *Political Communication* 23(2): 135–44.

Saeed, Saima. 2012. *Screening the Public Sphere: Media and Democracy in India*. New Delhi: Routledge.

_____. 2015. 'Phantom Journalism: Governing India's Proxy Media Owners.' *Journalism Studies* 16(5): 663–79.

Sahni, J. N. 1974. *Truth about the Indian Press*. Bombay: Allied Publishers.

Sainath, P. 2013. 'Yes We Spent Money on Paid News Ads.' *The Hindu*, 30 January. Accessed 14 September 2016. Available at http://www.thehindu.com/news/national/yes-we-spent-money-on-paid-news-ads/article4354575.ece.

Sanders, Karen and María José Canel. eds. 2013. *Government Communication: Cases and Challenges*. New York: Bloomsbury.

Sardesai, Rajdeep. 2014. *The Election that Changed India*. New Delhi: Penguin Viking.

Schlozman, Kay. L., Sidney Verba and Henry E. Brady. 2010. 'Weapon of the Strong? Participatory Inequality and the Internet.' *Perspectives on Politics* 8(2): 487–509.

Schuck, Andreas R. T. and Claes H. De Vreese. 2006. 'Between Risk and Opportunity: News Framing and its Effects on Public Support for EU Enlargement.' *European Journal of Communication* 21(1): 5–32.

Schudson, Michael. 1998. *The Good Citizen: A History of American Civic Life*. Cambridge, MA: Harvard University Press.

_____. 2011 (2003). *The Sociology of News*, second edition. New York: W. W. Norton & Company.

Schumpeter, Joseph A. 1952. *Capitalism, Socialism and Democracy*, Fourth Edition. London: Allen & Unwin.

Semetko, Holli A, Anup Kumar, Taberez A. Neyazi, Jonathan Mellon, Dhavan Shah, and Arash Sangar. 2016a. 'Social and Traditional Media Use and Influences on the Vote in India.' Paper presented at International Communication Association Meeting, Fukuoka, Japan, 9–13 June.

Semetko, Holli A, Anup Kumar, Taberez A. Neyazi and Jonathan Mellon. 2016b. 'Media Attention and Voting for New vs. Established Parties: Evidence from India.' Paper presented at American Political Science Association 112th Annual Meeting, Philadelphia, USA, 1–4 September.

Semetko, Holli A. 2004. 'Media, Public Opinion, and Political Action.' In *The Sage Handbook of Media Studies*, edited by John D. H. Downing, Denis McQuail, Philip Schlesinger and Ellen Wartella, 351–74. Thousand Oaks, CA: Sage Publications.

Semetko, Holli A. and Patti M. Valkenburg. 2000. 'Framing European Politics: A Content Analysis of Press and Television News.' *Journal of Communication* 2(50): 93–109.

Semetko, Holli A. and Klaus Schönbach. 1994. *Germany's Unity Election: Voters and the Media*. Cresskill, NJ: Hampton Press.

Semetko, Holli A., Jay G. Blumler, Michael Gurevitch and David Weaver. 1991. *The Formation of Campaign Agendas: A Comparative Analysis of Party and Media Roles in Recent American and British Elections*. London: Routledge.

Sen, Amartya. 1981. *Poverty and Famines: An Essay on Entitlement and Deprivation*. New Delhi: Oxford University Press.

_____. 2005. *The Argumentative Indian: Writings on Indian History, Culture and Identity*. New Delhi: Penguin.

Shah, Alpesh, Nimisha Jain and Shweta Bajpai. 2015. *India@Digital Bharat: Creating A $200 Billion Internet Economy*. Delhi: The Boston Consulting Group & Internet and Mobile Association of India.

Shah Commission of Inquiry. 1978. *Interim Report I* (11 March 1978) and *Interim Report II* (26 April 1978). New Delhi.

Shah, Dhavan V., Kathleen Bartzen Culver, Alexander Hanna, Timothy Macafee and Jung Hwan Yang. 2015. 'Computational Approaches to Online Political Expression: Rediscovering a "Science of the Social".' In *Handbook of Digital Politics*, edited by Stephen Coleman and Deen Freelon, 281–305. Cheltenham: Edward Elgar.

Shah, Ghanshayam. ed. 2013. *Caste and Democratic Politics in India*. New Delhi: Permanent Black.

Sharma, Anil K. 2015. 'Transformation in Indian Agriculture, Allied Sectors, and Rural India: Is There Less *Krishi* in Bharat?' *NCAER Report*. Accessed 14 December 2016. Available at www.ncaer.org/free-download.php?pID=245.

Sharma, Gopal. 1978. 'Hindi and the Composite Culture of India.' *Contribution to Asian Studies* 11: 57–68.

Sharma, Supriya. 2014. 'Why Modi Should Thank the Media for the Way It Has Covered this Election.' *Scroll*, 8 May. Accessed 7 May 2015. Available at http://scroll.in/article/663859/why-modi-should-thank-the-media-for-the-way-it-has-covered-this-election.

Sheth, D. L. 1995. 'The Great Language Debate: Politics of Metropolitan versus Vernacular India.' In *Crisis and Change in Contemporary India*, edited by Uppendra Baxi and Bikhu Parekh, 187–215. New Delhi: Sage Publications.

Singh, Gurharpal. 2000. *Ethnic Conflict in India: A Case Study of Punjab*. Houndmills: Palgrave Macmillan.

Singh, Indu B. 1980. 'The Indian Mass Media System: Before, During and after the National Emergency.' *Canadian Journal of Communication* 7(2): 39–49.

Singhal, Arvind and Everett M. Rogers. 1989. *India's Information Revolution*. New Delhi: Sage Publications.

Sivakumari, B. 2013. 'Half of India's Dalit Population Lives in 4 States'. *The Times of India*, 2 May. Accessed 24 May 2016. Available at http://timesofindia. indiatimes.com/india/Half-of-Indias-dalit-population-lives-in-4-states/ articleshow/19827757.cms.

Smith, Anthony. 1980. *Goodbye, Gutenberg: The Newspaper Revolution of the 1980s*. New York: Oxford University Press.

Soroka, Stuart and Stephen McAdams. 2015. 'News, Politics, and Negativity.' *Political Communication* 32(1): 1–22.

Soroka, Stuart N. 2002. *Agenda-setting Dynamics in Canada*. Vancouver, British Columbia, Canada: UBC Press.

_____. 2014. *Negativity in Democratic Politics: Causes and Consequences*. Cambridge: Cambridge University Press.

Sparrow, Bartholomew. H. 1999. *Uncertain Guardians: The News Media as a Political Institution*. Baltimore: Johns Hopkins University Press.

Sridharan, E. 2004. 'The Growth and Sectoral Composition of India's Middle Class: Its Impact on the Politics of Economic Liberalisation.' *India Review* 3(4): 405–28.

_____. 2008. 'The Political Economy of the Middle Classes in Liberalising India.' *ISAS Working Paper* (49) (22 September): 1–60.

Srinivas, M. N. 1962. *Caste in Modern India, and Other Essays*. Mumbai, New York: Asia Publishing House.

Sriram, Jayant. 2015. 'Regional Languages are the Lynchpin to India's Internet Boom.' *The Hindu*, 30 November. Accessed 15 December 2016. Available at http:// www.thehindu.com/business/Economy/regional-languages-are-the-lynchpin- to-indias-internet-boom/article7930285.ece.

Srivastava, Manish. 2000. *Hindi Patrakarita Mein Ayodhya Vivad*. New Delhi: Naman Prakashan.

Stahlberg, Per. 2002a. *Lucknow Daily: How a Hindi Newspaper Constructs Society*. Stockholm: Stockhlom Studies in Social Anthropology.

_____. 2002b. 'The Illicit Daughter: Hindi-language Newspapers and Regionalisation of the Public Sphere in India.' In *Contesting 'Good' Governance: Crosscultural Perspectives on Representation, Accountability and Public Space*, edited by Eva Poluha and Mona Rosendahl, 207–36. London: Curzon.

_____. 2013. *Writing Society through Media: Ethnography of a Hindi Daily*. New Delhi: Rawat Publication.

Standing Committee on Information Technology. 2013. *Issues Related to Paid News.* New Delhi: Ministry of Information and Broadcasting, Government of India.

Strömbäck, Jasper. 2008. 'Four Phases of Mediatization: An Analysis of the Mediatization of Politics.' *The International Journal of Press/Politics* 13(3): 228–46.

Strömbäck, Jasper and Adam Shehata. 2010. 'Media Malaise or a Virtuous Circle? Exploring the Causal Relationships between News Media Exposure, Political News Attention and Political Interest.' *European Journal of Political Research* 49(5): 575–97.

Stromer-Galley, Jennifer. 2014. *Presidential Campaigning in the Internet Age.* New York: Oxford University Press.

Subramanian, Narendra. 1999. *Ethnicity and Populist Mobilization: Political Parties, Citizens and Democracy in South India.* New York: Oxford University Press.

TAM Annual Universe Updates. 2015. TAM Media Research Pvt. Ltd.

Tanabe, Akio. 2007. 'Toward Vernacular Democracy: Moral Society and Post-postcolonial Transformation in Rural Orissa, India.' *American Ethnologist* 34(3): 558–74.

Tayagi, Shailendra. 2015. 'Agriculture Not the Main Source of Rural Income.' *The Guardian*, 25 July. Accessed 6 November 2016. Available at http://www.sunday-guardian.com/business/agriculture-not-the-main-source-of-rural-income.

Thachil, Tariq. 2014. *Elite Party, Poor Voters: How Social Services Win Votes in India.* Cambridge: Cambridge University of Press.

Thakurta, Paranjoy Guha and Subi Chaturvedi. 2012. 'Corporatisation of the Media: Implications of the RIL-Network 18-Eenadu Deal.' *Economic and Political Weekly* 47(7): 12–14.

Thakurta, Paranjoy Guha. 2014a. 'What Future for the Media in India?' *Economic and Political Weekly* 49(25): 13–17.

———. 2014b. 'Mass Media and the Modi "Wave".' *Himal*, 30 June. Accessed 6 May 2015. Available at http://himalmag.com/media-modi-elections.

Thirumal, P. and Gary Michael Tartakov. 2010. 'India's Dalits Search for a Democratic Opening in the Digital Divide.' In *International Exploration of Technology Equity and the Digital Divide: Critical, Historical and Social Perspectives*, edited by Patricia Randolph, 20–39. New York: International Science Reference.

Thomas, Pradip. 2014. 'The Ambivalent State and the Media in India: Between Elite Domination and the Public Interest.' *International Journal of Communication* 8: 466–82.

Thorsen, Einar and Sreedharan, Chindu. eds. 2015. *India Election 2014: First Reflections.* Bournemouth: The Centre for the Study of Journalism, Culture and Community, Bournemouth University.

Thorson, Kjerstin and Chris Wells. 2016. 'Curated Flows: A Framework for Mapping Media Exposure in the Digital Age.' *Communication Theory* 26(3): 309–28.

Thussu, Daya Kishan. 1998. 'Infotainment International: A View from the South.' In *Electronic Empires: Global Media and Local Resistance*, edited by D. K. Thussu, 63–83. London and New York: Hodder Education Publishers.

_____. 2006a. *International Communication: Continuity and Change*, second edition. New York: Bloomsbury Academic.

_____. 2006b. 'The Murdochization of News? The Case of Star TV in India.' *Media, Culture and Society* 29(4): 593–611.

_____. 2007. *News as Entertainment: The Rise of Global Infotainment*. London: Sage Publications.

Times News Network (TNN). 2011a. 'No Curbs, But Media Needs to Sensitise Itself: Ambika Soni.' *The Times of India*, 5 November. Accessed 29 November 2011. Available at http://timesofindia.indiatimes.com/india/No-curbs-but-media-needs-to-sensitize-itself-Ambika-Soni/articleshow/10613980.cms.

_____. 2011b. 'When Revolutions Go Viral.' *The Times of India*, 27 August. Accessed 14 December 2016. Available at http://timesofindia.indiatimes.com/ When-revolutions-go-viral/articleshow/21617491.cms.

_____. 2014a. '44% of Voters in India's Top Metropolises Say They Will Vote AAP for Lok Sabha: TOI Poll.' *The Times of India*, 9 January. Accessed 15 December 2016. Available at http://timesofindia.indiatimes.com/india/44-of-voters-in-Indias-top-metropolises-say-they-will-vote-AAP-for-Lok-Sabha-TOI-poll/articleshow/28566136.cms.

_____. 2014b. 'AAP to Bag 6 Delhi Lok Sabha Seats, Modi Top PM Choice: Poll.' *The Times of India*, 14 January. Accessed 15 December 2016. Available at http://timesofindia.indiatimes.com/india/AAP-to-bag-6-Delhi-Lok-Sabha-seats-Modi-top-PM-choice-Poll/articleshow/28764153.cms.

TRAI. 2011. *The Telecom Commercial Communication Customer Preference (Sixth Amendment) Regulations, 2011*. Accessed 21 October 2016. Available at file:/// Users/taberezneyazi/Downloads/20120530121051372589006th_amendement[1]. pdf.

_____. 2014. *Recommendation on Issues Related to Media Ownership*. New Delhi: Mahanagar Doorsanchar Bhawan.

_____. 2016. 'Telecom Subscription Data May 2016.' Accessed on 14 December 2016. Available at http://www.trai.gov.in/WriteReadData/PressRealease/Document /Press_Release_No74_Eng_29_july_2016.pdf.

Tripathi, Rahul. 2014. 'Communal Riots Rose by 25 Per Cent in 2013, Says MHA Data.' *The Indian Express*, 27 April. Accessed 15 December 2016. Available at http://indianexpress.com/article/india/india-others/communal-riots-rose-by-25-pc-in-2013-mha/.

Tufekci, Zeynep and Christopher Wilson. 2012. 'Social Media and the Decision to Participate in Political Protest: Observations from Tahrir Square.' *Journal of Communication* 62(2): 363–79.

Udupa, Sahana. 2015. *Making News in Global India: Media, Publics and Politics.* Cambridge: Cambridge University Press.

Vajpeyi, Ananya. 2011. 'The Grammar of Anarchy.' Accessed 16 June 2015. Available at http://india.blogs.nytimes.com/2011/09/16/the-grammar-of-anarchy/.

Valentino, Nicholas A. and Nardis, Yioryos. 2013. 'Political Communication: Form and Consequence of the Information Environment.' In *The Oxford Handbook of Political Psychology*, second edition, edited by Leonie Huddy, David O. Sears and Jack S. Levy, 1–25. Oxford: Oxford University Press.

Valkenburg, Patti M., Holli A. Semetko and Claes H. De Vreese. 1999. 'The Effects of News Frames on Readers' Thoughts and Recall.' *Communication Research* 26(5): 550–69.

Varshney, Ashutosh. 1993. 'Contested Meanings: Hindu Nationalism, India's National Identity, and the Politics of Anxiety.' *Daedalus* 122(3): 227–61.

_____. 1998. *Democracy, Development and the Countryside: Urban–Rural Struggles in India.* Cambridge: Cambridge University Press.

_____. 2000. 'Is India Becoming More Democratic?' *The Journal of Asian Studies* 59(1): 3–25.

Verba, Sidney and Norman H. Nie. 1972. *Participation in America.* New York: Harper Row.

Verba, Sidney, Kay Lehman Schlozman and Henry E. Brady. 1995. *Voice and Equality: Civic Voluntarism in American Politics.* Cambridge, MA: Harvard University Press.

Verghese, B. G. 2005. *Warrior of the Fourth Estate: Ramnath Goenka of the Express.* New Delhi: Penguin.

Verma, Rahul and Shreyas Sardesai. 2014. 'Does Media Exposure Affect Voting Behaviour and Political Preferences in India?' *Economic and Political Weekly* 49(39): 82–88.

Vernelis, Kazys. ed. 2008. *Networked Publics.* Cambridge: MIT Press.

Waisbord, Silvio. 2010. 'The Pragmatic Politics of Media Reform: Media Movements and Coalition-building in Latin America.' *Global Media and Communication* 6(2): 133–53.

Walgrave, Stefaan and Peter Van Aelst. 2006. 'The Contingency of the Mass Media's Political Agenda Setting Power: Toward a Preliminary Theory.' *Journal of Communication* 56(1): 88–109.

Walgrave, Stefaan, Peter Van Aelst and Lance Bennett. 2010. 'Beyond Agenda-setting. Towards a Broader Theory of Agenda Interactions between Political Actors and the Mass Media.' Paper prepared for the 2010 American Political Science

Association (APSA) Annual Meeting, Washington.

Weaver, David, Doris Graber, Maxwell McCombs, and Chaim Eyal. 1981. *Media Agenda-setting in a Presidential Election: Issues, Images, and Interest*. New York: Praeger.

Weiner, Myron. 1989. *The Indian Paradox: Essays in Indian Politics*. New Delhi: Sage Publications.

Willis, Derek. 2014. 'Narendra Modi, the Social Media Politician.' *The New York Times*, 25 September. Accessed 15 December 2016. Available at http://www.nytimes. com/2014/09/26/upshot/narendra-modi-the-social-media-politician.html?_r=0.

Wilmshurst, John and Adrian Mackay. 1999. *The Fundamentals of Advertising*, second edition. Boston: Butterworth-Heinemann.

Winseck, Dwayne. 2008. 'The State of Media Ownership and Media Markets: Competition or Concentration and Why Should We Care?' *Sociology Compass* 2(1): 34–47.

Witsoe, Jeffrey. 2011. 'Rethinking Postcolonial Democracy: An Examination of the Politics of Lower-Caste Empowerment in North India.' *American Ethnologist* 113(4): 619–31.

World Association of Newspapers and News Publishers. 2006. *World Press Trends 2006*. Paris, France: International Federation of Newspaper Publishers.

_____. 2014. *World Press Trends 2006*. Paris, France: International Federation of Newspaper Publishers.

Wu, Angela Xiao and Harsh Taneja. 2016. 'Reimagining Internet Geographies: A User-Centric Ethnological Mapping of the World Wide Web.' *Journal of Computer-Mediated Communication* 21(3): 230–46.

Yadav, Anumeha. 2014. 'Modi Critics Belong in Pakistan.' *The Hindu*, 19 April. Accessed 15 December 2016. Available at http://www.thehindu.com/ elections/loksabha2014/modis-critics-belong-in-pakistan/article5929009. ece?ref=relatedNews.

Yadav, Yogendra. 1996. 'Reconfiguration in Indian Politics: State Assembly Elections 1993–1995.' *Economic and Political Weekly* 31(2 and 3): 95–104.

_____. 2000. 'Understanding Second Democratic Upsurge: Trends of Bahujan Participation in Electoral Politics in the 1990s.' In *Transforming India: Social and Political Dynamics of Democracy*, edited by Francine Frankel, Z. Hasan, R. Bhargava and B. Arora, 120–45. New Delhi: Oxford University Press.

_____. 2006. 'Social Profile of Indian Media.' *The South Asian*, 12 June. Accessed 15 September 2009. Available at http://www.thesouthasian.org/archives/2006/ social_profile_of_indian_media.html.

Ziegfeld, Adam. 2012. 'Coalition Government and Party System Change: Explaining the Rise of Regional Political Parties in India.' *Comparative Politics* 45(1): 69–87.

Index

24×7, 13n7, 10, 20–21, 104, 146, 148, 159, 188

Aaj, 29, 42, 57n7, 66

Aaj Tak, 20, 148, 162–164, 172, 175–177, 179, 181–184

Aam Aadmi Party (AAP), 14, 139n3–140, 149, 159, 163–164, 167n7–168, 170–171, 173–177, 180, 184

advertising,
  advertising revenues, 13, 25, 67, 79n5, 104–105, 111, 115–117, 119, 121, 124, 126–128, 131, 134, 136 (see also Hindi newspapers)
  agency/ies, 112–113, 118, 120, 122–123, 129n42
  and consumerism, 112
  company, 112
  expenditure, 111
  income, 112
  industry, 104, 112
  markets, 25, 84, 105, 110–111, 119, 122, 127, 136
  political, 124, 126
  private, 111
  rate, 119–120n29, 135
  social role, 110

age of consensus, 49

agenda-setting, 26, 161–162, 164–166, 183, 187

All-India Language Conference, 58

Almond, Gabriel, 11

Amar Ujala, 52, 68

Amrit Bazar Patrika, 29, 35n12, 45

anti-corruption movement, 11, 14, 23, 25, 137–139n3, 140, 145–146, 148–150n16n18, 151–160, 188

Ayodhya movement/Also Ram Janmabhumi–Babri mosque controversy, 15–17, 51, 66, 68, 108

Bahujan Samaj Party (BSP), 75, 89–90, 179–180

Banerjee, Surendranath, 29

Barber, Benjamin, 143n6

Basumati, 46

Bengal Gazette, 32

Bengalee, 29, 45

Bennett, Lance W., 11, 103, 107, 132, 137, 183n19

Bharat Mitra, 32

Bharatiya Janata Party (BJP), 8, 14, 16–18, 108–109, 146, 150n18, 159, 161–162n2, 163–164, 166–171, 174–180, 183–185, 189, 194, 196n6

Bhasha Prachar Samiti, 39, 54

Birla, G. D., 45, 55, 107

Blitz, 50

Bombay Chronicle, 30, 46n28

British Raj, 35

censorship, 35, 37, 44, 46, 61–62, 157–158n26

Chadwick, Andrew, 7, 14, 26, 137, 141–142, 163, 166, 187

Chaturvedi, Makhanlal, 2, 33, 37–38, 42, 56–57n7, 105

Chhattisgarh Mitr, 37

City Bhaskar, 83–84n11, 91, 94, 127n40–128, 133

Civil Disobedience, 42

civic forum, 4–5

civil society, 3, 6, 12, 126, 139, 147, 156, 191

civil society activism, 3

Cohen, Bernard C., 163n5, 164

commodification of news, 3

communal,
  agenda, 185
  conflicts/violence/riots, 66–67, 108, 161
  discourse, 66
  harmony, 67n13
  leader, 36
  politics, 169
  rhetoric, 177
  tension, 180

communalism, 167, 179, 183–185

Congress system, 59

consumerism, 11, 25, 103–104, 110–113

Cook, Timothy. E., 9n5

corruption, 6–7, 11, 14, 23, 25–26, 60, 83, 95, 111, 127, 132, 137–138n2, 139n3–140, 142–146, 148–149n12, 150n18–160, 167–168, 182, 184, 188
  anti-corruption/campaign against, 11, 14, 23, 25, 137–139n3, 140, 142–143, 145–146, 148–150n16n18, 151–160, 188
  cause of, 95
  combat, 26
  corruption-fatigue, 144

  discourse on, 143
  government, 111
  reporting on, 111
  watchdog, 143
Corruption Perception Index (CPI), 143–144

Cow Protection Campaign, 51

Dainik Bhaskar, 8, 53, 67n12, 72, 80–81, 83–88, 91–93, 95–98, 100, 105–109, 112, 116–123, 125–135, 144, 149n12

Dahl, Robert A., 4, 12

Dainik Jagran, 8, 57n7, 66–67, 72, 80, 89n23, 105–109, 112n29, 126n36, 135, 149

Dalit, 45n26, 69, 74–75, 86–91, 99–102, 189–190n2n3

Dar, Pandit Bishan Narain, 36

De Vreese, Claes H., 99n36

democratisation, 12–13, 17, 68, 101

della Porta, Donatella, 11

deregulation, 111–112n9, 113

Deshasewak, 38

Deshbandhu, 53

developing democracy, 5

Doordarshan, 103, 165, 194–195

Dravida Munnetra Kazhagam (DMK), 60, 152

Druckman, James N., 99n36

Dwivedi, Mahabir Prasad, 32–33, 37

Eenadu, 79

Emergency, 39, 61–62n9n10, 63, 98

Empire, 44n24

English language media, 1, 67, 135

English newspapers, 15, 18, 24–25, 28,

32, 34n11–35, 38, 44–45n25, 46–47, 52–57, 59, 62, 65, 67–68n14, 71, 79, 87, 92–93, 104–105, 107, 113, 116, 121, 136, 148

English press, 17, 23–24, 28, 32, 34, 44, 47, 50–53n4, 56–57, 59–60, 64, 66–67, 94, 108, 126n36, 128, 186
debate between Hindi and, 24
distinction between vernacular press, 34, 186
domination of, 52
elite, 128
Hindi and, 28
Hindi vs., 44
mainstream, 64
national press, 17, 52, 59
relationship between Hindi press, 50

English-educated, 13, 24, 54–55, 57, 64, 75

Englishman, 44

English-speaking intelligentsia, 55

entertainment sector, 19

Entman, Robert M., 99n36, 103

Esser, Frank, 194

Ezhava, 60

Facebook, 150n16n17, 156, 163, 183, 187, 192

FICCI-KPMG, 104, 121

financial crisis, 1991, 9

Gagging Act, Also The Press Act of India, 34

Gamson, William, 99n36, 155

Gandhi, Indira, 61–63, 178

Gandhi, Mahatma, 29, 37, 40n18–41n21, 42, 45–48, 58, 153

Ghosh, Sisir Kumar, 29, 35n12

Goffman, Erving, 99n36

grassroots mobilisation, 1, 6, 13, 17, 24, 26, 75, 77–78, 94, 96, 101, 135–136, 138, 148, 159–161, 188

Gokhale, Gopal Krishna, 29, 38

Great Famine of 1876–78, 35

Guha, Ramachandra, 16n11, 61

Gupta, Shiv Prasad, 29, 42

Habermas, Jurgen, 132

Hallin, Daniel C., 77, 108n3

Hasan, Zoya, 9, 12, 15, 16n10, 64, 66n11, 68–69, 77n3, 152

Hazare, Anna, 6, 11, 14, 23, 26, 138n2–139 142–143, 145–159, 149n12, 188

Hindi Bangavasi, 33

Hindi belt, 24, 55–57, 59, 177

Hindi dailies, 8, 31–32, 37, 52, 57, 63–64, 66, 149

Hindi heartland, 8, 16–17, 34n9, 42, 57, 69, 161, 164

Hindi intelligentsia, 40

Hindi journalism, 31n6, 31–33, 36–37, 39–43, 78, 92–93

Hindi media, 1, 3–4, 7–8, 12–14, 16, 18, 24–25, 49, 52, 55, 64–68, 76, 78, 96, 99, 101–102, 106–107, 135, 181, 186–187
business/industry/conglomerates/ groups, 25, 55, 106–107, 135
contest between the English, 76
in regional and national politics, 24, 76
mediated democratic transformation, 3
mediated public arena, 99, 102
mobilising role of the/mobilising agent/grassroots mobilisation, 4, 12–14, 96, 186–187
platform for emerging political leaders, 52, 65, 76

reach of the, 8
rise of the, 7
subservient position, relative to the
    English media, 49
success of, 1
users, 55
Hindi news media (see also Hindi
    media), 7–8, 11, 20, 23–24, 76, 77,
    106, 163, 186
Hindi newspapers,
advertising revenues, 19, 25, 67, 79,
    104–105, 115–117, 119, 121,
    124, 126–128, 131, 134, 136
alternative platform of participation,
    18
Ayodhya movement/Also Ram
    Janmabhumi–Babri mosque
    controversy, 18, 66, 68
British rule, 38, 44–45
business, 10, 25, 68n15, 84, 105–
    106, 108–109, 116, 121, 129
challenged the dominance of
    English newspapers, 24, 52
circulation, 1, 8, 13, 16–18n14, 24,
    34, 43n22, 49, 52, 57, 63–64,
    70n15–72, 76, 78–80, 82n9, 84,
    106, 116, 119–120, 122–123,
    128–129n42, 130–132, 193
colonial period, 1, 24, 28, 40, 43–44,
    47, 51, 60, 64, 94, 134n53,
    158n26, 186
colonial rule, 23–24, 28, 31n6–32,
    44–45, 49–50n2, 158n26
colonial state, 44
communication revolution, 211
contesting the dominance of
    English newspapers , 59
credibility/credibility gap, 25, 54,
    56–58, 78, 126, 157, 184
Dalits, 45n26, 69, 74–75, 86–91,
    99–102, 189–190n2n3
defy the government's authority, 62

farmers, 9, 15n8, 101, 104, 115–116,
    135–136, 155–156
foreign coverage, 57n7
freedom movement/struggle, 4, 24,
    28, 31, 34, 38, 42, 44, 46n28, 49,
    56, 186
grassroots mobilisation, 1, 6, 13, 17,
    24, 26, 75, 77–78, 94, 96, 101,
    136, 138, 148, 159–161, 188
growth, 1, 7–8, 11–12, 14,
    17–18n14, 19, 21–22, 25–26,
    31–34n9, 38, 43–44, 51–52, 59,
    63, 68n14–70n15, 71–72, 76, 78,
    94, 101, 104–105, 107, 110, 112,
    115, 135–136, 142, 184, 187n1,
    189, 192–193, 195
identity politics, 17, 68–69
influence and political importance,
    15
interaction between the elites and
    mass public, 47
and local stringers, 80, 123
localisation, 24–25, 72, 77–86,
    94–97, 99, 101, 104, 118n26,
    123, 128
and MK Gandhi
Mandal reservation/also backward
    castes, 16n12
marginalised groups/sections, 9,
    12, 15, 25, 60n8, 66, 68–69, 76,
    78–79, 86, 88, 90, 101–104, 128,
    136, 152, 186, 189
mobilisation/mass mobilisation,
    9, 11, 13–15, 17–18, 23–28n2,
    32, 37, 40, 43, 47, 49, 59–61,
    64, 69–70n15, 73, 75–78, 94,
    96–98, 101, 115–116, 135–141,
    148–149n15, 155, 159–160, 179,
    186–189, 192–193, 195
nationalist causes, 32, 38, 41, 45n26,
    64
nationalism, 31–32, 35–37, 41n19–
    42, 47–48, 51, 77, 150n18

non-Hindi speaking areas, 43
owner/ownership, 10, 25, 29, 31, 36,
43–44n24, 45n25, 50n1, 53, 56–
57, 103, 105n1–106, 111, 135
owned by English language dailies,
57
political upheavals, 17
political causes, 36
political mobilisation, 4, 6–7, 11,
13–14, 17–18, 23–27, 43, 60–61,
70n15, 73, 75, 138, 141, 186–
187, 195
preoccupation with social, cultural
and religious issues, 36
presence in small towns, 15, 65
professionalism, 56, 133, 186
propaganda, 28–29n3, 43–44, 56,
110
public arena/sphere, 6, 9, 13, 15,
24–25, 44, 50, 52, 53–54, 56–57,
59, 64–68, 76–77n1, 78–79,
87–91, 94–95, 99, 101–104, 109,
132, 136, 157–159–160, 186,
188–191, 194
readership, 46, 56, 70n15, 83–84,
106, 116–117, 120–121, 128–
129n42, 131, 134, 136
regional and vernacular forces, 63
relationship with politics, 11, 14
rise in demand politics, 60–61
rural areas, 9, 15, 25, 57, 65, 68,
78–79, 83, 101, 104, 113–116,
123, 131, 136, 138, 148, 153n20,
192–193, 196
satellite press, 56, 67
social and religious issues, 28, 31
social media, 7, 23, 26, 137,
141–142, 150n17–151, 156,
161n1, 163–164, 168–174, 184,
188–189, 194–195
social transformation, 9, 64
state capitals, 57n7, 65, 76
upper caste, 16, 43, 51, 69, 75,
86–88, 90

women journalists, 91–94
World War I, 39, 44n24
Hindi press, 16–17, 25, 31–32, 44, 47,
50–52, 56–57, 64, 66, 68n14, 79, 86,
94, 103–104, 106, 115, 135–136,
186
advertising and ownership, 25
and the English press in
independent India, 50
Ayodhya movement, 17
communal and reactionary/
communal discourse, 51, 66
copied the English press, 56
highest number of dailies, 57
in colonial India, 31–32
localisation in, 79, 86
nationalist consciousness, 47
Political Economy of the, 25, 68n14,
103, 135
rise of new social classes, 25
vehicle of democratisation, 68
Hindi-medium schools, 55
Hindi Sahitya Sammelan, 39
Hindi-speaking states 8, 17, 52, 55, 64,
68, 72–74, 78
Hindu 30, 45n26
Hindustan 41, 41n21, 57, 62
Hindustan Times 45, 45n27, 55–57, 62,
105–107, 126n36, 133
Hindutva 15, 17, 30, 42, 66, 77–78, 108,
150n18
Hindutva politics, 17, 77
Hitavada, 29, 52
Hitvarta, 37
Howard, Philip N., 137
Huntington, Samuel P., 139
hybrid media environment, 22, 26, 137,
142, 161–164, 170, 183, 187–188,
196
Hybrid media systems, 195

identity politics, 17, 68–69

India Today, 168, 172

Indian Daily News, 44n24

Indian Express, 16n12, 46, 92, 129n42

Indian Language Internet Alliance
   (ILIA), 8, 192

Indian Mirror, 45

Indian National Congress, 14, 16n11,
   18, 28–29, 31–32, 34–36, 38,
   40n18–41n21, 42, 45–48, 58–61, 69,
   77, 140, 143n8, 145, 148, 158–159,
   161, 163, 167n7–170, 178n14, 180,
   183

Indian Nationalist Movement, 28n2,
   46, 51

Indian Press Act, 1910, 38–39, 42

Indigenous English media, 1

Internet,
   alternative media and voices, 190
   bypass mainstream media, 190
   campaign, 162, 187, 194
   content flows, 187, 195
   content in regional languages, 192
   Dalits, 190n2n3
   democratic framework, 158
   democratic politics, 137
   democratised the communication
      process, 196
   developing countries, 142n5, 157,
      160
   digital strategies, 187
   editorial offices Internet, 82
   fragmentation of media channels,
      137
   growing rapidly, 22, 192
   growth, 7, 142, 187n1, 192, 195
   Hindi language, 192
   Indian language, 8, 192
   influence traditional media, 157, 190
   localisation, 97

mainstream media, 74–75, 90, 101,
      189–191
   mediatised politics, 195
   mobile phones, 1, 6, 21, 26, 142,
      174, 184, 189
   mobilisation, 23, 98, 192
   mobilise support, 26, 90, 138, 142,
      146, 161–162, 179, 190
   mobilised disengaged citizens, 160
   mobilising beyond the locality, 25,
      78
   non-elite actors, 188–191
   political and civic engagement, 99,
      141
   public arena, 157–158
   public sphere, 157–158
   rural areas, 193, 196
   single daily news cycles, 166
   social and political mobilisation, 4,
      23, 141, 186
   strategic role, 159
   transnational mobilisation, 98
   use of computer technology, 68
   users, 141–142, 170n11, 187,
      192–193
   villages, 142, 193
   voters, 162n3, 163–164, 173–
      175n13, 184, 189
internet vernacularisation, 192–193, 196

Jaffrelot, Christophe, 9, 12, 16n11, 77,
   83

Jan Lokpal Andolan, 138

Jan Lokpal Bill, 26, 138, 145, 148, 150,
   154

Jansatta, 16n12, 151

Jauhar, Maulana Mohammad Ali, 30

Jeffrey, Robin, 2n1, 7, 13, 15, 79, 87,
   104, 106, 112, 129, 134, 143

JP Movement, 60

journalistic practices, 186

Kargil War, 108

Karamveer, 29, 37

Katz, Elihu, 162

Kavi Vachan Sudha, 31n6–32

Kesari, 30, 34, 38, 53, 68

Kohli, Atul , 79n5, 111n8

Lazarsfeld, Paul F., 5, 162

liberalisation, 7, 19, 25, 105, 111n8, 113
–114n17, 152–153, 166

Liberty, 46

Lipset, Seymor Martin, 12

local advertising, 79, 119, 122–123, 127,
135

localisation, 24–25, 72, 77–86, 94–97,
99, 101, 104, 118n26, 123, 128

Lohia, Ram Manohar, 53

Madhya Bharat, 37, 42

Mail, 45

mainstream media, 74–75, 90, 101,
189–191

Malviya, Madan Mohan, 30, 34n9, 36,
46

Mancini, Paolo, 10n6, 77, 108n3, 194n4

Mandal Commission, 16, 16n10

Mandal movement, 16, 18

Mandal politics, 15, 66

mass participation, 26, 166, 195

Mayawati, 64, 74, 89n23–90

McChesney, Robert W., 103

McCombs, Maxwell, 4, 165

media capture, 10n6, 111

media effects, 4, 137, 144, 158, 183

media ownership, 10, 103, 105n1, 106,
111

media trial, 10

Mehta, Sir Pherozeshah, 30, 38, 46

micro politics, 24

Mirat-ul-Akhbar, 34n10

mobilising agents, Hindi media, 4, 12

mobile phone/cell phone, 1, 6, 8n4,
21–22, 26, 138, 142, 149, 151, 155,
163, 167, 170, 172, 174–175n13,
184, 189

Modi, Narendra, 26, 149, 149n15, 161,
161n1, 163, 166–167, 167n7, 168,
169n9, 171–172, 176–179, 183–185,
194–195

Murdochisation of news, 3

Nai Duniya, 52, 57n7, 62, 107–108

National Herald, 30, 46, 57

Nationalist, 8, 28n2–29, 32, 36n16,
38–44n23, 45n26–49, 51, 55, 60,
64, 180
   cause, 32, 38, 41, 45n26, 64
   consciousness, 47
   English newspaper, 45, 55
   feeling, 43
   forces, 60
   issues, 36n16
   leaders, 29, 36, 40, 41, 47, 49
   movement, 28n2, 46, 51
   newspaper, 38–39, 45–46, 49
   organisation, 180
   politics, 42
   press, 36, 44n23, 49
   program, 42
   struggle, 46

Native Newspaper Reports, 43

native press, 34

Navbharat Times, 56–57

Navjivan, 57

NDTV, 13n7, 87, 148, 151

Negativity, 179–181

Nehru, Jawaharlal, 30, 46, 49, 50n1, 53, 60

Nehru, Motilal, 30, 46

neo-liberal state, 23

Nielsen, Rasmus K., 163, 167n7, 175n13

non-political elite, 27, 195

Norris, Pippa, 4–6n2, 141, 187

North-Western Province (NWP), 36n13

Oodunt Martand, 32

Official Language (Amendment) Bill, 58

online campaign, 187

opaque media ownership, 10, 103

Pal, Bipan Chandra, 30, 38

paid news, 10, 25, 109n4–110, 122, 135, 194

permanent campaign, 195

Pioneer, 45, 57

political advertising, 123–124, 126

political elite, 10, 12, 26–27, 53, 58, 68–69, 75, 103, 145, 166, 195

political journalism, 31

political mobilisation, 4, 6–7, 11, 13–14, 17–18, 23–27, 43, 60–61, 70n15, 73, 75, 138, 141, 186–187, 195

post-broadcast era, 26, 98, 190, 194

Prabhat Khabar, 68

Prasad, Rajendra, 53

Pratap, 30, 38

Press Commission, 13, 52, 57n6

Press Council of India, 62, 66, 109n4

Press in India, 8, 13, 24, 28, 52, 57, 63–64, 65, 70n15–71, 73, 110

Press Ordinance, 34n10, 42

Press Trust of India (PTI), 54, 56, 180n16, 192

pressure groups, 12, 59

public arena, 6, 9, 13, 15, 24–25, 52, 54, 64–65, 76–77n1, 78–79, 88, 90–91, 94–95, 99, 101–102, 157, 159–160, 188, 191, 194

public opinion, 4, 7, 21–24, 26, 28, 31, 34–37, 47, 60, 77, 94, 99, 137–138, 143, 146, 158n26, 159, 169, 186, 194–195

public policy, 26

public sphere, 44, 50, 53–54, 56, 59, 64, 66–68, 87, 89–90n24, 94, 103–104, 109, 132, 136, 157–158, 186, 189–190n3, 191

Punjab Kesari, 53, 68

Putnam, Robert, 5

Raj TV, 85n13

Rajasthan Patrika, 68

Rao, Shakuntala, 166

Rashtra Bhasha Prachar Samiti, 39

Report on Native Newspapers, 35

reservation, 16n12, 88, 91

Right to Information Act (RTI), 109, 44, 154, 188

right-wing, 15, 66, 180, 184

Samachar Sudhavarshan, 31n7–32

Sapre, Madhavrao, 37

Saraswati, 32–33, 37

satellite channels, 18n15–19, 79, 85, 104

Schudson, Michael, 132

Semetko, Holli A, 5, 99n36, 163, 165, 170–171, 181, 189

Sen, Amartya, 110

sensationalisation of news, 25, 78
sentiment analysis, 164
sentiment scores, 183
Shah Commission Report, 61n9n10
Social media, 7, 23, 26, 137, 141–142,
150n17–151, 156, 161n1, 163–164,
168–174, 184, 188–189, 194–195
traditional media and, 7
growth of, 7
data from, 23
highlighting the issue of corruption,
26
disruption caused by, 137
role in anti-corruption movement,
150
election, 161
Narendra Modi, campaign strategy,
161, 194
access to, 170
stories and controversies from, 171
regular use of, 173
internet and, 188
effect, on voting behaviour, 189
Sony TV, 19
Stahlberg, Per, 55, 65, 89n23, 92, 108
Star TV, 19
Statesman, 44–45n25, 50
Strömbäck, Jasper, 5, 194
Stromer-Galley, Jennifer, 162–163, 189
subaltern, 13, 75, 136, 140
Swadesh, 61
swaraj, 45
Swarajya, 46
Swatantra Bharat, 57, 66
Swatantra Chetna, 66

Team Anna, 143, 146–149, 151, 154–
156, 158–159, 188

Telecom Regulatory Authority of India
(TRAI), 22n16, 106, 149n14
television channels, 13n7, 85n14
television network, 13
Thussu, Daya Kishan, 2, 103, 132, 166
Tilak, Bal Gangadhar, 30, 34, 38–39,
41n19n20
Times, 45
Times of India, 45n25, 49–50n1, 56–57,
62, 105–107, 120n29, 126n36, 131,
144, 148–149, 167n7, 171, 179n15
Times News Network, 147, 151, 167n7
Tufekci, Zeynep, 157
Tribune, 45
Twitter, 143, 150n17–151n19, 156,
162–164, 166, 168, 170n12, 183,
187, 192, 194

United News of India (UNI), 54, 56
United Progressive Alliance (UPA), 14,
158n24–159, 167, 178n14
Upcountry City Bhaskar, 83, 91, 94,
127n40–128

Vajpayee, Atal Bihari, 64, 108
Vemula, Rohith, 190–191
Verba, Sidney, 5, 11, 139–140, 143n6,
152
vernacular language press, 8
vernacular media, 1, 3, 7, 10, 50, 60, 64
vernacular population, 21
Vernacular Press Act, 1878, 34–35n12
Vernacular print media, 121
Vidyarthi, Ganesh Shankar, 30, 38
Vir Prataap, 61
Viswamitra, 39
voter turnout, 7n3, 14, 24, 52, 68,
73–74, 76

Western media, 77

WhatsApp, 163, 172–174

WikiLeaks, 27, 137, 195

Women Bhaskar, 84n11n12, 91–92, 94

women journalists, 91–94

World Association of Newspapers and
    News Publishers, 120n29

Zee TV, 19, 151